MONSTROSITIES

MONSTROSITIES

BODIES AND BRITISH ROMANTICISM

Paul Youngquist

University of Minnesota Press
Minneapolis ✢ London

An earlier version of chapter 2 appeared as "Lyrical Bodies: Wordsworth's Physiological Aesthetics," *European Romantics Review* 10 (1999): 152–62; reprinted by permission of *European Romantics Review*. An earlier version of chapter 3 appeared as "The Face of Beauty: Reynolds, Camper, Blake," in *Word and Image*; reprinted by permission of Taylor and Francis Ltd. An earlier version of chapter 4 appeared as "Rehabilitating Coleridge: Poetry, Philosophy, Excess," *English Literary History* 66 (1999): 885–909; reprinted by permission of The Johns Hopkins University Press. An earlier version of chapter 5 appeared as "De Quincey's Crazy Body," *PMLA* 114 (1999): 346–58; reprinted by permission of the copyright owner, The Modern Language Association of America.

Published by the University of Minnesota Press
111 Third Avenue South, Suite 290
Minneapolis, MN 55401-2520
http://www.upress.umn.edu

Library of Congress Cataloging-in-Publication Data

Youngquist, Paul.
    Monstrosities : bodies and British romanticism / Paul Youngquist.
        p.   cm.
    Includes bibliographical references (p.) and index.
    ISBN 0-8166-3979-5 (alk. paper) — ISBN 0-8166-3980-9 (pbk. : alk. paper)
    1. English literature—18th century—History and criticism.   2. Abnor-
    malities, Human, in literature.   3. English literature—19th century—
    History and criticism.   4. Abnormalities, Human—Great Britain.
    5. Romanticism—Great Britain.   6. Body, Human, in literature.   I. Title.
    PR448.A25Y68 2003
    820.9'35—dc21

                                                                2003007994

Printed in the United States of America on acid-free paper

The University of Minnesota is an equal-opportunity educator and employer.

12 11 10 09 08 07 06 05 04 03   10 9 8 7 6 5 4 3 2 1

For Caitlin Rose
perfect monster

CONTENTS

ACKNOWLEDGMENTS

This hideous progeny, like Frankenstein's, deserves a better author. Luckily it has many in the extraordinary people who helped create it. Two in particular, while not responsible for its deformities, breathed life into its dead matter. Jeff Cox is so vital a colleague and friend that he has on more than one occasion resurrected my creative spirits. Henry Giroux taught me how to work in a way that brings scholarship alive. The soul of this book belongs to them. I built the body, such as it is, but not without the help of a host of others, too. I am indebted to the many archivists who put flesh on the bones of my argument: those at the British Museum, the British Library, the Bodleian, the Wellcome Institute Library for the History of Medicine, the Hunterian Museum at the Royal College of Surgeons, and the College of Physicians of Philadelphia. Their skullduggery and mine found support in the generosity of the Department of English, the Research and Graduate Studies Office, and the Institute for Arts and Humanities at Pennsylvania State University. I am grateful to Don Biolostosky for arranging a semester free from teaching so I could write and to Marie Secor for a last-minute infusion of funds for illustrations.

Then there are the friends, colleagues, and students whose conversation and sometimes concern drove my speculations. Susan Squier said just the right thing at just the right time. Jeff Nealon gave the nod to more than a few questionable claims. Danielle Conger, Eric Wiener, Tallissa Ford, Jim Masland, and Denise Gigante all gave great advice without knowing it, while Kirstin Collins did some especially dirty editorial dirtywork. The Cockneys were a godsend: Greg Kucich, Charles Snodgrass, Dan White, and Michael Gamer. Ratchet up the dose, boys. The astute, at times aghast, reactions of my readers at the University of Minnesota Press made this birth less monstrous than it otherwise would have been, especially Alan Bewell's thoughtful critique. Richard Morrison has been a patient and supportive editor, Lynn Walterick an inspired copy editor. Finally, I could never have finished this book without the kindness and support of my friends Jane Juffer, Billy Joe Harris, Cecil Giscombe, Stuart Selber, Julia Kasdorf, Ed Ballock, and Dave Klein. Wes Montgomery deserves thanks, too.

INTRODUCTION

Monstrosities haunt the human. "A flash of lightning illuminated the object, and discovered its shape plainly to me; its gigantic stature, and deformity of its aspect, more hideous than belongs to humanity" (Shelley 71). The words are Victor Frankenstein's, and they register the horror monstrosities can inspire. Some bodies disturb by their very difference from the aspect of humanity. Like Frankenstein, flesh is a prodigal creator. The myriad bodies it breeds don't always reduce to common proportions. Its freaks are identified by words that register their exceptionality—prodigy, curiosity, monstrosity, specimen—words that often obscure the social relations that enforce their meanings. Consider the force of the word "abnormal." To be called abnormal is to become subject to normality—a curiosity, perhaps a freak. Abnormality breeds interest, the kind of interest that circulates power. And yet the word "abnormal" is of surprisingly recent coinage. The OED dates its first appearance to an anatomical encyclopedia published in 1835 and explains it to mean "deviating from the originary rule or type; contrary to rule or system; irregular, unusual, aberrant." In its earliest uses, "abnormal" denotes monstrosity, deviation from a corporeal norm. That anatomy provides the precedent for this meaning suggests that medicine, at the historical moment of its emergence as a distinct institutional and professional practice, produces and enforces a cultural norm of human embodiment. Monstrosities offer medicine a material occasion for such operations.

"Her great antipathy is to Doctors; these have offended her by examining her too minutely, and whenever they are mentioned she doubles her filbert of a fist, and manifests her decided displeasure." So writes a contributor to the *Literary Gazette and Journal of the Belles Lettres* in 1824 of Mademoiselle Caroline Crachami, known to polite society as "the Sicilian Dwarf" for her remarkable tininess (17 April). Only ten at the time, Caroline had reason to be irritable. She had been brought to London from Ireland by one Dr. Gilligan, a quack, ostensibly to cure a cough. Her father, a Sicilian employed in a musical capacity at the Theatre Royal in Dublin, had been persuaded by Dr. Gilligan that the genial air of England would improve his daughter's health (Altick 257–60).

On arriving in the metropolis, however, Dr. Gilligan immediately began exhibiting the Sicilian Dwarf at his lodgings in Bond Street. He invited the public to view this diminutive prodigy for a shilling—handle her for another. And the public came, subjecting Caroline to a crush of curious eyes and hands. Physicians were among the curious, eager to examine so singular a human specimen. The author of a notice in the *Literary Gazette* measures that singularity with peculiar precision:

> I found that the real height of Miss Crachami is nineteen inches and a half; the length of her foot (Cinderella was a nobody!) three inches and one-eighth; and the length of her fore-finger (she would not give me the wedding one) one inch and seven eighths!!! Having thus gone my lengths, I was allowed to go my rounds; and they follow: Round the head, twelve inches three-eighths; round the waist, eleven inches and a quarter; round the neck, (only think of taking such a creature round the neck!) five inches and three-eighths; round the ancle, three inches and a quarter; and round the wrist, two inches and seven sixteenths!! These are, bona fide, the measurements of this most extraordinary Human Being. (15 May)

Caroline's measurements make her extraordinary for the way they deviate from a norm of embodiment. The strange eroticism that accompanies their determination (the author's preoccupation with wedding fingers and passionate embraces) suggests, however, that such deviance both disturbs and intensifies the authority of that norm. In her minuteness, Caroline embodies femininity in extremis. To know her is to love her; to know her physically is to love her intimately. It has even been suggested that the good Dr. Gilligan's personal examinations might have been more than merely medical, accounting for Caroline's antipathy toward medical men.

As it turned out, that antipathy was precocious. By June 1824 Caroline Crachami was dead, expiring, as the *Literary Gazette* put it, "after enduring the fatigue of receiving above 200 visitors" (12 June). Between her cough and her constitution, exhibition proved too much. But death didn't put an end to her attractions. In some ways death perfected them, since now the Sicilian Dwarf could be subjected to a medical examination of the most intimate kind. Deprived of his income, Dr. Gilligan made the best of a bad situation by approaching several prominent physicians with the opportunity, for a modest gratuity, to buy Caroline's body. Most refused, but in a deal whose particulars remain a mystery, the Royal College of Surgeons acquired the little cadaver— in the interests, no doubt, of anatomical science. When Caroline's distraught father learned of her fate, he rushed to the Hunterian Museum in Lincolns Inn Fields, only to find her remains in an advanced state of dissection. On the table lay the Sicilian Dwarf, her miniature monstrosity now fully exposed by the operations of medical knowledge. To calm the distraught father, the doctors promised they would dissect no further. Today, nearly two centuries later, her tiny skeleton is still on display (Figure 1).

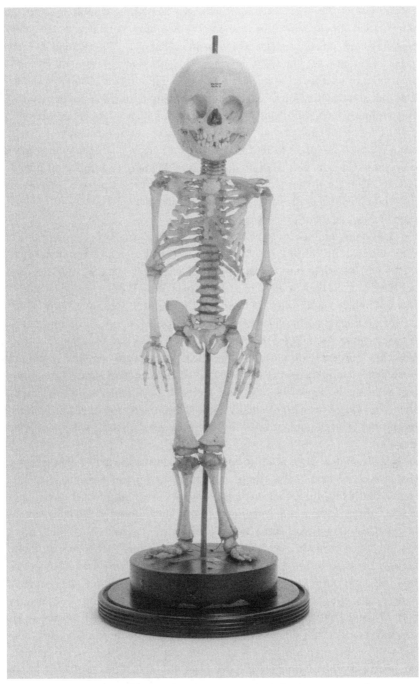

Figure 1. Skeleton of Caroline Crachami. Hunterian Museum, The Royal College of Surgeons of England.

The fate of Caroline Crachami illustrates something troubling about the intersection of flesh and culture during the Romantic period: singular bodies become subject to regulatory norms in liberal society. The Sicilian Dwarf's extreme tininess set her apart for special attention and treatment. But that treatment proved lethal, suggesting that the simple acts of observing and examining abnormality might be ways of managing it, maybe even eradicating it. Caroline Crachami's small but singular body shows how flesh relates to culture less as its object than its medium, the material through which relations of power circulate to reproduce cultural norms. Norms of embodiment coordinate the agencies of flesh, directing their energies toward normal behaviors. That a ten-year-old girl under two feet tall must be seen and valued as a miniature bride illustrates the force of such norms. They literally incarnate beliefs and values.

This book examines the part physical monstrosities play in the operation of such norms in British culture of the Romantic period, occasioning their reproduction or soliciting their transformation. Caroline Crachami's story is a sad one. Her singularity succumbs to common measures. But her story is nonetheless exemplary for the way it illustrates the material force of a norm of embodiment. Such a norm seeks an exception to prove its rule. It assimilates as it pathologizes, assimilates in a weird way *because* it pathologizes. And since Crachami's ordeal takes place at about the time the word "abnormal" acquires popularity, it illustrates the historicity of this normative logic. The norm of embodiment that both identifies and destroys the singularity of the Sicilian Dwarf circulates through the many bodies whose collective agencies produce, by the end of the eighteenth century, an increasingly liberal society in Great Britain.

British Romanticism needs to be approached from the materialist perspective of such developments. The time is past when it was possible to remain complacently faithful to its own idealizations.[1] Corporeally considered, the period of cultural history that corresponds with Romanticism in England saw the installation of a norm of embodiment—call it "the proper body"—that served (and in some ways still serves) to regulate the agencies of bodies in liberal society. Much of the work familiarly deemed Romantic involves a confrontation with that norm that goes unnoticed to eyes trained to see ideas as what matter most. But bodies also matter, to invoke a potent theoretical formula, and the pages that follow will take a few, perhaps halting, steps toward an account of the cultural politics of embodiment during the Romantic period. That end will require stepping beyond literature as a privileged idiom to consider the effects of other discourses and practices on some of Romanticism's major achievements. As themselves instances of cultural politics, those achievements participate directly in the reproduction or rupture of the norms they circulate. And because bodies really do matter, the measure of Romanticism's success will not be the spiritual consolation it provides so much as the material freedom it promotes.

The British Romantic period coincides with the cultural consolidation of a proper body.[2] As a norm of embodiment, the proper body regulates corporeal agencies, but not as a law or an originary principle. Such a norm is not a prescription so much as a performance of embodiment. It emerges out of what Judith Butler describes as an array of "complex cultural exchanges among bodies" to regulate their agencies (*Trouble* 127). So the proper body, and the cultural logic of embodiment more generally, arises as a performative effect of a multiplicity of discourses and practices that make such a norm possible without determining it absolutely. It acquires force as a regulative norm through material repetition, the reenactment of the "complex cultural exchanges" that enable it. It remains, then, to enumerate some (but undoubtedly not all) of the discourses and practices whose interplay gives rise to this norm of embodiment. But it should be understood that such a norm is in a sense nowhere and everywhere in British culture during the Romantic period, dispersed among a multiplicity of discourses and practices and reenacted in a variety of bodily behaviors. It is for this reason that monstrosities prove so troubling to liberal society. Not only do they jam cultural machinery that produces the norm of the proper body, but they challenge its performative authority, inserting the material fact of bodily difference into the circuit of its reenactment. Monstrosities afford an occasion for the cultural (re)production of the proper body.

As a cultural norm of embodiment, then, the proper body emerges as a means of regulating corporeal agencies in liberal society. Its production involves the interplay of at least four distinct discourses or practices: those of liberalism, free-market economics, British nationalism, and professionalized medicine. Michel Foucault has shown how European culture of the eighteenth century undertakes the extraordinary project of producing a manageable population from among a largely undefined, amorphous populace. For Foucault liberal society operates by means of a dispersed network of regulatory norms that discipline bodies toward the end of a socially serviceable docility.[3] The proper body serves culturally as a disciplinary strategy that regulates individual bodies and behaviors without reference to higher powers, secular or divine.

Liberalism, dubbed by C. B. Macpherson "the political theory of possessive individualism," provides theoretical and political impetus to the norm of the proper body.[4] Macpherson shows how liberal political theory takes the individual for the unit of civil society and the marketplace for its epitome. It does so on the basis of a brilliant if dubious description of the individual as a proprietor. As Macpherson puts it, "The individual was seen neither as a moral whole, nor as part of a larger social whole, but as an owner of himself, . . . free inasmuch as he is proprietor of his person and capacities" (3). An individual *is* what he (never she) possesses, and most fundamentally he possesses himself. Civil society as liberalism conceives it becomes an alliance of such proprietors, whose apparent autonomy gets reinforced by the operations of the marketplace: "Society becomes a lot of free equal individuals related to each other as proprietors of their own capacities and of what they have acquired by their exercise. Society consists of relations of exchange between proprietors" (3). If these possessive individuals owe allegiance to nothing beyond the anonymous laws of the market, then their freedom to exchange goods and accumulate property becomes the equivalent of their freedom as human beings. For the good liberal as Macpherson describes him, property makes the man.

But the belief that possession produces the individual arises from a theory of embodiment tacitly advanced by the foundational claims of liberalism. Property can make men only because men make property. The political theory of possessive individualism identifies economic with human activity on the basis of the way bodies work. A society modeled on the behaviors of autonomous property owners requires that each individual have ready access to the means of production. That access takes the material form of the body and comes through its labor. There will be more to say in the pages ahead about the relationship in liberalism between labor, property, and a norm of embodiment. Here what matters is to grasp the implications of taking labor for the engine of autonomy. John Locke, the most influential early theorist of liberal society, at least in England, shows how labor transfers what is common to humanity into the possession of the laboring individual:

> It is evident, that though the things of Nature are given in common, yet Man
> (by being Master of himself, and *Proprietor of his own Person,* and the Actions
> or *Labour* of it) had still in himself *the great Foundation of Property*; and that
> which made up the great part of what he applyed to the Support or Comfort of
> his being, when Invention and Arts had improved the conveniencies of Life,
> was perfectly his own, and did not belong in common to others. (Locke, *Two
> Treatises* 316–17)

The labor of the body legitimates not just property but the individual that possesses it. If there is a material basis for individual autonomy, it is the appropriating capacity of the laboring body. For with labor comes value, the real difference between a common thing and commodity, and with value comes possession, the right of ownership that substantiates the individual.

So persuaded is Locke of the link between labor and rightful ownership that he justifies a colonial policy of domination over bodies incapable of labor or whose labor accrues no value. That at least is the implication of his calculation of the relative value of land in England and in the New World:

> An Acre of Land that bears here Twenty Bushels of Wheat, and another in
> *America,* which, with the same Husbandry, would do the like, are without

doubt, of the same natural, intrinsick Value. But yet the Benefit Mankind receives from the one, in a Year, is worth 5 *l*. and from the other possibly not worth
a Penny, if all the Profit an *Indian* received from it were to be valued, and sold
here. (316)

Because Indians do not labor, their land lacks value and barely benefits mankind. Locke's colonialist accounting of labor and the value it produces subjects all bodies to an abstract standard. Indian and European bodies are the
same. Differences between them are not materially but morally produced. If
Indians won't work it is no fault of their bodies. The land they refuse to value
belongs, in advance, to bodies that *will*. By making individual autonomy an
effect of the appropriative capacity of labor, Locke measures singular material bodies against a norm of human embodiment. Not only do such measures
serve ideologically to justify colonial ambitions abroad, they also come culturally to reinforce regulative bodily practices at home.

The norm of the proper body serves just such purposes in liberal society,
but toward the end of maintaining class rather than colonial domination.
Macpherson shows how the character of the possessive individual shifts with
the introduction of money into human affairs. Where prior to that moment,
possession took its natural limit in subsistence, with money comes the possibility of unlimited accumulation. Money, after all, transmutes the decaying
fruits of human labor into permanent and plastic wealth. Money therefore
becomes one measure of Locke's abstract bodily standard. As the aim of the
possessive individual shifts from subsistence to accumulation, the appropriative capacity of labor turns increasingly abstract, until it becomes possible
to value bodies according to the relative *physicality* of their labor. Stated
simply, in liberal society bodies that perform the least physical labor warrant the most social prestige. Their noblest agency occurs in the abstract
and unlimited terms of accumulation rather than material and limited
terms of subsistence—when driven by reason rather than muscle. That's why
Macpherson argues that while for Locke "the labouring class is a necessary
part of the nation its members are not in fact full members of the body politic
and have no claim to be so" (221–22). Laboring bodies remain too material to
realize Locke's abstract standard. That norm coordinates individual economic
activity with collective social enterprise in a way that justifies the subordination of bodies that labor. The proper body thus legitimates class as well as
colonial domination. Macpherson states the case with morbid clarity: Locke
"justifies, as natural, a class differential in rights and in rationality, and by
doing so provides a positive moral basis for capitalist society" (221). In its
abstraction, the proper body breeds capital and shits class.

But liberal political theory alone doesn't account for the force of this
norm. A second legitimating discourse is that of free-market economics. If
Macpherson makes economic activity the raison d'etre of the possessive individual, that is because eighteenth-century economics insists on it. The great

theorist of the free market is of course Adam Smith, who readily assents to
Locke's assertion that labor produces property.[5] But in keeping with his project of anatomizing the wealth of nations, Smith emphasizes not merely the
productivity of labor but its characteristic divisibility: "It is the great multi-
plication of the productions of all the different arts, in consequence of the division of labor, which occasions, in a well-governed society, that universal opulence which extends itself to the lowest ranks of the people" (166). Leaving
aside for a moment the presumed pervasiveness of that opulence, it's clear
that Smith valorizes labor for its abstract capacity to be divided into units.
His famous account of the production of pins, illustrating the way property
is multiplied when labor is specialized, proves labor subject to quantification
as productivity becomes a mathematical rather than material operation. The
division of labor makes working men into abstract integers, variable parts
of an economic process that renders their agency fungible. With divisibility,
to put the point another way, comes exchangeability. The whole purpose of a
market economy is to maximize the efficacy of exchange:

> When the division of labour has been once thoroughly established, it is but a
> very small part of a man's wants which the produce of his own labour can sup-
> ply. He supplies the far greater part of them by exchanging that surplus part
> of the produce of his own labour, which is over and above his own consumption,
> for such parts of the produce of other men's labour as he has occasion for. Every
> man thus lives by exchanging, or becomes in some measure a merchant, and the
> society itself grows to be what is properly a commercial society. (172)

Smith adds the element of exchangeability to the cultural norm of embodiment. Bodies turn fungible in two ways, first by being divisible according to
units of labor, second by being exchangeable according to units of value. To
live by exchanging requires bodies capable of abstract equivalence at every
step of the economic process.

The norm of the proper body thus acquires an almost universal applicability, so long as human bodies prove capable of divisible, exchangeable labor.
Perhaps predictably, Smith identifies civilization with these capacities and
denies access to those others whose bodies assert their own substance, as in
his infamous comparison of the princely comforts of "the industrial, frugal
peasant" to those "of many an African king, the absolute master of the lives
and liberties of ten thousand naked savages" (168). As Mark Seltzer observes
in a different context, the relative disembodiment of exchangeable labor requires more deeply embodied bodies against which to measure its prestige.[6]
Colonization provides an occasion for measuring this prestige externally. Internally, British culture measures it by means of a universally applicable norm of
proper embodiment. Bodies not readily interchangeable—palpably improper
bodies—fail to achieve individuality and therefore humanity in a free-market

economy. Unless assimilated to that norm, they remain merest matter, monstrosities that come to trouble the universality of the human.

Foucault has shown how Smith's analysis of wealth bespeaks a classical episteme in its appeal to labor as a unit of value in total system of equivalences.[7] What distinguishes later theorists of political economy, in particular Thomas Malthus and David Ricardo, is their tendency instead to view labor not as the sign but the source of value. Wealth isn't simply there to measure, as for Smith. Rather it accumulates over time through the material conditions that give rise to production. The historicity of labor involves economics in a confrontation with human finitude, most spectacularly in Malthus's original version of *An Essay on the Principle of Population* (1798). As Catherine Gallagher points out, "In the *Essay,* concrete laboring bodies, and not abstract units of labor, are the measures of value" (96). Malthus biologizes labor as he historicizes it, emphasizing in his mordant way its poverty of means. His fatal dictum, that subsistence increases arithmetically while population increases geometrically, makes labor a losing proposition, since the production of food can never keep pace with the reproduction of people. Biology trumps economics in the game of life, which is why Foucault concludes that by the late eighteenth century "*Homo oeconomicus* is not the human being who represents his own needs to himself, and the objects capable of satisfying them; he is the human being who spends, wears out, and wastes his life in evading the imminence of death" (*Order* 257). With Malthus the possessive individual comes to be defined through a desperate and terminal confrontation with finitude.

But that only enhances the normative force of the proper body. Malthus's grim calculations materialize the abstract exchangeability of labor. That's why food serves as his privileged commodity: its value is a function of its ability to renew the laboring body. For Malthus that body incarnates a fatal tension between eating and intercourse, arithmetic and geometry. Or as he puts it, "The power of population is so superior to the power in the earth to produce subsistence for man, that premature death must in some shape or other visit the human race" (51–52). Viewed from a corporeal perspective, this statement describes an organism at odds with itself, torn apart by its own conflicting powers—a terminal congeries of forces. Gallagher observes how "the healthy body here has lost, in the very power of its fecundity, the integrity of its boundaries and hence comes to be a sign of its opposite" (85). But for Malthus the body is more than a sign. It is a natural organism that exceeds the limits of nature. Reproduction so outstrips production that an excess of the body's life menaces the life of the body. Left to its own energies, then, the body breeds monstrosities. In its excessive capacity for reproduction, it fatally deviates from a norm of health. By biologizing labor Malthus adds a physiological valence to the norm of the proper body.

The force of that valence shows up in his quibble with Condorcet regarding the plausibility of perfectibility. Condorcet's utopian dreams offend against physiological norms, which Malthus illustrates with an aside to the art of breeding: "In the famous Leicestershire breed of sheep, the object is to procure them with small heads and small legs. . . . it is evident that we might go on till the heads and legs were evanescent quantities, but this is so palpable an absurdity that we may be quite sure that the premises are not just and that there really is a limit, though we cannot see it or say exactly where it is" (61). Similarly, although we may not be able to see it or say it, there really is a limit to proper embodiment, a norm beyond which bodies cease to be socially productive. Such are the implications of Malthus's biologized economics, which reinforce that norm with the menace of reproductive monstrosity. The only proper recourse is to labor within the limits of the norm, as in Malthus's strange example of "the ancient family of the Bickerstaffs, who are said to have been very successful in whitening the skins, and increasing the height of their race by prudent marriages, particularly by that very judicious cross with Maud, the milk-maid, by which some capital defects in the constitutions of the family were corrected" (63). Such are the rewards of proper embodiment: for the genteel, heightened whiteness, and for the commoner, upward mobility.

There are other rewards too, not least among them the pride of being British. Another discourse through which the norm of the proper body circulates is that of British nationalism. If, as Benedict Anderson so usefully suggests, a nation is "an imagined political community," eighteenth-century England witnesses the creation of a community of Britons.[8] With the emergence of liberal society arises the prospect of British national identity. And part of what makes that identity possible is a pervasive sense of common embodiment that mobilizes feelings of national belonging. Linda Colley has done much to document the rise and reward of becoming British. She shows meticulously how, beginning with the Act of Union that joined England, Scotland, and Wales in 1707, the cultural project of creating Great Britain involved producing terms of inclusiveness to unite a diverse populace into an identifiable population. As another historian, Gerald Newman, puts it, "The English nationalist movement was essentially cultural in origin, a cultural and ideological growth without any clear political purpose at all at its beginning" (168). That England avoided the revolutionary unrest that convulsed France testifies to the effectiveness of that cultural project, all the more astonishing for not being a willful policy of the British state. Nationalism arose in England as if by consensus among an aspiring bourgeoisie. That's much too free a formulation, but it indicates something of the role played by liberalism and free-market economics in the rise of British nationalism.

These discourses interact to assert a kind of cultural imperative of national belonging that the norm of the proper body affirms in corporeal terms. Colley insists that this imperative was not among the machinations of a ruling class: "much of the growing sensitivity and receptivity to the nation which undoubtedly existed was spontaneously generated from below" ("Class" 109). British nationalism is better understood as a discourse that distributes relations of power not by imposing but by producing them. Becoming British was not an ideology but an opportunity for participation in an imagined community and affirmation of a collective identity. There are obvious historical reasons for its effectiveness. Not only did becoming British turn possessive individualism into a patriotic cause, nationalizing liberalism (making commerce the quintessential English activity), it provided a referent for other practices that extended the membership of that community. With a population on the increase (doubling between 1780 and 1836), with a press proliferating all kinds of reading material, with a monarchy reorienting its rule toward the mobilization of public opinion, British culture saw conditions arise that were peculiarly conducive to a national identity that promoted membership in liberal society while manufacturing consensus within it. Nationalism became, in John Womack's words,

> a kind of liberal education for traditional individuals on the move out of tradition . . . promising them the excitement of exercising their wills like anyone else of "the people." It . . . felt to them like liberation. Nationalism has also served as a kind of professional education for individuals on the move into the bourgeoisie . . . promising them the excitement of imposing their wills in championing "the people." It . . . felt to them like responsibility. (quoted in Colley, "Class" 109–10)

British nationalism imagined a community of possessive individuals united by common causes.

And no cause was so common by the late eighteenth century as war with France. Colley insists on the role war played in the production of British national identity. England was at war from 1756 to 1763, from 1775 to 1783, from 1793 to 1802, and from 1803 to 1815. It would not be too much to say that the identity of the Briton was forged in the furnace of war. Perhaps politics—even cultural politics—is another name for war because war is so conducive to national, and in this case liberal, identity. That seems at least to have been the case in eighteenth-century England. Pervasive warfare provided an occasion for forging a nation. Most obviously it offered a cause to rally the population. Wars can of course be unpopular, but in this instance their historical coincidence with the emergence of an increasingly inclusive bourgeoisie provided an opportunity for an otherwise politically disenfranchised populace to acquire a say in the life of the nation. As Colley puts it, "Being a patriot was a way of claiming the right to participate in British political life, and ultimately a means of demanding a much broader access to citizenship" (*Britons* 6). From the point of view of the individual patriot, war was a way into liberal society.

From the point of view of the state, war was a way of managing it. This strategy proved especially useful during the wars with revolutionary and Napoleonic France, which as Colley puts it, "compelled a reluctant and fundamentally oligarchic British government to recruit the nation in an unprecedented fashion" ("Class" 101). With the threat of French invasion between 1803 and 1805 the number of adult men in Great Britain involved in military service was one in five, showing how effectively a very real military threat consolidates an imagined community. It also shows how such communities get built over the bodies, often dead bodies, of some menacing Other. France was that Other during the war, but before and after, too. Becoming British meant something culturally superior to being classed among the French, whose characteristic Catholicism, rationalism, republicanism, and cuisine all smacked of corruption. The British cult of sincerity and culture of common sense, as David Simpson has shown so well, comprise an aggressive rejection of French difference that mobilizes feelings of belonging toward an affirmation of national identity.[9] Extended war with the French only confirmed their menacing otherness. A British nation of possessive individuals identifies itself against a foppish, frog-eating people.

That eating should enter into such distinctions shows how nationalism involves and invests its believers' bodies. The discourse of British national identity adds a valence of collective belonging to the cultural norm of the proper body. Proper embodiment becomes a matter of national inclusiveness that incorporates the Briton to the very bones. The force of its operation can be clearly observed in popular cultural practices such as caricature.[10] With the rise of liberal society comes a public culture openly at play with the proper body, challenging its normalizing force even while affirming its cultural function. Caricature exploits the tendency of norms to produce deviations. Grotesque images only appear so by tacitly invoking the norms from which they deviate. It seems appropriate, then, that the consolidation of liberal society, wherein normative discourses all but saturate bodied agency, should be accompanied by an outburst of grotesque caricature. Thomas Rowlandson, James Gillray, George Cruikshank, and a host of lesser-known caricaturists foment a rage for disorder that makes perfect political sense in a world of increasing normalizations. An article in the *Morning Chronicle* from 1796 illustrates the point handily: "The taste of the day leans entirely to caricature. . . . We are no longer satisfied with propriety and neatness, we must have something grotesque and disproportioned, cumbrous with ornament and gigantic in its dimensions." What this observer fails to notice, however, is the link between propriety and disproportion. In a cultural context of nationalist ideology and normative discourse the grotesque serves the double function of transgressing and affirming the proprieties that make it possible.

Such at least is the way Gillray's caricatures work. Their notorious grotesqueness and vulgarity transgress a norm such as that of the proper body ultimately to affirm it and the national identity it asserts. This logic appears clearest in frankly nationalist prints, as for instance the one titled "The King of Brobdingnag and Gulliver" (1803), in which a super-sized George III holds Little Boney on the palm of his hand and views the tiny tyrant through a spyglass. The giant and the mite both deviate monstrously from the norm of human stature, but this double transgression only confirms the Britishness embodied in the king, who in a neat reversal towers as Gulliver over the so-called king of Brobdingnag. British identity beats French by the measure of the national, monarchal body. More typical of such encounters, and reproducing a nationalist agenda, is a print Gillray published in 1792 titled "French Liberty/British Slavery" (Figure 2). It contrasts a Frenchman eating onions over a smoldering fire with a Briton eating beef at a burgeoning table. The physical difference between them is unequivocal.[11] Gillray invokes stereotypes that in his arch view sum up national differences between French and British bodies. The former are pointed, lank, and scrawny, the latter round, thick, and fleshy. While neither is a paragon of health (French liberty is emaciated while British slavery obese), the Briton has the better meal and the living luxury of mistaking abundance for privation. Both bodies represent a deviation from the proper norm, but the Briton is in a better position to remedy it, since he suffers from an excess of flesh in need only of better management. The Frenchman can't put on the proper body because he hasn't the means available. His puny diet cannot incorporate the norm of human health. Proper embodiment belongs to Britain as a natural, national endowment, and Gillray's print violates that integrity only to reaffirm its moral and material authority. The somatic lesson of "British slavery" is to submit a superabundant flesh to better management. The French haven't the physique to endure the disciplines of true liberty. As so often is the case, Gillray's caricature promotes national identity by depicting its deformities. The norm's exception proves the rule that proper bodies incorporate the Briton. In just this way the discourse of nationalism, which so many of Gillray's caricatures promote, mobilizes feelings of collective belonging to reinforce a bodied norm.

Finally, as with the discourses of liberalism, economics, and nationalism, the norm of the proper body moves through the practices of an increasingly professionalized medicine. The advancing availability of treatments of all kinds makes medicine a means of embodying a moral economy of health, one whose congenial fit with the marketplace persists into the present. But medicine in the late eighteenth century was no one thing. Roy and Dorothy Porter have shown definitively how multiple were its practices and how various its practitioners. The traditional view of an increasingly coherent medical profession divided hierarchically into three groups (physicians, surgeons, and apothecaries), and regulated directly by three corresponding corporate bodies (the College of Physicians, the Corporation of Surgeons, and the Society of Apothecaries), belies the profusion of medical options available to the sick in the eighteenth century.[12] There were highly trained professionals like William

Figure 2. James Gillray, *French Liberty/British Slavery* (21 December 1792). Copyright The British Museum.

Hunter, the renowned anatomist and man midwife to the queen, or William Cheselden, whose mercifully swift lithotomies (cutting for bladder stones) were the stuff of legend. Such men made their careers by catering to the rich. But there were populists too, like William Buchan, whose *Domestic Medicine* became a standard reference in households throughout Britain. And there were plenty of quacks, like the infamous Dr. Katterfelto, whose necromantic black cats gave off salubrious sparks while he hawked remedies for influenza, which was spread, he insisted, by microscopic insects.[13] To fall ill in liberal society was to enter a marketplace of treatments ranging from scientific to superstitious and including everything in between.

The Porters emphasize the openness of that market, its promotion of genuine medical alternatives rather than prescription of treatment on the basis of income, gender, or social status: "because no single group of doctors could reliably cure, patients inevitably shopped around" (27). The commercial *Medical Register,* first published in 1779, lists three thousand medical practitioners in England, a figure since proved too low but indicating the wide availability of services for those in need. In this open market of medicine the sick contracted for treatment as individuals, consulting experts and quacks alike on a personal basis for private relief. Their afflictions were singular and their remedies were contingent, often less the object of institutional knowledge than an occasion for practical know-how. Christopher Lawrence has suggested that in the "face-to-face society" of eighteenth-century England such personal medical relationships were one means of maintaining social order: "people were

known and made their way in the world by and through their personal con-
nections. To be known in this way was to be subject to various obligations and
these were the ties that bound eighteenth-century society together. Personal
knowledge was social control" (*Medicine* 44). Practical medicine created personal relationships that reinforced a network of obligation binding individuals together in one body politic.

But Lawrence also suggests that by the last decades of the eighteenth
century this means of maintaining social order was giving way to another, one
that worked through operative norms rather than contingent needs. Medicine, while not solely responsible for this shift, advanced it by promoting a
new view of illness. According to Lawrence,

> Rational medicine in the eighteenth century had a language for constituting a
> person in terms of his life history and experiences. It could describe a person's
> own *natural* state and (sometimes) restore him to it if he fell sick. Nineteenth-
> century medical men were developing a language (which we still use) for situ-
> ating all people in relation to each other, for measuring their deviation from the
> *normal,* and, increasingly, for managing their deviations from that norm. (45)

The last decades of the eighteenth century witness the installation of this
turn from contingency to norm, rendering bodies proper and a medium for
the circulation of power. Foucault describes a similar development in post-
revolutionary France and shows how medical discourse contributes to the
production of a docile body susceptible to disciplinary practices that constrain
its force and limit its mobility.[14] While British society of the time differs significantly from that of the French, particularly in its ideological commitments
to liberalism and a free market, it betrays a related tendency to manage its
population by way of normative discourses and practices. Medicine cannot
but become complicit in that process; its object is the human body and its aim
is human health. To the extent that it achieves such ends by way of a norm
it (re)produces *normal* and therefore proper bodies. Just because it promotes
health along the way does not mean it operates in a power vacuum. Health
is not without political effects. Lawrence puts the point concretely: "Doctors,
after all, dealt with the basic stuff out of which societies are made—men's
and women's bodies—and they made those bodies into the sorts of objects of
knowledge that helped to make it possible for . . . industrial society to function in the way it did" (45). By the late eighteenth century, medical knowledge
and practice were promoting a proper body suited to the norms of life in a
liberal, commercial, increasingly bourgeois society.

In *The Birth of the Clinic,* Foucault examines the history that assigns
medicine this cultural vocation. Thanks to a reorganization of the medical gaze
and its institutionalization in clinical practice, "In the ordering of human
existence [medicine] assumes a normative posture, which authorized it not
only to distribute advice as to healthy life, but also to dictate standards for

physical and moral relations of the individual and of the society in which he lives" (34). The emergence of liberal society becomes possible by means of material—and medical—norms that coordinate the agencies of individual and collective bodies. That Jürgen Habermas ignores the function of such norms in his influential study of eighteenth-century culture, *The Structural Transformation of the Public Sphere,* betrays his own deep allegiance to liberalism, his easy belief that critical reflection trumps material practice. But that reflection acquires force only through the operation of cultural norms such as that of the proper body. Such norms normalize. One of the effects of critical reflection is to occlude their operation.

As the preceding account suggests, a cultural norm of embodiment amounts less to a clearly defined conceptual paradigm than to a loose ensemble of discursive effects. It advances the logistics of what Foucault elsewhere calls "political anatomy," a "mechanics of power" that produces material bodies subject to self-management. As such, political anatomy involves "a multiplicity of often minor processes, of different origin and scattered location, which overlap, repeat, or imitate one another, support one another, distinguish themselves from one another according to their domain of application, converge and gradually produce a blueprint of a general method" (*Discipline* 138). The political anatomy of the proper body involves the convergence of an array of discourses and practices, among which liberalism, free-market economics, British nationalism, and professionalized medicine seem particularly productive. The bodily norm that arises through their interaction is so familiar as to be all but transparent: a private body whose labor produces property and is therefore fungible, a British body whose health reproduces propriety and is therefore normative.

The pages that follow will confront other characteristics of this transparent, compulsory body: its whiteness, its rationality, its masculinity, its able-bodied bulk. Emphasis will fall not only on the norm that reproduces such qualities but also on those corporeal deviations that disrupt its operation: monstrosities. That bodies turn docile in liberal society seems by now, thanks to Foucault, to go almost without saying. But that monstrosities don't always, or often can't, should occasion an examination of the limits of docility. Monstrosities often trouble the operation of the proper body, materially diverting forces of normalization away from (stereo)typical ends. They haunt the political anatomy of the human in British Romantic culture. That is why the work of Judith Butler proves so useful to the task of affirming their disturbing life. Butler theorizes the materialization of sexed bodies and the coincidental production of a gendered subject: what she calls the physical and psychological "girling of the girl." Hence her claim that "bodies only endure, only live within the productive constraints of certain highly gendered regulatory schemas" (*Bodies* xi). Remove the word "gendered" from this sentence and it precisely describes the operation of the cultural norm of the proper body. As an ensemble of discursive effects, it is a regulatory norm that produces the material bodies it legitimates. In liberal society, the norm of the proper body constrains the cultural (re)production of individual bodies.

In Butler's sense, then, that norm is performative, an instance of "a reiterative and citational practice by which discourse produces the effects that it names" (2). Such practices need not be discursive in a strict sense but might include material practices as well, such as eating or giving birth or correcting a congenital deformity—the kinds of practices that medicine makes the occasion of its operations. Where Butler's sense of the performative is thus broadened, it becomes a powerful tool of cultural analysis, showing not only how the force of such repeatable practices incorporates cultural norms but also how those norms become disrupted by materially deviant—and therefore monstrous—bodies. Butler's exclusive focus on the formation of the subject somewhat distracts from the material practices that produce it, but her description of the logic of their operation bears repeating: "the subject is constituted through the force of exclusion and abjection, one which produces a constitutive outside to the subject, an abjected outside, which is, after all 'inside' the subject as its own founding repudiation" (3). Simply put, a performative norm both produces and excludes, produces by excluding. The norm of the proper body thus constitutes monstrosities through exclusion.

No wonder they haunt the human. Monstrosities materialize its constitutive repudiation. As Butler puts it, "the human is not only produced over and against the inhuman, but through a set of foreclosures, radical erasures, that are, strictly speaking, refused the possibility of cultural articulation" (8). The point here is not that the inhuman is the logical double of the human, but that the forces which produce the latter actively refuse the possibility and therefore life of the former. Monstrosities in this sense *cannot live* except through assimilation to the norm of the proper body. What is lost in that process is the value in liberal society of life that deviates materially from the norm. And that's why monstrosities provide a material occasion not just for observing norms of embodiment in action but also for advancing their disruption and transformation. Performative bodies never completely materialize, or rather their materializations are never completely achieved. Possibilities persist that escape the norm's refusal. The trick is to put them into play, to make monstrosities matter. That's the force of Butler's troubling and promising question: "What challenge does that excluded and abjected realm produce . . . that might force a radical rearticulation of what qualifies as bodies that matter, ways of living that count as 'life,' lives worth protecting, lives worth saving, lives worth grieving?" (16).

It has fallen to queer theory, race studies, and disability studies to offer substantive answers to that question—perhaps inevitably, since the lives of gays and lesbians, racial minorities, and disabled people have failed, culturally speaking, to pass the test of proper embodiment. Michael Warner has written eloquently about the operation of such norms in contemporary culture. In his view the trouble with "normal" is that it circulates power and distributes bodies accordingly, conferring respectability on those whose behaviors, for instance sexual behaviors, accommodate prevailing norms. Warner ties the rise of normality in mass culture to the rule of statistics over lives and bodies, the appeal of which comes through the identifications they produce. People are "constantly bombarded by the images of statistical populations and their norms, continually invited to make an implicit comparison between themselves and the mass of other bodies" (53–54). Such identities are seductive because they seem shared, but the normality they produce has pathologized actual sexual behavior ever since "normal came to mean right, proper, healthy" (57). Identity trumps activity as a way of valuing physical life.

Warner calls for a new kind of normality, one that affirms not identity but variation. Drawing on the work of the historian of medicine Georges Canguilhem, he suggests that deviations from a norm might not necessarily signal pathology. Canguilhem's understanding of physical health involves the capacity to establish new norms in new circumstances: "Man feels in good health—which is health itself—only when he feels more than normal—that is, adapted to the environment and its demands—but normative, capable of following new norms of life" (200). Becoming normative in this sense would require a transformation of the regulatory discourses that reproduce proper embodiment. It would hazard an affirmation of the abject, pathologized life of monstrosities. When being deemed less than normal becomes an occasion for becoming more, norms aren't transcended so much as transformed—toward the possibilities of new embodiments. The proper body becomes a humanist skin, shed to materialize new kinds of life, higher kinds of health. Theorists committed to such possibilities—Warner and Eve Sedgwick in queer theory, Paul Gilroy and David Theo Goldberg in race studies, Rosmarie Garland Thomson and Michael Bérubé in disability studies—force a reevaluation of which bodies really matter and how they materialize, and their example proves invaluable to the future of studies in Romanticism. Monstrosities may haunt the human, but they hound it too—toward other embodiments.

That's why, as Steven Shaviro maintains, there can be nothing utopian or redemptive about the new life of monstrosities. Whatever freedom they might assert from the norm of the proper body amounts only to the freedom to struggle toward new incarnations, physically and politically. It seems questionable, therefore, to associate monstrosity with visions of excess or dreams of utopia, as has been the habit of poststructuralists such as Jacques Derrida.[15] Monstrosities symbolize nothing; they materialize afflictions, politicize subjections. Only because they come into carnality through relations of power in the first place can they challenge those relations, transforming their regulatory force. Shaviro emphasizes the materiality of such disruptions, which alone accounts for their political possibilities: "The body is a potential site of resistance, not in spite of but *because* of its being a necessary relay, target, and support of power. The flesh is perpetually monstrous, unstable, out of control" (143–44). Hence the regulatory force of norms such as that of the proper body. Monstrosities can redeploy their powers, inspiring social reforms, creating new solidarities, promoting a politics of inclusiveness. And in doing so they might make possible the "special sort of sociability" that Warner associates with contemporary queer culture, "a relation to others" that "begins in an acknowledgment of all that is most abject and least reputable" (35).

One way to advance the project of such a sociability is to examine the history of the culture of normality that Warner describes so well. That the proper body still functions to some extent today as a regulatory norm attests to its force as a way of making bodies matter in liberal society. Describing its historical emergence challenges its authority, reiterating its present function with the difference of the past. Such normalizing discourses have a history that shows their consolidation to be a complicated process involving resistances as well as constraints. By investigating that history it becomes possible to see how those discourses came to function so naturally. Where Butler and Warner in their different ways address the operative logic of normalization, neither attends much to the details of its history, those discursive and material practices that constitute the cultural politics of embodiment in liberal society. The preceding account provides a general background for the way culture materializes bodies, or more particularly the way liberalism, free-market economics, British nationalism, and professionalized medicine interact to constrain, regulate, and reproduce them.

The monstrosities that culture breeds also become material terms for its transformation. This book promotes that possibility by examining the relationship between British Romantic writers and the discourses and practices that set the terms for proper embodiment. The Romantics were the first to respond fully to the material conditions of life in liberal society, and thanks to the example of the French revolution, some were keenly invested in the prospect of its radical transformation. If that prospect never materialized, it is partly because of the affective appeal and regulatory force of cultural norms such as that of the proper body. The task of a historically oriented cultural criticism would be to show how that norm came to take hold of British bodies—to make them matter, in Butler's phrase—and how particular Romantic writers responded to its force. The traditional association between Romanticism and monstrosity (a.k.a. "Romantic Agony") has less to do with psychological trauma or emotional excess than with the social project of proper embodiment in liberal society. The monstrosities of Romanticism trouble the matter of normality. So the aims here are twofold: first to examine further the emergence of the proper body as a regulatory norm, and second to show

how monstrosities of various kinds become occasions for advancing, resisting, or transforming its operations in British culture of the late eighteenth and early nineteenth centuries.

Warner urges a sociability that begins by acknowledging the abject and disreputable. This book tries to advance such a sociability by forcing an encounter with forms of life and ways of living that traditional literary and cultural criticism of British Romanticism disregards. It examines the anatomy of Romantic abjection, incompletely of course, but toward the end of making bodies a matter of cultural politics. By approaching monstrosities as the "constitutive outside" of the proper body, a criticism becomes possible that troubles such distinctions—and perhaps too the political order they reinforce. The chapters that follow fall into three sections, three examinations, assessing different functions of abjection.

The first section, "Incorporations," examines the cultural production during the Romantic period of the proper body and its constitutive monstrosities. Chapter 1 pursues in more detail the role medicine plays in incorporating and legitimating a cultural norm of embodiment. The work of John Hunter (1728–93), the great comparative anatomist and father of modern surgery, shows how late-eighteenth-century medicine built a body strangely conducive to the needs of liberal society. Physiology becomes a regulatory discourse that produces bodily health by appealing to operational norms, making it a means of incorporating—materially—liberalism. Chapter 2 examines a range of practices showing how monstrosities occasion the production and subversion of human values in liberal society. Humanitarian treatments of singular bodies demonstrate the moral force of proper embodiment, while the annual festivities of Bartholomew Fair prove that monstrosities can produce a space of their own. Chapter 3 focuses on the way the proper body gets raced in liberal society, advancing the superior virtue of whiteness as much as health. Black African bodies prove deviant by this standard. The curious cultural fact that at just this moment anatomists and physicians advance themselves as experts in artistic expression shows how medicine and aesthetics converge to maintain this racial exclusion.

"Habituations," the second section of this book, investigates the relationship between drug use and proper embodiment. Junkie bodies are abject bodies—a judgment hard to argue with even today. This judgment first acquires social force during the Romantic period, and abjection has been the junkie's lot ever since. Samuel Taylor Coleridge's opium habit is the subject of chapter 4, which argues not merely that such a habit troubles the norm of the proper body but also that it enhances the transformative effect of Coleridge's poetry. Coleridge is interesting for his inability to affirm his habit. Instead he elaborates a philosophy that reinforces regulatory social norms. Not so Thomas De Quincey. Once hooked, he becomes a magus of self-medication. Chapter 5 shows how De Quincey tests philosophical idealism against bodily life in his

Confessions of an English Opium Eater. Any critique of pure reason turns out to be a high-flown apology for the proper body, one De Quincey refuses in his faithfulness to the material effects of eating opium.

The book's final section, "Appropriations," examines the ways in which abject body parts incarnate power relations. The parts in question, the placenta in one case and a deformed foot in the other, expose bodies to the operations of a medicine that appropriates what it treats. Women are the monstrosities treated in chapter 6, or rather one woman in particular: Mary Wollstonecraft. The relationship between her liberal feminist politics and the medical practice of obstetrics illustrates the fate of generative flesh in liberal society. Chapter 7 diagnoses the similar fate of Lord Byron's deformed foot. The focus here is less on Byron's deformity per se or his personal feelings about it than the prosthetic devices he used to heal or to hide it. Prosthetics in early-nineteenth-century England served partly to incorporate national identity, embodying the Briton where prosthesis meets flesh. Byron's boot makes his efforts at creating new norms of embodiment and forms of sociability all the more monstrous for their deviation from the patriotic norm.

Such are the cultural politics of embodiment in the increasingly liberal society of late-eighteenth- and early-nineteenth-century Britain. Discourses and practices as diverse as liberalism, economics, nationalism, and medicine interact to promote regulatory norms that, invisibly but materially, constrain the lives of abject bodies. The proper body measures deviant flesh and finds it wanting. Hence William Blake's baleful remark about the advancing *normality* of Britons: "since the French Revolution Englishmen are all Intermeasurable One by Another Certainly a happy state of Agreement to which I for One do not Agree" (783). If proper embodiment is a matter of agreement, one of the lessons of British Romanticism is that monstrosities will disagree. As Blake insists, not all bodies are so proper as they are presumed to be. Deviant flesh provides a material occasion for the (re)production of new norms—and forms—of life, breeding a sociability that acknowledges the abject and the disreputable. The promise of monstrosities is that they multiply lives that matter.

PART I
INCORPORATIONS

CHAPTER 1

BUILDING BODIES

. . . our body is but a social structure
composed of many souls . . .
—*Nietzsche,* Beyond Good and Evil

"I lately got a *tall man*." The remark is John Hunter's, renowned anatomist and physician. It concerns the skeleton of Charles Byrne, a.k.a. the Irish Giant, procured some two years earlier under questionable circumstances. Hunter continues: "at the time I could make no particular observations. I hope next summer to be able to show him" (Kobler 244). Show him he did. Fixed upright in a glass cabinet, the tall man became a kind of centerpiece for Hunter's museum of anatomical specimens, a colossal monument to the intelligible if sometimes deviant ways of nature. Brown like a fossil saurian and leeringly aloof, Byrne's skeleton presides to this day over the tumors and the stomachs, the tissues and the fetuses—all neatly tagged and sequenced—that comprise the Hunterian Museum: a monument to medical science, one that displays its normalizing force.[1] Master of comparative anatomy and founding father of modern surgery, Hunter builds a proper body that unites politics with physiology, incorporating liberalism in the flesh.

THE REACH OF THE CHIRURGICAL FRATERNITY

Byrne didn't want to become a medical specimen. Born in Littlebridge, Ireland, to parents of small means and middling stature (who conceived him, it was said, on top of a very tall stack of hay), he lived and died in fear that the anatomists would get his prodigious body. It was his prize possession, literally his life and livelihood. He began exhibiting it for money under the tutelage of one Joe Vance in Scotland and came to London in April of 1782 to try his large hand at the metropolitan trade. He was a huge success. After a month of appearances at a cane shop next to Cox's Museum, Spring Gardens, Byrne received this favorable puff in the *Morning Herald*:

> However striking a curiosity may be, there is generally some difficulty in engag-ing the attention of the public; but even this was not the case with the modern living Colossus, or wonderful Irish Giant; for no sooner was he arrived at an elegant apartment at the cane-shop . . . than the curious of all degrees resorted to see him, being sensible that a prodigy like this never made its appearance among us before; and the most penetrating have frankly declared, that neither the tongue of the most fluid orator, or pen of the most ingenious writer, can suf-ficiently describe the elegance, symmetry and proportion of this wonderful phe-nomenon in nature, and thus all description must fall infinitely short of giving that satisfaction which may be obtained on a judicious inspection. (Kobler 239)

Byrne was a prodigy, a spectacle to beggar description, a sight to behold—for half a crown. To see him was to purchase and consume the wonder of mon-strosity. His income mounted with his renown, which reached such heights that it inspired a pantomime at the Haymarket Theater, *Harlequin Teague or the Giant's Causeway*. He was befriended by other celebrities, most notably that wry little aristocrat Count Borulawski. As if to compound his success, Byrne grew even taller. London seemed a place where a country lad with a little wit and a lot of heart might rise above his expectations (Figure 3).

But this particular country lad was not in the best of health. For all his pon-derable bulk, he seemed somehow blighted. Silas Neville remarked of Byrne in his diary that "he stoops, is not well-shaped, his flesh is loose, and his ap-pearance far from wholesome" (Kobler 239). That ill appearance would later be attributed to the combined effects of consumption and drink, the latter a habit Byrne indulged passionately. He showed signs of an early demise—quite promising signs to the eye of an anatomist. Compounding ill health was the emotional blow of the theft of all his worldly property—some seven hundred pounds. It seemed clear that the Irish Giant was not long for this world. That was Hunter's professional opinion, which he reached discreetly and advanced consolingly. Hunter dispatched his assistant Howison, skilled in the practices of anatomy, to make a monetary offer for Byrne's spectacular corpse. Such a contract was by no means unprecedented. Hunter often bargained with his patients for their remains in the event of surgical misadventure. But Byrne shunned it with horror, unwilling to submit his extraordinary body to the second death and desecration of dissection.[2]

He took steps. It is said that he ordered a lead coffin, engaged his Irish cronies to watch his corpse, and hatched a plan to spirit it away. The inde-fatigable Howison was not, however, to be so easily bested. He nagged Byrne

Figure 3. J. Kay, *Charles Byrne, George Cranstoun, and Three Normal Sized Men* (1794). The Wellcome Library, London.

like the gout. He would come by the cane shop, just to say hello. He would stand outside Byrne's residence in Cockspur Street, just to catch a glimpse. He would fix the giant with his eye and nod with knowing, professional approval: it was only a matter of time. Stalked by the anatomist, numbed by the bottle, Byrne spent his last days drenched in gin and fear. When on the evening of May 30, 1782, death seemed imminent, Howison was just outside to receive the news. He immediately communicated it to Hunter along with the added intelligence that Byrne's cronies were awaiting the end at an alehouse off Cockspur Street. Hunter took the situation into his own hands and made a dash for the pub. With Howison's help he cornered one of the corpse watchers and began buying drinks. Then came the proposition: 50 pounds for the delivery of Byrne's corpse—not bad pay for a night's work. The man was agreeable, but his colleagues saw the weakness of Hunter's position. He didn't possess the body, but they did—or would in a matter of hours. If it was worth 50 pounds to the crafty surgeon, why not 100? And if 100, why not 150? It was a simple matter of supply and demand. The haggling continued toward an agreeable price, 500 pounds by some accounts, 800 by others—a value approximating that of the property lost when the Irish Giant was robbed. Byrne was worth about as much dead as alive, with the difference that he couldn't now claim the profits of his singular anatomy.

The bargain struck, the parties dispersed to their appointed tasks: Byrne's cronies to retrieve the corpse, Howison to secure the cash, and Hunter to await them all at some appropriately dark corner. When the wagon bearing the colossal coffin arrived, Hunter had only to jimmy the lid, strip the clothes (to avoid a property violation), make the exchange, and Byrne's spectacular body was his. It was not the first human corpse he acquired in a clandestine manner, but it was certainly the tallest. With Howison's help he jockeyed it into his coach, taking a seat beside the naked wonder on its journey to new life as pathological specimen. Its immediate destination was Hunter's quiet country residence at Earl's Court, or, more precisely, a copper cauldron. Working quickly, Hunter chopped up the body and boiled away the flesh, leaving only bones, stained deep brown but still prodigious. When resurrected to full stature they would make a remarkable skeleton, a specimen like no other in Hunter's possession.

Just how remarkable can be surmised from the obituary for Byrne that appeared in the *Annual Register* of 1783:

> Our philosophical readers may not be displeased to know, on the credit of an ingenious correspondent who had opportunity of informing himself, that Mr. Byrne, in August 1780 measured eight feet; that in 1782 he had gained two inches; and that after he was dead he measured eight feet four inches. (210)

No wonder Byrne was so renowned a wonder, and to this day remains so spectacular a specimen. He was, indeed, a tall man. A visit to the Hunterian

Museum proves his enduring capacity to awe (Figure 4). But there is something wistful too in the fate of this tall man, dead of tuberculosis and alcoholism at the age of twenty-two, something troubling that his obituary registers about the relationship between medicine and monstrosity:

> In his last moments (it has been said) he requested that his ponderous remains might be thrown into the sea, in order that his bones might be placed far out of the reach of the chirurgical fraternity; in consequence of which, the body was shipped on board a vessel to be conveyed to the Downs, to be sunk in 20 fathom water. We have reason, however, to believe that this report is merely *a tub* thrown out to *the whale*. (209)

As indeed Byrne's own bones confirm. To the eye of the anatomist, there are no last requests. Byrne's extraordinary body becomes a field of contest between competing interests, the physical space of an encounter among forces that regulate the matter of embodiment. What is wistful in this body's fate is the poverty of its agency. Try as he might, Byrne cannot evade the reach of the chirurgical fraternity. It *will* have his body, with or without his consent. Its entitlement comes from his body's monstrosity, which commands knowledge, influence, and cash. Those brown bones in their display case at the Royal College of Surgeons attest to much more than the pituitary malfunction to which medical knowledge now attributes their extravagant size. They demonstrate the normalizing force of modern medicine as a means of producing proper bodies.

PRODIGY, PATHOLOGY, PROGENY

If one of the cultural projects of liberal society, with its individualist and capitalist commitments, is to build a proper body that circulates a norm for human health and wholeness, monstrosities prove a challenge, a carnal turn toward some unutterable otherness.[3] Embodying such otherness, the Irish Giant stood at an intersection of cultural formations in late-eighteenth-century England. In one he was a spectacle, a miraculous sign of something wondrous in the ways of God or nature. But in another he was a specimen, less prodigy than pathology. For centuries a culture of monstrosity flourished on the fringes of polite society, in the back streets of the metropolis or the stalls of country fairs. It served to segregate and often celebrate the uncanny force of physical deformity.[4] As the Irish Giant, nationally and physically other, Byrne inhabited a space traditionally reserved for such singularities. There he could live and even flourish, not an outcast from society so much as its exception, a prodigy anatomically beyond the bodied lot of human kind. With the appearance of Hunter's henchman at his window, however, his singularity came to be seen in scientific terms. To the anatomist, the Irish Giant

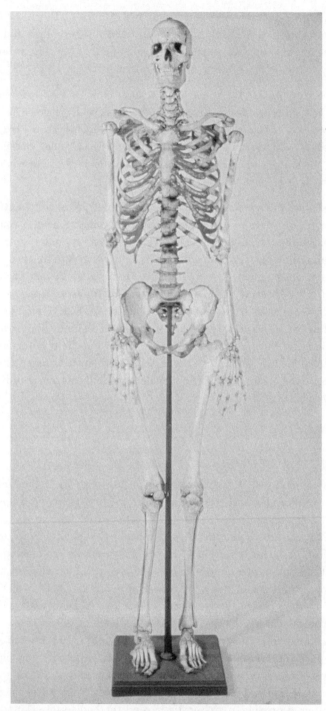

Figure 4. Skeleton of Charles Byrne. Hunterian Museum, The
Royal College of Surgeons of England.

appeared a huge deviation from nature's principles of embodiment. Byrne's singular anatomy thus incarnates an encounter between monstrosity and medicine in liberal society, laying bare the material and discursive practices that produce bodies that matter.

From prodigy to pathology: the phrase describes the strange career of Charles Byrne's body as it lived and died between two cultures, one affirming its social exceptionality and another measuring its physical deformity. That 1783 was the year of Byrne's transformation from prodigious spectacle to pathological specimen shows that by the late eighteenth century medical science was consolidating its authority over deviant flesh. As Rosemarie Garland Thomson observes, "the monster's power to inspire terror, awe, wonder, and divination was being eroded by science, which sought to classify and master rather than revere the extraordinary body" (*Bodies* 57). This mastery may come in the name of health, but that in no way lessens its bodily effect. Nor are extraordinary bodies alone in feeling its force. Monstrosities provide an occasion for the cultural production of the proper body in the late eighteenth century, a project that medicine advances through material practices like anatomy and discursive knowledges like physiology. During the nineteenth century, as Erin O'Connor observes, "monstrosity was professionalized." Medical curiosities became freaks, and "the spectacle of disfigurement ministered to a historically specific need to interrogate the contours of human identity" (150). For British culture during the Romantic period, however, monstrosities presented less a psychological than a somatic challenge. Medicine met it by measuring deformity against the rule of health, helping to materialize a norm of proper embodiment. Having said that, however, it is important not to overestimate the victory of medicine over monstrosities. The story that Thomson tells of their cultural containment ("a conversion of wondrous, ominous pre-Enlightenment monsters to fascinating freaks . . . and, finally, to medical cases" [*Bodies* 79]) reduces a dynamic history to a telic fate, minimizing in the process the resistance of deviant flesh to the claims of medical science and the proper body.

Closer to the material record is Stephen Pender's conclusion that "the marvelous and the scientific coexisted in the reception and study of monsters and continued to do so long after the monster's absorption by 'legitimate' scientific discourse in the eighteenth century" (150). Monstrosities retain the mark of the marvelous in spite of the efforts of medicine to master them, so much so in fact that they acquire a new and potentially menacing aspect that augurs unprecedented cultural formations. Prodigy cedes to pathology only to raise the possibility of new progeny. Monstrosities confront the proper body with its immanent, progenitive transformation. They are not just a sign of transcendent marvels or a medium for the miracles of medicine. They also materialize transformative forces, haunting the proper body in the abject shape of change.

THE ANATOMY OF DEVIANCE

John Hunter was a body builder. His voracious curiosity about all living things impelled him not only to amass the astonishing collection of anatomical specimens that includes Byrne's tall skeleton but more importantly to reinvent the animal body from the bones up. As an anatomist he was without peer, and his many distinctions announced it. He was made surgeon-extraordinary to King George III, appointed surgeon-general, and inspector of the regimental hospitals in the army, and of course elected to the Royal Society of London for Improving Natural Knowledge. His rise to prominence from a modest start as son of a Scottish grain merchant was living proof that industry and ability would yield a proper recompense.[5] But there were also scientific reasons for believing such things. Hunter's anatomical investigations produced a knowledge of the animal body that emphasized its functional organization toward the ends of preservation and increase. Not a Great Chain of Being but a normative principle of action determines a creature's standing among creatures. As that norm increases in complexity, so an animal increases in perfection. It is perhaps not surprising that complexity and perfection meet in an animal traditionally called Man.

But because all animals appear to have certain functions in common, anatomy for Hunter became a comparative enterprise. Sea urchins, eels, chameleons, emus, buffalo, and people all have stomachs. To understand the animal body requires an understanding of the functions that advance its vitality. Hunter ceased to view the body simply as a machine that worked according to mechanical laws and saw it instead as an organism that lived by means of coordinate functions. It was not enough to observe the body's substance, as anatomists had for centuries. Hunter brought physiological theory to bear on anatomical observation.[6] Hence the two foundational assumptions of Hunterian anatomy: first, that organs are defined by their physiological function in an organism, and second, that a principle of life animates all parts while making possible their coordinate activity.

The first of these assumptions leads Hunter to emphasize the functional similarity of apparently different animal bodies. Rather than classify them according to taxonomic category, he relates them according to anatomical function.[7] Thus the basic structural principle of Hunter's comparative anatomy is that of the anatomical series. The common characteristic of a stomach proves that as animals, crocodiles and people are related. What makes them different kinds of animals is the different ways their stomachs function, both alone and in relation to other vital organs. Crocodiles therefore do not differ from people because their bodies differ in kind or quality, but because their vital organs function according to different operative norms. The aim of comparative anatomy, then, is first to reduce animal bodies to their vital functions, then to formulate the normative principles that regulate their distinct operations. In this regard Hunter is the Immanuel Kant of modern anatomy, reducing particular appearances to general functions in what might be called a transcendental critique of animal cadavers. Just so does Everard Home, Hunter's brother-in-law, describe his anatomical practice: "It was not his intention to make dissections of particular animals, but to institute an inquiry into the various organizations by which the functions of life are performed, that he may thereby acquire some knowledge of general principles" (*Treatise* vi).

Hence the second assumption of Hunterian anatomy, the existence of a vital principle. If anatomy alone has never produced a knowledge of life, it may be because a living body is so much more difficult to dissect than a dead one. Because both possess the same anatomical organization, that alone cannot account for the difference between them. Hunter's physiology of vital function attempts to explain that difference by referring organization to principles of action that regulate its persistence and regeneration. It is not simply that Hunter postulates a transcendent vitality that animates all living things. His tries to show instead how life gives rise to material agency. His first move is to suggest that life characterizes animal matter down to the smallest particle: "every individual particle of the animal matter . . . is possessed of life, and the least imaginable part which we can separate is as much alive as the whole" (*Lectures* 289). Thus the blood, which circulates throughout the body to enliven it and coagulates when necessary to rebuild it, is alive.

But this particulate vitality cannot of itself account for material agency. Hunter appeals to an architectonics of function to show how bodies act as physical organisms. Moving beyond traditional metaphors of mechanical operation, he describes an animal body whose vital functions are integrative and dynamic:

> The principle of life has been compared to the spring of a watch, or the moving powers of other machinery; but this is not the case with an animal; animal matter has a principle of action in every part, independent of the others, and whenever the action of one part (which is always the effect of the living principle,) becomes the cause of an action in another, it is by stimulating the living principle of that other part, the action in the second part being as much the effect of the living principle of that part as the action of the first was of the living principle in it. (*Lectures* 289)

Hunter's prose is thick, but his point seems to be that, although life inhabits all parts of animal matter, a principle of action coordinates their dynamic interplay, sustaining and regulating vital functions. Historian of science François Duchesneau describes this process, which gives rise to diverse but functionally typical animal bodies, as a kind of feedback loop: "The feedback process . . . adjust[s] the activity of the whole according to the species of action intervening in various parts. Action is a stimulus for further action of a more harmonious kind; it is through retroactive stimuli that the dispositions of the elementary parts are set in regulative operation" (289). Hunter builds a body whose vital functions are an effect of this self-regulative principle of action. His is a physiology of the functional norm, materialized in the mute interiors of vital tissues. That he took nonvoluntary bodily functions for the subject of his science makes him one of the prime architects of the proper body. Foucault's technologies of discipline would never work without bodies to work on. Hunter's vital organism, functionally normative and physiologically self-regulating, provides a material substrate for the subject of discipline.

But what of monstrosities? It is Hunter's physiology that makes it possible to speak at all of *deviance* in regard to material bodies. The traditional medical term for bodily anomaly, "monstrosity," shows how close medicine once stood to superstition in its attempts to fathom disfigurement.[8] A pamphlet published in the late seventeenth century, for instance, catalogs the strange and various causes that produce monstrosities: "for though Nature in working intends her own business, yet because diverse obstacles often happen in respect of the first agent; the Seed, the Constitution of the Heavens, the formative Virtue, Imagination, Heat, it is no wonder if she err sometimes" (*Collection* BL). Hunterian physiology advances a simpler explanation. Bodily anomaly originates simply if sometimes frightfully in material deviation from the norm of the natural function of an organism's parts or interaction among them:

> Nature being pretty constant in the kind and number of the different parts peculiar to each species of animal, as also in the situation, formation, and construction of such parts, we call everything that deviates from that uniformity a "monster." . . . There must be some principle for those deviations from the regular course of Nature, in the economy of such species as they occur in. (*Essays* 1: 239)

Two points are worth noting here: first, that monstrosity occurs materially as a deviation from a functional norm; and second, that this deviation becomes intelligible as a monstrous instance of the very norm it violates. Deviations only become visible to Hunter when they materialize a prior uniformity, an assumption that becomes clearer in his remarks on the medical value of monstrosities: "many of their parts can explain nothing with regard to their formation, or the animal economy in general. . . . However, some of their structures may explain something in the physiology of the more perfect animals" (*Essays* 1: 249). Monstrosities mean nothing in themselves. Their value for medicine derives solely from their relationship to the functional norms of more perfect organisms. Where such deviance seems most disturbing—in its physical singularity—it is in fact most benign, an atypical occurrence of typical vital functions. Hunter's reduction of pathology to proper function renders deviant flesh strangely transparent to the norms it embodies.

If Canguilhem has shown that one of the effects of the sciences of life is to normalize deviation through the assumption that "pathological phenomena are identical to normal phenomena save for quantitative variations" (35), then Hunter's physiology of vital function writes that equation into flesh, providing a material foundation for the belief that, so to speak, deviance doesn't matter, that people are all the same under the skin because they embody uniform vital functions—a physiology peculiarly appropriate to liberal society. As Canguilhem describes this liberal logic, "the conviction that one can scientifically restore the norm is such that in the end it annuls the pathological" (42). Material difference means physical transparency, the disappearance of deviant flesh into its functional norms. For Charles Byrne, death was the condition of that disappearance; for John Hunter it produced the science of life.

The force of Hunter's explanations underwrites the emergence of pathological anatomy as not only a specialized medical knowledge but also a physically and morally regulative discourse. The work of Hunter's nephew, Matthew Baillie, is instructive in this regard. His important study *The Morbid Anatomy of Some of the Most Important Parts of the Human Body* (1797, 2d ed.) fully adheres to Hunter's principles, since "the object of this work is to explain, more minutely than has hitherto been done, the changes of structure arising from morbid actions in some of the most important parts of the human body" (1).[9] Morbid actions produce monstrosities and monstrosities illustrate normal functions—while sometimes providing an occasion for a moral evaluation of such deviance. In a separately published article titled "Of a Remarkable Deviation from the Natural Structure in the Urinary Bladder and Organs of Generation of a Male," Baillie associates deviant flesh with deviant behavior in a way that pathologizes the life of the lower class. This particular monstrosity is especially remarkable because it manifests a morbid action in the function of the penis (Figure 5), and Baillie is clearly disturbed by the manner in which the afflicted individual lived this deviance:

> The person in whom this variety was found was a man of about forty years of age, of a short stature, of a robust habit, and of a very dissolute life. Having occasionally got a good deal of money by exhibiting himself to public curiosity, and having acquired habits of idleness, he very readily fell into drunkenness, the most prevailing vice among the lower class of people. He was at length very rarely sober, and in one of his fits of inebriety he died. (*Transactions* 189)

Baillie comes close here to identifying physiological with moral deviance, by no means an unprecedented prejudice, but one that in this case illustrates the social efficacy of an emergent medical science. Like deviant flesh, attendant social pathologies (idleness, drunkenness) are basically deviations from natural functional norms. Identifying a physiological origin for this man's affliction relieves Baillie of confronting its social conditions and effects. It comes as no surprise, then, that Baillie should conclude that this apparent monstrosity conceals the normal function of the organ in question: "yet I have no doubt that titillating the glans, so as to produce erection promoted the secretion of the semen as in common men. We are led to this opinion from considering the general structure of his organs" (197). Medically speaking, monstrosities only confirm the norm of proper embodiment.

Hunterian physiology thus advances the cultural production of bodies susceptible to the imperatives of liberalism. Those bodies are social structures composed, in Nietzsche's terms, of many souls, and their physiological functions neatly accommodate cultural norms. Consider in this regard Hunter's distinction between immediate and accessory actions. The first involves the body's internal operation, the second the coordination of its vital functions toward other ends, but both conveniently legitimate the making of the English working class: "the second kind may be called laborers, being subservient to the first, which, as being engaged in laying down and taking up parts, may be called bricklayers. It is the first which compose the movements of the true animal, being those which are immediately employed about itself. It is the operations of these which properly constitute the animal oeconomy" (*Lectures* 243). Physiologically considered, the body is a laborer, but one characterized by a principle of self-regulation. The working class has its functional epitome

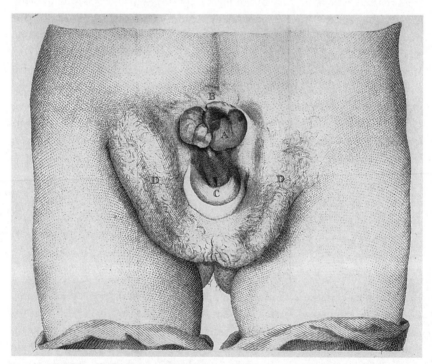

Figure 5. Deformed penis, *Transactions of a Society for the Improvement of Medical and Chirurgical Knowledge* **(1793). The Wellcome Library, London.**

in normative bodily operations. Physiology thus provides a material connection between individual and social organization.

That explains Hunter's confidence in the reciprocal stability of both: "The more complicated a machine is, the more nice its operations are, and, of course, the greater dependence each part has upon the other; and, therefore, there is a more intimate connexion through the whole. This holds good in society. It also holds good in the animal oeconomy" (*Essays* 1: 119). If complexity and perfection meet in the human body, and if the human body is a paradigm of social structure, then its normal function becomes the measure of a just society. Hunter's physiology of function incarnates a politics of normality. That no amount of deviation can really disrupt normal function is the lesson of the strange tale Hunter tells of his monstrous horse. However deviant the flesh, the mind prevails as the index of normal function and natural behavior:

> Do not monsters show that the mind and the formation of the body do not necessarily correspond?—that is to say, that the formation of the mind does not arise out of the formation of the parts; for although the body may be strangely formed, yet the mind, if properly formed, shall have all the natural dispositions for the natural actions of the body . . . My monstrous horse, although the penis stood out behind, when erected, and did not come along the belly, yet leaped upon the mare to cover her, which he certainly would not have done if the instinctive principle of action had arisen out of the construction of the parts. (*Essays* 1: 248).

On this account monstrosities cannot disrupt the overall function of the animal economy, which in this case remains reasonable in spite of obvious anatomical complications. Normal function rides triumphant, eliminating in advance any need to address problems of material difference. Social reform becomes a monstrous horse whose misdirected virility cannot trouble the ways of nature.

THE GREAT UNWRITTEN BOOK

When an acquaintance of Hunter asked if a friend could visit his anatomical museum in Leicester Square, this was his reply: "if your friend is in London in October (and not a Democrat) he is welcome to see it; but I would rather see it in a blaze, like the Bastille, than show it to a Democrat, let his country be what it may" (Kobler 105). An odd comparison, perhaps—that between a medical museum and a prison. One is an institution for the advancement of knowledge, the other an instrument of state power. But maybe Hunter knows of what he speaks, or at least intuits the ways in which such knowledge circulates power.[10] His physiology would be so much empty theorizing without material practices to distribute its authority and force among living bodies. Charles Byrne lived his last days in fear of one such practice, and in that he was not alone. Dissection was disparaged by the common populace as a desecration of the flesh. Riots were a frequent feature of the festival of execution in the early eighteenth century as family and friends fought with agents of the anatomists for the corpses of executed criminals. The Murder Act of 1752 formalized the state policy of supplying bodies of condemned felons to the Company of Surgeons, and its preamble made clear that its purpose was more political than scientific: "it has become necessary that some further Terror and peculiar Mark of Infamy be added to the Punishment" (Linebaugh 76–77). Dissection was that terror. With the removal of the gallows from the public eye at Tyburn to the private grounds of Newgate prison in 1783, the anatomists could get their dead with a minimum of interference. Grave robbing was still a flourishing trade and would be until the Anatomy Act of 1832, that sinister companion of the Reform Bill, advanced the policy of state-sponsored dissection to include the unclaimed corpses of the poor who died in hospitals. The underclass knew dissection for what it was, an instrument of power that advanced a knowledge to which they became materially subject. As Peter Linebaugh has said, "anatomy depended as much upon eighteenth-century penal practices as it did upon the idealist transmission of knowledge" (69).

Dissection cuts knowledge into flesh, building the proper body by tearing down dead ones. It incarnates the truths it exhumes from the dim recesses of the corpse through surgical practices such as the standard "Y" incision that begins at each shoulder, meets below the sternum, and ends at the synthesis pubis; the craniotomy that removes the top of the skull to reveal the meninges and the brain within; the evisceration that requires breadloafing—lateral slicing—of vital organs to discover hidden traumas; the inspection of the stomach that establishes a cadaver's final meal. Such practices sustain whole cultures through the knowledges they incarnate. In late-eighteenth-century Britain, they help produce a proper body whose vital functions articulate with those of society. Michel de Certeau emphasizes the complexity of this cultural project: "A long historical development stretching from the fifteenth to the eighteenth century was required before the individual body could be 'isolated' in the way one 'isolates' an element in chemistry or microphysics; before it could become the basic unit of a society" (142). Anatomical dissection isolates the dead body to produce a living unit functionally continuous with others. That such a practice received state sanction underscores its efficacy as an instrument of power.

For Hunter, anatomical dissection became something of an industry, making his fabulous museum a kind of corporate headquarters of the body business. The defining structural principle behind his practice, that of the anatomical series, required multiple dissections for the purpose of comparing specimens. Hunter was nothing if not tireless, and the products of his amazing labors found their way into his museum preserved in alcohol, pumped with colored wax, or painstakingly dry-mounted—over 13,000 specimens in all. There were curiosities (whale skeletons suspended from the ceiling), conjugations (animal pairs mounted in flagrante delicto), and congenital deformities (conjoint twins preserved in jars, Figure 6). But what distinguished Hunter's museum from others like Rackrow's in Fleet Street was the systematic presentation of its specimens. Hunter hammered the chaos of the traditional cabinet of curiosities into a structure built in the image of physiological knowledge. "My design, gentlemen, in the formation of this museum," he is said to have confessed to visitors, "was to display throughout the chain of organized beings the various structures in which the functions of life are carried on" (Kobler 234).

This display came in three divisions, the first devoted to anatomical structures securing survival of the individual, the second to those serving regeneration of the species, and the third to those illustrating pathological functions. Through the principle of anatomical series, visibly documented in graded arrangement of stomachs, teeth, embryos, etc., Hunter posits a functional integration *among* as well as *within* animal bodies. To dissection, which consolidates the body as individual unit, his museum adds the practice of gradation, which creates functional and progressive relationships between such units. The cultural effects of such practices can be seen in beliefs as apparently natural as evolution, innate ability, and unbridled economic growth. Hunter's museum opens up a conceptual universe in which bodies relate functionally through a graded scale of complexity, capacity, and perfection. It institutionalizes what one commentator calls "the imperialism of the anatomical space of the animal species," a space so saturated by proper function that deviant flesh, such as that of Hunter's fascinating monstrosities, just disappears, nothing in itself but a negative allegory of vital function (Cross 10).

The Hunterian Museum, then, is also a body Bible. It scripts relations of power that legitimate the proper body and regulate its functions.[11] Famously described once in *The Lancet* as a "great unwritten book," it is a holy text whose lessons are more physical than spiritual (F. Jones 778). Although its language of series and gradation "obeyed the grammatical rules of organic nature itself," its rhetorical effects were—and remain—deeply social (Cross 16). At his death in 1793 Hunter owned 160 pounds' worth of books. When his anatomical collection was finally sold to the government in 1799, it brought 15,000 pounds (Kobler 93; Qvist 70). Its acquisition formalized its institutional function as a book for building and regulating the proper body. It is not merely that the anatomical collection advanced the cause of medicine as a privileged form of knowledge. While Hunter was alive it was open to visitors only twice a year, in October to qualified specialists and in May to "noblemen and gentlemen" (Kobler 233), but even so it became internationally renowned.

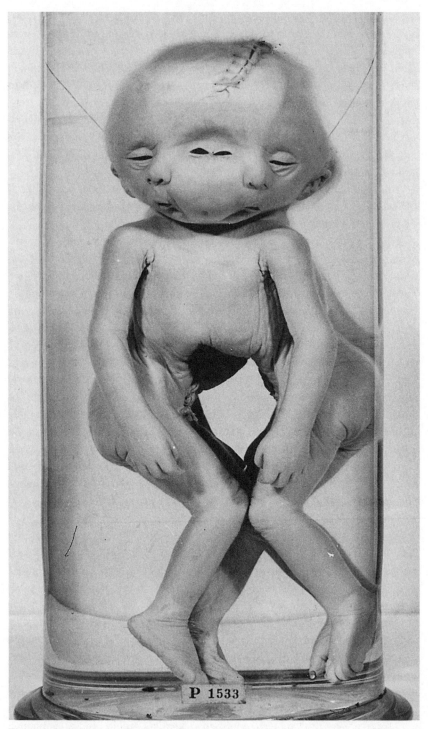

P 1533

Figure 6. Conjoint twins. Hunterian Museum, The Royal College of Surgeons of England.

After acquiring its custody the Company of Surgeons applied for a new charter as the Royal College of Surgeons in order not only to receive funds for its maintenance but also to grant diplomas by examination. As a social practice the museum disseminates Hunter's physiology of normal function, advancing its cultural authority. As a database of diagnosis, the museum teaches medical professionals how to identify deviant function.

The result is an institutionalized knowledge that eradicates singularity in advance, since normal function is typical, while pathological function is, carefully considered, even more so. Housed in a royal college and funded by government subventions, the Hunterian Museum helps make possible the new species of politics that de Certeau associates with modern medicine: "a change in sociocultural axioms occurs when the unit referred to gradually ceases to be the body politic in order to become the individual body, and when the reign of a *juridical* politics begins to be replaced by the reign of a *medical* politics, that of the representation, administration, and well-being of individuals" (142). Hunter's physiology builds bodies susceptible to such politics, and his great book of a museum institutionally scripts their function. In one sense at least, then, Hunter was a voracious reader. Gesturing once toward a room full of cadavers, he remarked to the father of the fatefully named Dr. Philip Physick, "These are the books. The others are fit for vurra little" (Kobler 194).

PROPER BODY

Not quite all traditional books are so empty, however. Books of liberal political theory would fit nicely in Hunter's museum. Hunterian physiology is body politics. It legitimates a body peculiarly suited to the purposes of liberalism, capitalism, and bourgeois society. Carole Pateman has shown how the social contract that enables liberal politics presumes a prior sexual contract whose occlusion prevents the full participation of women in civil society. Something similar happens at the level of the body in the foundational statements of the political theory of possessive individualism. If women are excluded from the social contract it is partly on the basis of bodily deviance from a masculine standard, an assumption whose authority runs back to Aristotle. Liberal political theory presumes a standard that renders all such deviant flesh innocuous. Hunter's physiology thus articulates with political liberalism to reinforce the cultural norm of the proper body, a body physically, even physiologically qualified to participate in civil society. If Pateman proves that body masculine (while not addressing its apparent whiteness), it becomes important to notice how its masculinity serves also to devalue any body irreducible to its functions.

According to Locke, the proper body owns property—*is* property that pro-duces ownership.[12] The simple brilliance of this view of man is to view him (not her, obviously) as a property owner. No matter how little else a person possesses, *he possesses his body* and with it the right to use it as he sees fit: "Though the Earth, and all inferior Creatures be common to all Men, yet every Man has a *Property* in his own *Person*. This no Body has any Right to but himself" (Locke, *Two Treatises* 305). Locke isolates the individual as property owner from social relations that would otherwise determine his status by making his body the sole means of establishing identity. It's an astonishing move for the way it materializes the individual. Identity becomes the product of a possession, the body, that functions to produce possessions. The body is thus property without a proprietor until its actions produce one. Locke col-lapses the individual into actions that identify it, rendering his body's mate-riality less substantive than functional. A man is what his body does, and a proper body accumulates property.

It can do so, as shown earlier, because labor legitimates appropriation: "The *Labour* of his Body, and the *Work* of his Hands, we may say, are properly his. Whatsoever then he removes out of the State that Nature hath provided and left it in, he hath mixed his *Labour* with, and joyned to it something that is his own, and thereby makes it his *Property*" (305–06). Labor is a mobile al-chemy that transmutes what belongs to all into what belongs to one. The body functions to produce property through this activity of material appropriation, laboring to assimilate to itself the common matter that sustains it. In a sense, then, the proper body is infinitely prosthetic, accumulating bulk and stature with every acquisition. But rather than emphasize the physical specificity of such bodies, their wildly various power and value, Locke focuses instead on their functional equivalence. Not possessions but the ability to possess is what qualifies the individual for participation in civil society. It is because a man has a right to the free use of his body that he can accumulate property, which civil society then develops to protect. As property, in other words, the proper body is a commodity. Its labor can be exchanged for other possessions, for instance money. The suitability of so fungible a body to the twin interests of liberalism and capitalism is succinctly rendered in Macpherson's sum-mary of Locke's position: "To Locke a man's labour is so unquestionably his own property that he may freely sell it for wages. . . . The labour thus sold becomes the property of the buyer, who is then entitled to appropriate the produce of that labour" (215). As a commodity that can be bought and sold, the (labor of the) proper body represents a functional equivalence that wages measure and appropriate to the ends of further accumulation.

Marx's assessment of commodities thus applies as well to the proper body: "There, the existence of things *qua* commodities, and the value relations between the products of labour which stamps them as commodities, have absolutely no connection with their physical properties and with the material relations arising therefrom" (446). Locke's proper body is a commodity whose functional equivalence with others dematerializes its specificity—even while establishing a material basis for identity. Bodies in all their physical variety and contingent history must acquire a form capable of exchange if they are to participate in the relationships that give rise to civil society. Deviant flesh, especially where incapable of labor, remains outside the social contract. A body that cannot be exchanged for wages or other property cannot achieve individuality in Locke's sense. It remains incapable of free agency, restricted to a relationship of dependency on others. That this relationship never receives the formal recognition accorded even to the sexual contract only exaggerates its social force. Bodies irreducible to functional norms live beyond the pale of liberal politics, the objects perhaps of charity and affection but not quite persons, not quite proper. They remain too dependent to be full participants in civil society. Monstrosities wear the stigmata of social and material relations that the proper body labors to transcend. Hence their threat: the monstrosities of interdependency and obligation trouble the propriety of the free, fungible individual.

It should be clear that Hunter's advances in anatomy produce a physiology of the proper body. The emphasis on the normative function of organs and self-regulating action of organisms neatly accommodates a politics of free and equal individuals laboring to sustain a liberal society. Seeing deviance as a special instance of normal function provides physiological grounds for solving the problem of improper embodiment. To the extent that monstrosities incorporate the cultural norm of the proper body, to that extent they achieve participation in civil society. Their singularity disappears into the normative truth of physiological and political function. Hunter's physiology builds a body perfectly suited to the needs of liberal politics and free-market economics, one whose agency is independent, whose labor is alienable, and whose physical specificity is overcome by its functional equivalence with others. This is a body susceptible to the biopolitics of discipline that Foucault describes so relentlessly, a body of multiply measurable forces and collectively manageable mobilities.

That physiology is the proper venue for the legitimation of such strategies is the lesson of Hunter's odd remarks on digestion. The body itself, it turns out, runs on an economy of free exchange. Digestion involves a kind of contract between individual agents:

> The remote cause of absorption of whole and living parts implies the existence of two conditions, the first of which is a consciousness, in the part to be absorbed . . . [and] the second [of which] is a consciousness of the absorbents of such a state of the parts. Both these concurring, they have nothing to do but to fall to work. (*Lectures* 1: 255)

Hunter distributes consciousness throughout the body and turns its internal economy into a civil society of cooperating capitalists. His physiology interacts with liberalism to legitimate the proper body as a cultural norm. A note by Hunter's Victorian editor commenting on the passage above registers the political force of such conjunctions: "It were devoutly to be wished that the body politic possessed a similar consciousness of what ought to be done, and an equal will and power to carry its resolutions to effect" (1: 255).

BURKE'S ANATOMY, PAINE'S DWARF

Such statements turn physiology into a political discourse, one taken up by conservative and radical theorists of liberalism alike. The old trope of the body politic makes the move from medical to political knowledge almost inevitable, allowing Hunter's physiology of function to articulate readily with the claims of contemporary liberalism. It wasn't Locke, after all, but Locke's political heirs who set the social agenda for the proper body. If the French Revolution put aristocratic privilege to the guillotine, British reaction brought the proper body into power. Foucault has argued that one of the distinguishing features of this new dispensation is its ability to produce and manage large masses of individuals through normalizing evaluations. Where earlier an exemplary body was unique (the luxuriant courtier, the indomitable king), from now on it would be normal (the common citizen, the average man). An unmarked standard becomes the means of determining an individual's value.[13] The able-bodiedness presumed by the political theory of possessive individualism thus *incorporates* a norm whose force goes unfelt by those it empowers. Hence its appeal to later theorists of liberalism and its success in consolidating liberal society. In the social ferment that followed the French Revolution, the proper body solves the problem of perceived distinction, and Locke's heirs, Edmund Burke and Thomas Paine, both write to identify its functions with those of liberal society conceived as an aggregate of individuals.

Hunter's physiology lends medical and scientific credibility to both of their political projects. That these men were political enemies goes without saying: Burke the archconservative, architect of an organic conservatism, Paine the equally archradical, advocate of a progressive republicanism. Burke defended what Paine abhorred, the entitlements of birth. Both make their case, however, by appealing to the cultural norm of the proper body. This is not to say that their politics are ultimately commensurable, that deep down they share the same vision. But Stuart Hall has shown how each emphasizes different elements of the liberalism that descends from Locke. Different emphases produce different liberalisms, proving its ideological diversity:

The radical and subversive strand, represented by Paine's emphases, flowed into working class radicalism and later became a key element in the formation of English socialism. The traditionalist and *laissez-faire* emphases of Burke's ideas were absorbed into English conservatism. *Both* were premised on the liberal principles of political economy. (57)

And both were grounded in the liberal presupposition of the proper body. The liberalisms they advocate, however diverse their aims, interact with a physiology of function to build a body politic susceptible to normative strategies of evaluation and management. Liberal polities regulate the proper body they empower. As Thomson puts it, "in its complex social codification, power is veiled by a rhetoric of neutrality that creates the illusion of meritocracy" (*Bodies* 40).

In his polemics against the French republic Burke often styles himself a physician, not of the individual citizen but of the corporate body of British society. Medical tropes allow him effortlessly to assimilate individual to social health, as in the following passage from his *Letters on a Regicide Peace* (1796): "the constitution of any political being, as well as that of any physical being, ought to be known, before one can venture to say what is fit for its conservation, or what is the proper means of its power" (214). That the constitutions in question are known to Hunterian physiology is among the assumptions at play in Burke's *Reflections on the Revolution in France* (1791). Burke's purpose is to defend, against the diseased example of revolutionary France, the fundamental health of a hereditary British monarchy and its constituent social organization. In Burke's words, "No experience has taught us, that in any other course or method than that of an *hereditary crown,* our liberties can be regularly perpetuated and preserved sacred as our *hereditary right*" (*Reflections* 25). That such rights are less supernaturally than naturally given puts Burke squarely in the lineage of possessive individualism that descends from Locke.

To secure its authority and to make the case for the heritability of natural rights, Burke deploys a physiology of function that assures the normative operation of the British body politic over time. For him that body is a historical organism that functions according to normative principles. The trouble with the "new doctors of the rights of men" and their convulsive French medicines is that they "take the deviation from the principle for the principle," mistaking aberrant for normal function (23). Burke approaches such problems in the manner of a trained physiologist, interpreting these deviations in light of the principle they exemplify:

It is far from impossible to reconcile . . . the use both of a fixed rule and an occasional deviation; the sacredness of an hereditary principle of succession in our government, with a power of change in its application in cases of extreme emergency. Even in that extremity . . . the change is to be confined to the peccant part only; to the part which produced the necessary deviation; and even then it is to be effected without a decomposition of the whole civil and political mass. (21)

As a physiologist of the social body, Burke views deviation from the functional norm of hereditary succession as an occasion for reasserting the integrity of that norm. Quack advocates of revolution fail to perceive the real lesson of deviation, its illustration of the vital functions of British society as a historical organism.

Burke's anatomy of the proper body is thus closely in keeping with Hunter's, for both are "founded on the idea that Nature's general principles are right, and all the corresponding parts adapted to one another, except when monstrous, either in form or action" (Hunter, *Observations* 218). When Burke speaks of monstrosities, he similarly means deviant parts of a social body, Jacobins for instance, ill adapted to function healthfully within the whole organism. It is against the functional integrity of the whole that governments must be measured. The constitutional monarchy of Britain is preferable to the new republic of France for the way it coordinates and regulates the various agencies of its constituent parts:

> With us, when we elect popular representatives, we send them to a council, in which each man individually is a subject, and submitted to a government complete in all its ordinary functions. . . . With us the representative, separated from the other parts, can have no action and no existence. The government is the point of reference of the several members and districts of our representation. This is the center of our unity. This government of reference is a trustee for the *whole,* and not for the parts. (188)

Good government collectively incorporates a physiology of function. Individual parts act vitally in relation to the whole organism, whose persistence and regeneration it becomes the purpose of government to direct. Burke's organic conservatism acquires force not merely for its allegiance to historical tradition but also for the way it articulates with contemporary medical knowledge.

Little wonder, then, that to defend the status quo Burke turns comparative anatomist. Viewed historically, the social body includes

> many diversities amongst men, according to their birth, their education, their profession, the periods of their lives, their residence in towns or in the country, their several ways of acquiring and of fixing property, and according to the quality of the property itself, all which rendered them as it were so many different species of animals. From thence [legislators] thought themselves obliged to dispose their citizens into such classes, and to place them in situations in the state as their peculiar habits might qualify them to fill, and to allot to them such appropriated privileges as might secure to them what their specific occasions required, and which might furnish to each description such force as might

protect it in the conflict caused by the diversity of interest, that must exist in all complex society. (185)

Burke's liberalism takes full if oblique advantage of comparative anatomy and functionalist physiology to promote the cultural norm of a proper body whose labor is historically cumulative and whose organization is internally regulative. It is within the terms of this embodied Britishness that individual Britons must be measured. Under such circumstances monstrosities can only augur subversion, which is why "the body of the people must not find the principles of natural subordination by art rooted out of their minds" (246). Burke's proper body guards against such monstrous prospects.

At first glance it might appear as if Paine eschews the norm of the proper body. When he speaks of monstrosities in *The Rights of Man* (1792), his counterblast to Burke's *Reflections,* he means those of hereditary government and title.[14] Contrary to Burke's comparative anatomy of the body politic and its patent complacency toward social inequities, Paine propounds a fundamental—and natural—equality among human beings: "as there is but one species of man, there can be but one element of human power, and that element is man himself" (139). In keeping with Locke, Paine takes that element of human power to be the individual. Man may be of one species, but he only acts autonomously. That is why Paine so detests hereditary title. It unjustly empowers one individual over another. Because every birth is a creation ex nihilo, there can be nothing cumulative about it: "all men are born equal and with equal natural rights, in the same manner as if posterity had been continued by *creation* instead of *generation*" (77). Rejecting generation as a condition of agency, Paine rescinds Burke's historical determination of the proper body.

But that does not mean that Paine's more radical liberalism rescinds the proper body as a cultural norm. On the contrary, *The Rights of Man* helps reinforce its legitimacy. For all its sedition Paine's polemic, with its radical commitment to equality, reinforces the able-bodiedness tacitly presumed by the theory of possessive individualism. Consider Paine's account of the origins of civil society. A man enters into social relationships only when he is unable to execute his natural rights as an individual: "The natural rights which he retains [in civil society] are all those in which the power to execute is as perfect in the individual as the right itself. . . . The natural rights which are not retained are all those in which, though the right is perfect in the individual, the power to execute them is defective" (79). Paine's example of a right not retained in civil society is that of judgment. Lacking the power to redress wrong, an individual deposits the right of judgment with society, which makes it collectively available to all who have done likewise. Thus "civil power, properly considered as such, is made up of the aggregate of that class of the natural rights of man which becomes defective in the individual in point of power"

(79). Civil society arises out of defects in individual power—defects that all individuals share. Paine's description of civil society presumes an equality of power *and* defect among individuals. Viewed corporeally, that presumption puts deviant flesh beyond the pale of civil participation. Bodies whose powers are not equal, whose defects are not shared, cannot deposit their natural rights in the common stock of society. They lack the cultural capital that the able-bodied so effortlessly command. So while Paine can honestly assert that "every man is a proprietor in society, and draws on the capital as a matter of right," that right really belongs to the proper body, a proprietor whose powers and defects are shared by all. Not to accommodate that proper body is to be something other than "every man."

In Paine's terms, it is to be a dwarf. At two points in his polemic, Paine invokes the figure of a dwarf to embody a limit to human possibility, and thus to participation in civil society. Regarding France, Paine takes revolution as an instance of natural, normal human development: "France has not leveled, it has exalted. It has put down the dwarf to set up the man" (89). Regarding aristocracy, he views degeneration as a natural consequence of abnormal breeding: "Aristocracy has not been able to keep a proportionate pace with democracy. The artificial *noble* shrinks into a dwarf before the *noble* of nature" (92). In both instances physical abnormality incarnates a limit, marring the humanity of man, menacing the natural power of the proper body. If civil society were really open, if the proper body included *all* bodies, then why would a dwarf serve Paine as so potent a gargoyle? Even a radical liberal politics recapitulates the biases of its forebears. The corporeal investments of liberalism are indeed as imperious as Thomson describes them: "within such an ideological framework, the figure whose body is a neutral instrument of the self-governing will becomes a free agent in contractual relations, [while] the disabled figure represents the incomplete, unbounded, compromised, and subjected body susceptible to external forces: property badly managed" (*Bodies* 45). Between them Burke and Paine consolidate the force of the proper body as a cultural norm. Their various liberalisms make deviant flesh the dark other of solid citizenship.[15] Whether conceived historically or individually, the proper body measures flesh and disciplines what it doesn't affirm. The only tolerable deviance is no deviance at all, or one whose true principles are those of the bodied norm. Hence Paine's ideal form of government in a well-built republic, uniting all human faculties into one "gigantic manliness" (137).

Such, then, is the political fulfillment of the promise of Charles Byrne's bones, whose gigantic manliness provides the skeletal structure that the theory of possessive individualism fleshes out. Hunter's anatomical interest in monstrosities as an exaggerated instance of normal function allows liberalism, conservative or radical, to saturate the social agencies of human bodies.

Physiology incorporates politics, making bodies matter in a way that eliminates physical differences in advance. Hence the humane belief that we are all alike under the skin. Bodies unassimilable to that belief don't quite count as human, at least not materially. That's the hard lesson of Hunter's body building: in liberal society, only proper bodies really matter.

CHAPTER 2

TROUBLING MEASURES

"Walk in, walk in, ladies and gentlemen, just going to begin,
the splendid romantic pastoral gallimaufry of the
Horrible Secret, or, Monstrosities made Public . . . "
—Bartholomew Fair: A Musical Drama *(1823)*

What is the fate of monstrosities in liberal society? Mary Shelley's *Frankenstein* offers a harrowing portrayal of its treatment of deviant flesh. Victor Frankenstein is a good liberal, or at least tries to be. Sure, he abandons his creature, but not without reason. The monster is physically hideous, subject to "contortions that ever and anon convulsed & deformed his unhuman features" (52). Frankenstein shirks his paternal responsibilities—the archetypal deadbeat dad—but comes to see the error of his ways when his creature hunts him down to demand his human due, a companion. Victor's response is revealing: "His words had a strange effect upon me. I compassionated him, and sometimes felt a wish to console him; but when I looked upon him . . . my feelings were altered to horror and hatred" (143). The monster's monstrosity undoes all humanity. His emotional appeal for companionship inspires an ambivalence that ultimately turns violent. Shelley's novel will prove useful in the following pages for examining the fate of monstrosities in liberal society, where they afford an occasion for the cultural (re)production of the proper body. But first comes an examination of a range of related practices: Wordsworth's healing humanist poetry, the display of several famous monstrosities, and that ancient and annual saturnalia, Bartholomew Fair. As the latter in particular shows, the appearance of monstrosities in public troubles and redoubles the measures taken to manage them. In such a cultural context, the ordeal of Frankenstein's monster dramatizes the full normative force of proper embodiment.

LYRICAL BODIES

Wordsworth is in some ways the poet laureate of the proper body. He practices a physiological aesthetics that aims as much at normalizing bodies as soothing souls. There's a long critical tradition that takes Wordsworth for a healer. Myer Abrams describes it in some detail in *Natural Supernaturalism*: Wordsworth's recovery from his own spiritual crisis, his salubrious mature poetry, its healing effects on the minds of John Stuart Mill, William Cullen Bryant, and William James.[1] Wordsworth becomes a therapist to the stars, the great physician of the liberal soul. He's a healer of men's minds—and, it turns out, their bodies too. Abrams ignores this possibility, preferring, in his Judeo-Christian way, the claims of spiritual to physical health. But in his early poetry especially, Wordsworth practices a more material sort of healing. The poems of *Lyrical Ballads* as well as its famous "Preface" communicate a surprisingly physical sense of what poetry does. They speak directly to the body and seek to cultivate its health. In doing so, they interact with the more openly political liberalisms of Burke and Paine to reinforce a norm of proper embodiment. Poetry proves a powerful agent of cultural politics as Wordsworth literally plays the healer.

He can only do so because he has absorbed the latest advances in physiology. The late eighteenth century was a time of ferment in a field that witnessed the emergence of a new solution to the old crux of the mind's relation to the body. The year of the publication of *Lyrical Ballads,* 1798, also saw the publication of two texts that define the traditional poles of debate. John Haslam's *Observations on Insanity* and Alexander Chrichton's *Inquiry into the Nature and Origin of Mental Derangement* advance rival descriptions of the causes and cures of insanity. Haslam, who had served for many years as the attending physician at Bethlem Hospital, took the traditional materialist view of the body as a mechanism subject to physical breakdown. Chrichton, on the other hand, advocated a more idealist view, approaching madness as an affliction of the "mind," an aggregate of faculties and principles irreducible to physical mechanism. Between them Haslam and Chrichton illustrate the persistence of the mind-body debate in medicine contemporary with Wordsworth. Dualism dies hard, and still sets the terms for much medical practice.

But there was another way emerging among more adventuresome physicians, one that would open up new possibilities not only for medicine but for poetry too. The Scottish school of medicine at the University of Edinburgh had followed the example of Hunter, a fellow Scot, in advancing a physiology of normative function that puts the mind fully in the body and the body fully in the world. In the words of Lawrence, "in physiological theory Scottish medicine was characterized by its stress on the total integration of body function, the perceptive capacity or sensibility of the organism, and a preoccupation with the nervous system as the structural basis for these properties"

("Nervous System" 19). It was Robert Whytt, appointed professor of medicine in 1747, who first assimilated mind to body in physiological terms.[2] He viewed bodily responses to stimuli as purposeful, not mechanical, locating their source in what he called "the sentient principle," an immaterial substance that could feel and react. His successors at the university developed this notion further: William Cullen by replacing the immaterial sentient principle with a material fluid that, when in an excited state, produced "nervous energy," the chief constituent of life, and Alexander Monro by putting Whytt and Cullen together to claim that, where a sentient principle received stimuli, an electric nervous energy managed the ensuing agency. Hunter's vital principle involves a related attempt to make life an effect of the agency of a self-regulating organism. The point here is not to ponder the peculiarities of physiological speculation but simply to see how Scottish medicine makes the mind run the whole length of the human body through a tender network of nerves. *Sensibility* is a property of the nervous system and *sympathy* the means of coordinating its operation both within and between bodies. The literature of sensibility that flourishes in the last half of the eighteenth century owes everything to physiology. Feeling becomes the new evangel because the body knows best.

That's why Jerome McGann, without drawing directly on this material, can emphasize the physicality of such literature. In it "the body's elementary and spontaneous mechanisms come to measure persons themselves as well as their social relations" (*Poetics of Sensibility* 7). The recent work of Alan Richardson shows how deeply Romantic literature too is touched by contemporary physiology.[3] Wordsworth is no exception. His poetry and poetics are both indebted to Scottish medicine. His preoccupation with the growth of the poet's mind as a dynamic effect of the body's life would be impossible without it. But it's worth asking just how those bodily mechanisms measure persons and relations. A closer look at Wordsworth's practice reveals its tendency to advance the norm of the proper body as the measure of human health. Deviant flesh proves problematic to a poetry of feeling, the occasion either of a sympathy that assimilates or a disavowal that dismisses its material difference. Either way, monstrosities succumb to the measure of humanity. Wordsworth may not have been a physician, but he played one in his poems, equipped with the *materia medica* of a physiological aesthetics.

Erasmus Darwin's *Zoonomia* is Wordsworth's most obvious source for such an aesthetics, but its plausibility derives from the work of John Brown.[4] Brown was another in the line of Scottish medical luminaries, the star student of Cullen. In 1780 Brown published, in Latin, the infamous *Elementa Medicinae,* which was translated into English with revisions in 1795. Its contribution to medicine inspired desperate allegiances. In Edinburgh there were duels between supporters and detractors. On the continent there were riots, one of which at the University of Göttingen in 1802 lasted two days. Novalis and Schelling were deeply impressed with Brown's work, and through them traces of it appear in Nietzsche. Brown took from Cullen the idea that living things were distinguished by a characteristic state of nervous excitement. But rather than linking this state causally to a material fluid, he preferred to view it as an effect of a relation between forces of excitation. With this move he constructed a theory of health and illness as normative as it is elegant: if excitation produces health, then too little or too much produces illness. "All life consists in stimulus" (19), says Brown, and health is its equilibrium, its normal state. Although he calls the capacity to react to stimuli "excitability," he considers it neither substance nor essence, avoiding the tendency of his teachers to hypostatize a material or immaterial origin for life. "Excitement" is simply the state that characterizes living tissue, whether animal or vegetable, and it arises through the interplay of "exciting powers" acting on "excitability." Brown posits no causal relations among these constituents. The appeal of his physiology is that, while it accepts the assimilation of mind to body characteristic of Scottish medicine, it takes health to be the normal effect of an interplay among force relations irreducible to matter or spirit.

The following passage clarifies Brown's peculiarly postmodern physiology:

> Excitement, the effect of the exciting powers, the true cause of life, is, within certain boundaries, produced in a degree proportioned to the degree of stimulus. The degree of stimulus, when moderate, produces health; in a higher degree it gives occasion to diseases of excessive stimulus; in lower degree, or ultimately low, it induces those that depend upon deficiency of stimulus or debility. And, as what has been mentioned, is the cause both of diseases and perfect health; that which restores the morbid to the healthy state, is a diminution of excitement *in the case of* diseases of excessive stimulus, and encrease *of the same excitement* for the removal of diseases of debility. (9)

The simplicity of Brown's theory is seductive. Stimuli produce excitement and excitement is life; too much or too little and a body deviates from the norm of health and falls ill. On this account, normal and pathological bodies are functionally equivalent, making health a condition that is not just normal but normative. In Brown's physiology proper embodiment becomes a matter of mathematics as health proves a quantifiable measure of excitement. As Canguilhem puts the point, "To define the abnormal as too much or too little is to recognize the normative character of the so-called normal state. This normal or physiological state is no longer simply a disposition which can be revealed and explained as a fact, but a manifestation of an attachment to some value" (56–57). Brown turns health into a value that reinforces the cultural norm of the proper body, since all bodies, even sick ones, are equally excitable.

It would appear, then, that what menaces life is life itself. Sickness and health are effects of the same interplay of forces, variations on the state of excitement that differ only in degree. The stimuli that cause disease or its predisposition can cure it too, which is why Brown divides disease into two categories, the *sthenic* and the *asthenic,* depending on whether it results from an excess or a deficiency of stimuli. Treatment in either case involves an adjustment of stimuli, down for sthenic and up for asthenic diseases, but since most tend ultimately toward the exhaustion of excitability, the usual and best medicines are stimulants. Brown's personal favorites were alcohol and opium. The physician's job is to observe and modify the play of forces responsible for pathological levels of excitement, in Brown's words "to consider the deviation of excitement from the healthy standard in order to remove it by proper means" (79). Healing involves the (re)embodiment of a norm of excitement. But because life thrives as the effect of so complex an interplay of stimuli, that norm proves its vitality more in the breech than the rule. Such is implied by Brown's dark suggestion that "Life is a forced state[;] that the tendency of animals of every moment is to dissolution; that they are kept from it, by foreign powers, *and by these* with difficulty and only for a little; and then, from the necessity of their fate, give way to death" (34). The same forces that produce life dissolve it. Brown's physiology affirms life as a state of excitement wholly without recourse to its persistence as either spirit or matter. One is reminded of Nietzsche's caveat: "Let us beware of saying that death is opposed to life. The living is merely a type of what is dead, and a very rare type" (*Gay Science* 168).

It is toward the enhancement of this type that Wordsworth directs his early poetry. Brown's physiology stands behind this effort, providing the theoretical foundation for both a physiological aesthetics and its corollary that the poet can play the physician. If Wordsworth is a healer not just of the human mind but also of the proper body, then his poetry must have healthful—which is to say normalizing—effects. His belief that it does appears most openly in the famous "Preface" he added to the 1800 edition of *Lyrical Ballads*. It is easy to read this document, with its spontaneous overflow of powerful feeling and its Man speaking to men, as an early articulation and defense of Romantic ideology. More circumspectly, McGann has recently described it as "a sentimental manifesto in the strictest sense" (*Poetics of Sensibility* 121). But an even more nuanced reading would see it as divided in its commitments—split between sentimentality and sensibility, to use McGann's terms, or better yet between competing explanations of what poetry is and what it does. On the one hand there's all the familiar language about "the essential passions of the heart," and "the manners of rural life," and "the beautiful and permanent forms of nature." But beyond this characteristically Romantic language is another kind that owes more to contemporary medicine than to critical stereotype. It's worth noting that the "Preface" bears little trace of the faculty that psychology associated with so much Romanticism. The word "imagination" appears only three times, once to describe the source of "a certain coloring" cast over ordinary things, once as a pejorative to describe the source of false descriptions, and once to raise the issue of its physiological effects: "I wished to draw attention to the truth that the power of the human imagination is sufficient to produce such changes even in our physical nature as might almost appear miraculous" (*Selected Poems* 461n).[5] Shifting the emphasis from the first part of this sentence to the last, from imagination to physical nature, begins to recover the physiological agenda of Wordsworth's "Preface," its commitment to a poetry of bodily effect and physical healing.

In other words, Wordsworth views his poetry as a stimulant to life and measures its value against its bodily effects—as long as they are normal, healthy effects. Wordsworth advances his physiological agenda by putting a Brunonian spin on his diagnosis of contemporary society. The "state of almost savage torpor" that he sees around him describes the characteristic debility of asthenic disease, the reduction of stimuli to a potentially fatal minimum. When Wordsworth makes the odd remark that "the mind is capable of being excited without the application of gross and violent stimulants" (449), he is practicing good medicine. In cases of asthenia Brown recommends moderate treatment: "The indication of cure is to increase excitement. . . . here it is necessary to begin with a small degree of stimulus and increase gradually" ("Table of Excitability" n.p.). No wonder Wordsworth distrusts "sickly and stupid German Tragedies" that excite only a "degrading thirst after outrageous stimulation" (449). It's not the works themselves but their bodily effects that concern him. Outrageous stimulation threatens an already debilitated nervous system with exhaustion. Physiologically speaking, German literature is bad for your health. By implication Wordsworth's own poetry is a stimulant too, but one that works more moderately than those sickly tragedies to restore a debilitated body to the healthy norm.

Consider in this regard Wordsworth's description of what poetry does: "The end of Poetry is to produce excitement in co-existence with an overbalance of pleasure" (459). This use of the word "excitement" ties Wordsworth's aesthetics directly to Brown's physiology, since excitement is the state that characterizes living tissue. To produce it through poetry is to enhance life, to advance vitality in unequivocally bodily ways. Poetry may in essence *be* a powerful overflow of spontaneous feeling recollected in tranquility, but in effect it *produces* life, the healthy life of the body in its normal state. As stimulant, poetry excites living tissues. Wordsworth comes surprisingly close in the "Preface" to Brown's sense of the body as an effect of the interplay of force relations. In Wordsworth's estimation, the Poet's understanding of humanity differs from other people's in that "He considers man and the objects that surround him as acting and re-acting upon each other, so as to produce an infinite complexity of pain and pleasure" (455). This infinite complexity of affects constitutes the proper body, which poetry medicates as a stimulant, making the poet the physician of what for lack of a better term can be called the bodied mind. The old tradition of taking Wordsworth for a spiritual healer is about half right. The spirit he tries to heal with his earliest work is the all too human one of the living body, a lyrical body assimilable to a norm of health through the operations of his physiological aesthetics.

But Wordsworth's physiological aesthetics is at odds with his more familiarly Romantic commitments to nature, mind, and their ennobling interchange. McGann is probably correct to classify him with sentimental writers for whom feeling is "an effect of sympathetic understanding gained through conscious attention and reflection" (*Poetics of Sensibility* 33). But Wordsworth succumbs to the sentimental only after testing the darker possibilities of his physiological aesthetics. The problem emerges around what Wordsworth calls "the grand elementary principle of pleasure, by which [humanity] knows, and feels, and lives, and moves" (455). Pleasure is Wordsworth's equivalent of Brown's "excitability," Cullen's "nervous energy," or Hunter's "vital principle." It is the driving force of life, the power that produces and is produced by living tissue. But unlike Brown, Wordsworth would prefer this force to have only healthy effects. Although he insists that the excitement poetry produces must be accompanied by "an overbalance of pleasure," he fears "there is some danger that the excitement may be carried beyond its proper bounds" (459). The possibility exists, in other words, that *his* poetry might produce sickness too, since "excitement is an unusual and irregular state of the mind" (459).

Wordsworth must keep poetry's overbalance of pleasure within the normal bounds of excitement if he means to maintain the health of the proper body. He tries to do so by using meter to add "the co-presence of something regular" to the stimulant effects of poetry. Meter normalizes those effects both physiologically and morally by introducing "something to which the mind has been accustomed . . . in a less excited state" (459). Its purpose is to produce a "dissimilitude" from what Wordsworth calls "the vulgarity and meanness of ordinary life," a dissimilitude that is "altogether sufficient for the gratification of a rational mind" (452). Poetry must produce pleasure and meter must secure health, but to reach those proper ends requires not just physiology but philosophy too—the rational mind that ultimately grounds Wordsworth's practice.[6] Wordsworth needs a guarantee for his treatments, so he turns sentimental to secure it, requiring poetry to originate in "that sane state of feeling which arises out of thought" (462). He rejects, in other words, Brown's suggestion that sickness and health are variations on the same state of excitement and insists on their opposition. As Wordsworth moves from the physiological to the philosophic mind, his poetry prefers moral to bodily effects. It betrays a nostalgia for the very dualism that a physiological aesthetics would do without. This, then, is the Wordsworthian decadence: the requirement that poetry have only healthy effects, that the body breed not life but mind. Is Wordsworth's poetry ultimately too mild a stimulant to affirm life fully, too balanced and thoughtful for bodily good? What of Nietzsche's reminder that

"It is exceptional states that condition the artist—all of them profoundly related to and interlaced with morbid phenomena—so it seems impossible to be
an artist and not to be sick" (*Gay Science* 428)?

That Wordsworth had an interest in the relationship between disease and
poetry is one of the lessons of *Lyrical Ballads*. It's full of sick people: mad
mothers, deranged vagrants, decrepit old men. His attention to their plight
is part of what gives his lyrics their social force. But so too is his sense of
how poetry might ameliorate distress. A liberal politics attends Wordsworth's
physiological aesthetics, one that appeals to a norm of health to find an index
of social justice. Wordsworth tries for a while to write a poetry that speaks
directly to the body, not for it, and improves its health. The possibility that
language spoken by real men and women affects people physiologically is the
obvious point of the poem Wordsworth called "one of the rudest" in his collection, "Goody Blake and Harry Gill." Goody Blake is poor and cold, Harry
Gill is warm and rich. Goody Blake's curse at being caught in the act of filch-
ing a few sticks plays straight on Harry Gill's pulses and undoes them: "And
Harry's flesh it fell away; / And all who see him say 'tis plain, / That, live as
long as live he may, / He never will be warm again" (ll. 117–18). Goody Blake's
words amount to a stimulant so violent that it exhausts Harry Gill's excitability, producing the classic symptom, according to Brown, of physiological
debility: extreme cold. Wordsworth imagines for his poetry a similar if more
moderate effect. It should act on the body to produce a physiological excitement that affirms the legitimacy of Goody Blake's curse. As stimulant, it mobilizes physical life to challenge class-based injustice.

Something similar happens in "The Idiot Boy," where old Susan Gale's
stomachache seems to require a man's attention, preferably a doctor's. Neigh-
bor Betty Foy's husband is away and only her beloved idiot boy can make the
trip into town. The little comedy of sympathies that ensues attests of course
to the healthiness of domestic affection. But it illustrates as well the physiological effects of language as a physical stimulant. When Betty finally leaves
to seek the fate of her errant child, Susan starts to worry about her friends,
and physically improves in the process: "And as her mind grew worse and
worse, / Her body it grew better" (100). Mental excitement has positive bodily
effects, a perfect illustration of Brown's prescription for the treatment of asthenic disease, of which he takes hysteria to be an instance. But it requires
speech to produce a full cure, Susan's spontaneous announcement of unen-
durable fears: "The word scarce said, / Did Susan rise up from her bed, / As if
by magic cured" (ll. 434–36). Once again words have bodily effects, a stimulant
to health that works like magic. And once again Wordsworth can quietly
trouble cultural hierarchies, this time of gender, through a poetry that illustrates and reenacts healing.

The trouble is that Wordsworth doesn't really trust such an aesthetics.
It is too intimately associated with things whose dwelling is not the light of

setting suns. His belief in poetry as a stimulant to life falters when the body does, or when sickness becomes the only kind of health the body can sustain. The poem that best illustrates this difficulty in *Lyrical Ballads* is "Simon Lee, the Old Huntsman," whose speaker, presumably Wordsworth, comes face to face with the disease of extreme old age. David Simpson has nicely parsed the poem's grammar of place and time, choosing to focus on "circumstances, apart from those of youth and health, that enabled the poet to come to the aid of the struggling old man" (*Wordsworth's Historical Imagination* 69). But it's worth considering those circumstances of youth and health too. For Simon Lee, the once robust and virile huntsman, is sick, but in a way that is indivisible from what remains to him of health: "And he is lean and he is sick, / His little body's half awry / His ancles they are swoln and thick; / His legs are thin and dry" (ll. 33–36). Confronted with such sickness, the poet does what he can to help, snapping with a quick blow the old root Simon has been wrestling. But the poem he writes about the encounter affirms life in moral rather than physiological terms. Simon's excessive gratitude becomes a sign not of excitement in the midst of decay and death, not of the slow health of dying, but moral truth: "Alas! the gratitude of men, / Has oftener left me mourning" (103–04). When sickness becomes the condition of health, when health is by definition diseased, as in the simple case of old age, Wordsworth turns to moral medicine. He speaks *for* the proper body and no longer *to* it, and his poetry solicits a philosophical response.

Wordsworth refuses the tragic implications that physiology forced on Brown: "that there is in no living system, whether of the animal or vegetable kind, any inherent power necessary to the preservation of life; that the same powers which form life at first, and afterwards support it, have at last a tendency to produce its dissolution; that life, the prolongation of life, its decay and death, are all states equally natural" (206). There are facts of physical life, it appears, that Wordsworth's poetry of the proper body cannot affirm. His physiological aesthetics turns sentimental, and moral reflection comes to regulate a diseased and dying body. His poems work quietly to incarnate a cultural norm of embodiment. It is worth remembering and perhaps repeating what Wordsworth wanted his poems to do: "I have wished to keep the reader in the company of flesh and blood" (450).

But not just any flesh and blood. When Wordsworth turns from diseased to deviant flesh, the normalizing force of his poetry becomes obvious. The pretense of the physician sucumbs to the pronouncements of the philosopher. In the famous account of Bartholomew Fair that closes book 7 of *The Prelude,* Wordsworth confronts flesh and blood en masse and retreats in mild disgust to the cleaner consolations of the proper body. Peter Stallybrass and Allon White show how Wordsworth delivers his description of the fair from a perspective, available only with the muse's help, "Above the press and danger of the crowd" (*Prelude* 1805, 7.657). Doing so, he recapitulates a classical poetics and politics that maintains a distance between the poet and the riot of humanity he sees beneath him (Stallybrass and White 122–23). That distance also reinforces the more material and contemporary norm of proper embodiment, allowing Wordsworth to devalue deviant flesh from the perspective of moral privilege.

From on high Bartholomew Fair seems nothing more than a "Parliament of Monsters" (7.691), a carnivalesque inversion of good governance and human health. However fascinated Wordsworth might be by "The silver-collared Negro with his timbre," the "Albinos, painted Indians, Dwarfs," or "Giants, Ventriloquists, [and] the Invisible Girl," he ultimately deems them "far-fetched, perverted things, / All freaks of nature" (7.676, 680, 683, 687–88). And he does so by appealing unabashedly to a moral norm that pathologizes material difference. The danger embodied in the fairgoing mob is its subversion of such norms through the production of a space of sociality where they no longer apply, where the distinctions they enforce become "All jumbled up together" (7.690). Stallybrass and White suggest that such spaces "become the very content of the bourgeois unconscious" as the filth and excess they encode shadow the subjectivity of the solid citizen (124). The same can be said for the bodies such spaces glorify. Monstrosities announce their singularity through "Dumb proclamations of the Prodigies," meaningless vauntings of material difference irreducible to bodied norms (7.666). Confronted with this glorious deviance Wordsworth turns doctor of philosophy, assimilating such singularities to "the same perpetual flow / Of trivial objects, melted and reduced / To one identity" (7.701–03). Deviant flesh possesses no moral value because it manifests only "differences / That have no law, no meaning, and no end" (7.703–04). It takes a norm to make such differences meaningful—which is to say morally and even materially equivalent. When it comes to bodies, Wordsworth "sees the parts / As parts, but with a feeling of the [proper] whole" (7.711–12).

That emphasis on feeling should be enough to indicate how Wordsworth justifies the norm of embodiment his poetry advances. The true standard of material and moral value thrives beyond the London metropolis with its fairs and freaks and fire-eating women. Proper bodies are natural bodies, and the philosophic mind best feels their sublime force: "Such virtue have the forms / Perennial of the ancient hills" (7.725). The norm of the proper body refers directly back to nature's forms, the ground of all that is morally and materially valuable. Wordsworth ultimately abandons physiology for the firmer ground of nature to reinforce a cultural norm of embodiment that morally devalues monstrosities. Moutains are what really matter, since "The mountain's outline and its steady form, / Gives a pure grandeur, and its presence shapes / The measure and the prospect of the soul / To majesty" (7.722–24). Proper bodies are natural forms, which makes mountains the measure of humanity.

ASTONISHING PRODIGY OF HUMAN DIMENSIONS

If ever there were a mountain of a man, Daniel Lambert was it (Figure 7). Fully grown he tipped the scales at upwards of fifty stone—at fourteen pounds to the stone, that's over seven hundred pounds. His massive body presents a challenge to such norms as Wordsworth naturalizes. Lambert's reputation as the largest human on record stood for well over a century, making his name a byword for the prodigious, as in Herbert Spencer's description in *Study of Sociology* of a "Daniel Lambert of learning." Born at Leicester in 1770 to normally proportioned parents and athletically inclined in youth, he began to gain weight in his early twenties, burgeoning to an enormous girth.[7] He was apprenticed to the button trade in Birmingham but gave it up to succeed his father as the keeper of Leicester jail, until it occurred to him that his extraordinary mass might present something of a career opportunity. Resigning his position at the prison on an annuity of fifty pounds, he embarked for London in 1806, hoping, in the words of the *Dictionary of National Biography*, "to turn to profit the fame for corpulence which had hitherto brought him merely annoyance" (11: 448–49). What his experience reveals is the capacity of so singular a body at least to disturb if not wholly to subvert the regulatory norms that determine its value.

Figure 7. Daniel Lambert. The Wellcome Library, London.

In London Daniel Lambert was a major success. Taking up residence at 53 Piccadilly, he received company daily from three to five at a shilling a head, quickly gaining celebrity as an astonishing prodigy of superhuman dimensions. He made a living just by sitting in his parlor, offering his body to amazed gazes, at the ready in repartee. Having so much property in his own person, Lambert didn't labor to acquire more. Part of what qualifies him as a prodigy is his material exemption from the need to labor, which for Locke legitimates the acquisition and accumulation of property. In its massive singularity, Lambert's body escapes the commodification of labor that enables wage relations and engenders civil society. People pay him to see the wonder of a body irreducible to labor, incapable of exchange. Here's a man so big that he makes money for doing nothing at all. His flesh embodies the negation of labor and merits fiscal reward, not for its fungibility but for its very substance. Giving money for a glimpse of it is paying tribute rather than wages, producing subsistence rather than capital. Lambert's monstrosity lays bare the operative logic of labor in a market economy to render singular bodies all the same.

Culturally speaking, then, the work of such monstrosities is double, troubling a norm that can reinscribe them. That the spectacle of this massive man presents a challenge to the proper body is part of what makes him so fascinating, as a contemporary advertisement attested: "When sitting he appears to be a stupendous mass of flesh, for his thighs are so covered by his belly that nothing but his knees are to be seen, while the flesh of his legs, which resemble pillows, projects in such a manner as to nearly bury his feet" (*DNB* 11: 448). Here's a body irreducible to propriety in either economic or moral terms. But other advertisements suggest just the opposite, that Lambert's huge body is remarkable for its very normality. As a physiological monstrosity, it can as easily afford an occasion for the (re)production of the norm from which it deviates, reinforcing rather than troubling its legitimacy. That's the effect of the copy accompanying Lambert's image (Figure 7). It treats Lambert's bulk as a kind of human ideal, bearing "NO BLEMISH WHATEVER" and enjoying "an excellent state of health." Functionally considered, this gigantic man is for the most part like any other: "His diet is plain and the quantity very moderate, for he does not eat more than the generality of men. . . . He sleeps well, but scarcely so much as other people; and his respiration is as free as that of any moderate-sized person." For all its troubling singularity, this particular monstrosity reinforces the cultural norm of the proper body. Once you get to know him, Daniel Lambert is just like you, only more so: "His countenance is manly and intelligent, he possesses great information, much ready politeness, and manners most affable and pleasing, with a perfect ease and facility in conversation." It comes as no surprise, then, that this prodigy turns out to be so personable, that beneath his bulk lurks a fundamental

similarity with others. Lambert's singular body functions culturally both to
trouble and to reinforce such beliefs.

This double work of deviance is exactly that of what Slovoj Žižek calls the
sublime object of ideology, which he describes as "a positive, material object
elevated to the status of the impossible Thing" (71). The sublime object gives
negation a material presence (the impossible Thing), but in such a way that
it communicates a terrifying delight. It can come to serve therefore as a site
for the overdetermination of ideological meaning. Žižek's example of such
an object is the sunken, silent wreck of the *Titanic.* The material fact of its
disaster is both psychologically fascinating and culturally symbolic for most
Westerners. The monstrosity of this titanic man produces similar psychological and cultural effects. In an increasingly liberal and capitalist social
context, Lambert's lumbering body communicates an impossible delight by
materializing the negation of labor, a desideratum whose conditions—what
bulk!—frighten as they fascinate. At the same time, it becomes the site of
ideological overdetermination, reproducing the cultural norm of the proper
body through that anxiety. Nowhere is this double work more apparent than
in the several political cartoons that appropriate the image of the Goliath
Lambert to affirm the patriotism of John Bull. In one titled *Bone and Flesh
or John Bull in Moderate Condition,* that familiar image placidly confronts
a thin but classically posed Napoleon in a manner reminiscent of Gillray's
national bodily stereotypes (Figure 8). The French adversary announces the

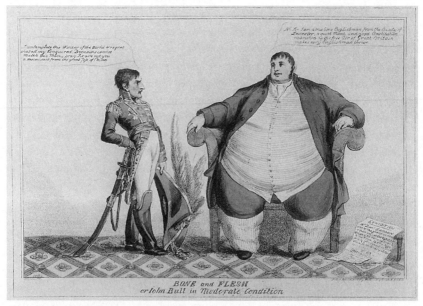

Figure 8. *Bone and Flesh or John Bull in Moderate Condition* (15 April 1806). Copyright
The British Museum.

frightful fascination Lambert's body provokes ("I contemplate this Wonder of the World"), while Lambert himself pronounces its ideological reinscription: "No Sir, I am a true born Englishman from the County of Leicester" (George 8: 426). The cartoon neatly documents the double work of deviant flesh first to trouble then to reproduce the cultural norm of the proper body, with the added lesson in this instance of its nationalist implications. The biggest man in Britain is the most British of men. His very deviance embodies national identity. Monstrosities apparently can have normalizing effects.[8]

Born without Hands or Arms

Monstrosities are legion, however, and do not always occasion such effects by materializing a negation of labor. On the contrary, some bodies affirm the value of labor as a means of overcoming a disabling singularity. Typical in this regard is the prodigy of the armless artisan, who wondrously performs tasks whose difficulty can be easy to take for granted. In her day, Miss Sarah Biffin made something of a name for herself through the unusually high quality of her fancy drawing and miniatures on ivory (Figure 9). She was born without hands or arms in East Qantoxhead in 1784, and her parents were poor. By dint of "indomitable perseverance," she taught herself to paint, using her mouth in place of her fingers to hold pen, pencil, and brush (*DNB* 2: 481). With the help of a man named Dukes, reputed to have withheld most of her earnings, she exhibited her unusual abilities at fairs and markets, settling for a time first in London and then Birmingham. After attracting the attention of the earl of Morton, she received formal instruction in painting from a popular keepsake illustrator, Mr. Craig, and came eventually to find sponsors in the impressive cadre of worthies listed on one of her handbills: the king of Holland, Her late Royal Highness the Princess Augusta, His Late Majesty George the Third, William the Fourth, His Royal Highness the Duke of York, "and almost all the Nobility of that day" (Morley, *Scrapbook*). Not bad for an armless artist from Somerset, though her later years were hard, and she died in poverty mitigated only by a friend's benevolence.

The singular body of Miss Biffin becomes an occasion for the production of social virtues. Through her labor at the canvas she could pledge allegiance to the proper body, affirming its legitimacy as a norm against which to measure her exceptional abilities. But more important perhaps is the role her body plays in the legitimation of class privilege and the advancement of a secular humanitarian pathos that ennobles all who are able to feel it. On the same handbill appears a testimonial offered by the duke of Sussex during the presentation of a medal from the Society of Artists in 1821: "I beg to call your attention to a Picture, which I consider deserves the greatest commendation had it been executed with every advantage, but more particularly so being

Figure 9. Sarah Biffin. Engraved by R. W. Sievier after Sarah Biffin (1821). The Wellcome Library, London.

the production of a Female Without Hands Or Arms. I recommend you to visit her, comfort her, and patronize her." Visit, comfort, patronize: monstrosities can conjure social virtues, the more so when capable of commendable productions. They register a dependency that the proper body occludes, the indelible trace of social relations, and thereby provide an opportunity for class largesse. Nobility may set an example, but in a social context that has the middle class forging a secular ethic of humanitarian obligation, deviant flesh affords an occasion for the production of virtues for the proper body. As an armless artist, Miss Biffin produces more than remarkable miniatures.

Her odd body helps to produce a humanitarian narrative written in flesh. Thomas Laqueur has shown how such a narrative might arise from medical practices like the case history and the autopsy that enable an imaginative appreciation of the depths of another's suffering.[9] Deviant flesh puts that appreciation to work socially. A humanitarian narrative comes to regulate the relation between the proper body and monstrosities, assuring their status as both deviation from and special instance of that norm. Laqueur suggests that such narratives "create a sense of property in the objects of compassion," that humanitarians "claim a proprietary interest in those whom they aid" ("Bodies" 179, 180). It should come as no revelation that the virtues of the proper body are proprietary. A humanitarian narrative simply legitimates the social appropriation of deviant flesh, its treatment as a kind of common moral property of little inherent value except in relation to a humane standard.

Such is the lesson of a sad if telling broadside bearing the image of a child born armless (Figure 10). "Nature," reads the text, written by a Dr. Bell, "has thrown this Infant on the care of the humane, with little other pretensions to be hailed as a brother by human beings, than his capacity of suffering. He has a head and body, organs of the senses, and a soul to suffer or to feel gratitude, but he is without all means of ministering to his own wants, of resistance, or even of motion. He seems to be delivered to the kindness of the world" *(John Johnson Collection)*. A residual capacity for suffering is all that relates this child to the proper body, yet it is enough to justify the world's kindness. His deformity may be manifest, but a humanitarian narrative manages its assimilation to that norm: not as a singular person defined by his physical difference, but as a kind of moral property acquired through the labor of love. It would appear that Laqueur is right, that humanitarian habits are those of the physician. Such a narrative treats its object the way John Hunter treated Charles Byrne. Monstrosities belong to their betters, materializing the virtues of proper embodiment.

THE DEVIOUS PATHS

With the emergence of liberal society, the proper body comes increasingly to serve as its cultural norm. But there remained in the late eighteenth and early nineteenth centuries spaces that contested that normative function. A close inspection of Thomas Rowlandson's lively colored print of Bartholomew Fair (1799) reveals, amidst the crowd and the attractions, a banner bearing the armless image of the amazing Miss Biffin (Figure 11). Part of the appeal of the annual fair, held at Smithfield for three days beginning on September 3, St. Bartholomew's Day, was the reign it gave to the spectacle of bodily difference. In the wry words of a pamphlet published in 1810, "There you might behold the astonishing gigantic infant girl, not more than *thirty* years old; the wonderful ventriloquist, the gigantic Irish youth, the surprising Miss Biffin, who, without legs or arms, writes a most beautiful *hand* with her *mouth,* and performs other most miraculous operations, terrific to the beholders"

Born, near Ide-hill – Sundridge – Co Kent – 1813.

NATURE has thrown this Infant on the care of the humane, with little other preten-sions to be hailed as a brother by human beings, than his capacity of suffering. He has a head and body, organs of the senses, and a soul to suffer or to feel gratitude, but he is without all means of ministering to his own wants, of resistance, or even of motion. He seems to be delivered to the kindness of the world.

The Philosopher may contemplate the progress of this Infant's mind with interest, for it must ever remain without those ideas which we receive through the united operation of the sense, of touch, and of motion.

How little knowledge is received by the eye and ear, there are few who consider; yet that the ideas which seem to be bestowed upon us through the power of vision, are in fact obtained through the sense of touch, and the motion of the fingers and limbs, there can be no doubt. This is the reason that the sense of touch is called the Geometrical sense: It corrects the others; it gives precision to the ideas otherwise undefined. It brings us acquainted with the hardness and softness, the roughness, smoothness, irregularity and distance of objects. Of how many aids to the understanding then must this Infant be deprived of! and it may be curious to observe how Nature will work to supply these defi-ciencies.

Nature, ever bountiful, may give to this soul, so nearly cut off from human communi-cation, powers or faculties of the internal sense, an equivalent for the want of those enjoy-ments common to the lowest human creature. But there are other considerations more pressing upon the Parents of this unfortunate Child—the helplessness of infancy is the link of endearment to the Parents. Here is a helpless thing, that must be ever an infant; and Nature has implanted in the Parent's breast a proportioned energy of affection.

Who then would wish to separate the Child from the Parent? who would give this little being to the care of any one but the Parent? The Parent must therefore be sup-ported; and that which the charitable may give, they are requested to note in the book, that those who have taken an interest in the welfare of this Child, may see it protected. Alas! how incapable must every exertion be, to bestow on this solitary thing, enjoyment equal to the lowest of God's creatures.

Born ocbr. 1813 – ob. april. 1816 – at 2½ years.
Lady Amhurst sent the child to be exhibited in London, & Dr Bell, had the above published.

London: Printed by R. M'Millan, Bow Street, Covent Garden.

Figure 10. Handbill (1813). Bodleian Library, Oxford University. J. Johnson Collection. Human Freaks 2.

(*Historical Account* 25). Bartholomew Fair was a space of deviance, a collective social practice that for a few days each year challenged the normative force of the proper body. In this it provides an instance of those "other spaces" Foucault calls "heterotopias of deviation," spaces "in which individuals whose behavior is deviant in relation to the required mean or norm are placed" ("Spaces" 22). Bodies as much as behaviors qualify for such placement. Fairs like the one at Smithfield provide a space, if only temporarily, for monstrosities to matter in a way that troubles the force of proper embodiment.[10]

Figure 11. Detail from Thomas Rowlandson, *Bartholomew Fair* (1799). Guildhall Library, Corporation of London.

Singular bodies had their day during Bartholomew Fair. Jeffrey Dunstan turned up there in 1783, a foundling cripple who "had acquired notoriety by his grotesque figure," becoming for a time the fair's presiding genius, to the point that he was made mayor of Garret (*A Peep* 10; Figure 12). Punch lorded over the motions with a form as twisted as his habits (Figure 13). And there were monstrosities of the sort that made Wordsworth so uncomfortable.

Figure 12. Jeffrey Dunstan. *The Wonderful and Scientific Museum: or Magazine of Remarkable Characters* (1803). The Wellcome Library, London.

Bartholomew Fair was a space "where John Bull and his merry family might see, for sixpence, such monsters, prodigies, and curiosities, as they could not see in any other part of the habitable globe for one thousand guineas" (*Historical Account* 24). It was a time "when all giants in the land, and the dwarfs too, make a general muster" to participate in a "Saturnalia of nondescript noise and nonconformity" (Hone, *Every-Day* 2: 1195). The obvious frivolity of these descriptions conveys the fair's countercultural force, its efficacy as a space of deviance that suspends habitual proprieties. There monstrosities could be valued for their singularity, their positive otherness to the proper body: "human monsters, shall acquire renown, / the spotted Negro—and the armless maid!" (quoted in Hone, *Every-Day* 2: 1206; Figure 14).[11]

While it is important not to romanticize that renown (the spotted Negro

Figure 13. Detail, *Punch's Puppet Show* (1792). Reprinted by permission of The British Library.

The Beautiful Spotted
Negro Boy

DURING THE FAIR.

In his Travelling Pavilion.

Will be exhibited the truly Wonderful and Beautiful

Spotted Negro
BOY,

FROM THE

Carribee Islands, in the West Indies,

Aged Three Years and a Half.

He is one of those wonderful productions of Nature, which excite the curiosity, and gratify the beholder with the surprising works of the Creator ; he is the progeny of Negroes, being beautifully covered over by a diversity of spots of transparent brown and white; his hair is interwoven, black and white alternately, in a most astonishing manner ; his countenance is interesting, with limbs admirably proportioned ; his ideas are quick and penetrating, yet his infantine simplicity is truly captivating. He must be seen, to convince it is not in the power of language to convey an adequate description of this Fanciful Child of Nature, formed in her most playful mood, and allowed by every lady and gentleman that has seen it, the greatest curiosity ever beheld.

May be seen from Ten in the Morning till Ten in the Evening,

Admittance for Ladies & Gentlemen 1s. Servants & Children Half-price.

N.B. Ladies and Gentlemen wishing to see this Wonderful Child at their own Houses, may be accommodated by giving a few hours notice.

Copper-plate Likenesses of the Boy to be had at the Place of Exhibition.

T. Romney, Printer, Bridge-road, Lambeth.

Figure 14. The Beautiful Spotted Negro Boy (1790s). Reprinted by permission of The British Library.

died in childhood, the armless maid sank into poverty), it is just as important not to dismiss this homage paid to monstrosities. In this regard Bartholomew Fair and others like it differ from the American freak show. Thomson has compellingly argued that the latter displays "America's need to ratify a dominant, normative identity by ritually displaying in public those perceived as the embodiment of what collective America took itself *not* to be" (*Bodies* 59). That fairs can produce similar effects needs to be acknowledged. That they necessarily do is another question. Bartholomew Fair was a social event in ways that the American freak show never was. The decontextualized spectacle of the freak turns him, her, or even *it* into a pure instance of pathological deviance. In Thomson's words, "freaks and prodigies were solely bodies, without the humanity social structures confer upon more ordinary people" (*Bodies* 57). Bartholomew Fair, in contrast, was a recurring heterotopia capable of conferring positive value on such bodies. Tony Bennett nicely captures its symbolic implications: "In the late eighteenth and early nineteenth centuries, the fair had served as the very emblem for the disorderly forms of conduct associated with all sites of popular assembly" (4). But its cultural function is more than merely symbolic. A space of deviance, the fair embodies a populous irreducible to an aggregate of individuals. It opens a place for deviations irreducible to a proper norm. As Stallybrass and White have shown so well, the fair does not simply oppose the festive to the mundane, the popular to the bourgeois, the grotesque to the classical. Rather, its practices "are intrinsic to the dialectics of social classification as such. The 'carnivalesque' mediates between a classical/classificatory [i.e. proper] body and its negations, its Others, what it excludes to create its identity as such" (26). Bartholomew Fair performs, so to speak, the cultural possibility of monstrosities.

And it has for centuries. Its history as a space of deviance spans back to the twelfth century when Henry the First granted his jester-turned-monk, Rayer, land in West Smithfield for the Priory of St. Bartholomew, later to become a hospital for the sick poor. Rayer built a space that persisted for some seven hundred years, whose boundaries were marked with the virtues of mirth and folk medicine. The hospital drew the sick and the lame, while the priory drew itinerant merchants, allowing compassion for bodily suffering to mix with concern for a decent trade. The fair that came annually to inhabit this space partook of its virtues, memorializing a culture that would run counter to that of liberal society. Trade was its original business but ceased to play a primary role before the late eighteenth century, as the pamphlet titled *A Peep at Bartholomew Fair* (circa 1810) attests: "although Bartholomew Fair was originally established for commercial purposes, that feature has long been obliterated; and it has for more than a century been distinguished merely for shows and interludes, and for noise, mirth, and a grotesque display of low fun and vulgar humor" (4). By the early nineteenth century it came to be called the Cockney Carnival, but it was still characterized by its own distinctive and long-standing cultural traditions: the ritual tumult of Lady Holland's mob on the eve of its commencement, the court of *pied poudre* that dispensed its own unappealable justice, the savory sausage (in earlier days pigmeat) that tempted the fairgoer at the entrance of Smithfield (the place dubbed Wilke's Parlor).

That these were mostly folk traditions often at odds with the proprieties of middle-class society is the sentiment that permeates Henry Morley's monumental and very moving *Memoirs of Bartholomew Fair* (1859). The book is an extended eulogy for a social practice those proprieties ultimately expunged, and it emphasizes the fair's affirmation of lives otherwise without material value: "enough has been read of the story of the Fair to show that it was as truly as the House of Commons, part of the Representation of the English People; not, indeed, its Lower, but its Lowest House" (254). Bartholomew Fair was a space open to all including the most common, the least proper: "journeymen and apprentices of all trades, sweeps, dustmen, and coal-heavers, sailors, Jews, and pickpockets, carmen and constables, giggling spinsters with their gadding mothers, milliners' apprentices, and servant maids, all mixed the throng, and every thing in the shape of modesty and delicacy was disbanded for the night" (*Historical Account* 26). That such a space should offer prominence of place to deviant flesh is in keeping with its characteristic economy of transgression. But as Stallybrass and White insist, and contrary to the spirit of Morley's understandable nostalgia, that economy is not simply one of opposition, of, for instance, folk to modern traditions. More menacingly perhaps, it is one that augurs change: "Indeed fairs were as much an agent of transformation as of 'popular tradition', since they brought together the exotic and the familiar, the villager and the townsman, the professional performer and the bourgeois observer. Fairs actually promoted a conjuncture of discourses and objects favourable to innovations" (36). In a space of deviance, monstrosities breed new forms of life. Where a space like the Hunterian Museum contains deviance to master it medically, that of Bartholomew Fair frees it to transgress the ways of proper embodiment.[12]

The fair may have been a licensed space, but it was not therefore divested of opportunities for transgression and transformation of proper embodiment and behavior.[13] Quite the contrary. De Certeau argues that the class most subject to the operations of power must "play on and with a terrain imposed on it and organized by the law of a foreign power. . . . It must vigilantly make use of the cracks that particular conjunctions open in the surveillance of the propriety powers" (37). As a space of deviance, Bartholomew Fair provided an opportunity for play on and with the field of power, for stepping on and through the cracks of a progressively normalized society toward new formations. In this it revives something of the life of becoming that Mikhail Bakhtin associates with the crowd of the traditional carnival:

> Man experiences this flow of time in the festive marketplace, in the carnival
> crowd, as he comes into contact with other bodies of varying age and social
> caste. He is aware of being a member of a continually growing and renewed
> people. This is why festive folk laughter presents an element of victory not only
> over supernatural awe, over the sacred, over death; it also means the defeat of
> power, of earthly kings, or the earthly upper classes, of all that oppresses and
> restricts. (92)

Bakhtin's utopian idealism may be inappropriate to the facts of fairgoing life
in the late eighteenth and early nineteenth centuries. The memory of the
festive marketplace may indeed live on in the persistence of folk traditions
at Bartholomew Fair. But monstrosities differ from what Bakhtin calls "the
great generic body" of the grotesque in their singularity (89). Their becoming
is a contingent matter that cultural norms like the proper body impede. As a
space of deviance, the annual fair at least exonerates these lives irreducible
to the proper body, less grotesque than truly monstrous in their singularity,
their physical otherness.

As the nineteenth century advances, however, museums displace fairs as
preferred places of amusement and recreation. Bennet shows how this move
institutionalizes a public pedagogy of the proper body, producing progressive liberal subjects by managing their physical encounter with culture and
knowledge.[14] The fair's space of deviance and the lives that matter there turn
nomadic, shifting to the fringes and the underworlds. It would be wrong therefore to conclude that such heterotopias have been eliminated from liberal
society. They have pitched their motley tents elsewhere than its most public
places. That the transformative force of deviant flesh presents a menace to
proper embodiment and its preferred public spaces is the true message of
Morley's *Memoirs*. By 1855 Bartholomew Fair was no more, its space rebuilt to
suit more mannerly functions: "There is a silence now on the historic ground
over which, century after century, the hearts of our forefathers have throbbed
with the outspoken joys of life" (493). All that remains of that historic ground
today is a small green and an underground carpark.[15]

Transformations become less likely without spaces in which to occur. Eliminating the space of Smithfield disperses the menace of its monstrosities. Even
the populist William Hone can testify to the increasing urgency of that bourgeois agenda: "no person of respectability . . . visits [Bartholomew Fair], but
as a curious spectator of an annual congregation of ignorance and depravity"
(*Every-Day* 1: 1252). The relative triumph of the proper body was not without
its battles, however, even if they were waged invisibly. In 1817 an insurrection against the government planned for Smithfield was called off partly for
lack of popular support.[16] Government mobilization of dragoons didn't help
the conspirators' plans, in which, according to the *Morning Chronicle*, "a
multitude of persons were to assemble at Bartholomew Fair in the evening,

armed with pikes and other weapons, with which they intended to sally forth,
attack the Bank and other public buildings, and finally excite and produce
a General Insurrection" (8 Sept. 1817; quoted in Hone, *Insurrection* 2). As a
space of deviance, Bartholomew Fair could turn palpably and politically menacing. On that night in 1817 an invisible skirmish took place between forces
of normalization and their singular opponents. In a brilliant, biting homage
to the dangerous powers of deviant flesh, Hone imagines what might have
happened:

> The main body of the conspirators was to march to the city, led by Askins the
> Ventriloquist, who, mounted on the *large horse,* nineteen hands high, was to
> stop at the top of Cornhill, with his face towards Shoreditch Church, and order
> an attack on the *Old Woman* (Bank) with one side of his mouth, and summon
> the *Old Man* (the Tower) with the other. If the *Old Man* made resistance, and
> fired red-hot shot, Signora Girdelli, the female *Salamander,* was to perform the
> important service of catching them in her mouth, and discharging them back
> at the besieged hotter than she had them. To the astonishing Youth, only seven
> years of age, was assigned the duty of blocking up London Bridge, by laying
> the Monument across it. The Irish Giant was stationed at Blackfriars Bridge,
> to throw the soldiers into the Thames by armfuls, if they ventured near him;
> and the Stone-eater was to be dispatched to the Strand Bridge, for the purpose
> of swallowing that edifice in the short space of one hour, and battering down
> Westminster Bridge with the fragments, which his zeal for the service prompt-
> ed him to engage he would do within the limited time. Boys were to be placed
> at every pump in London, and at a certain hour they were all to begin pumping
> for the purpose of inundating the metropolis, which it was calculated could be
> effectually done in one hour and twenty minutes; whilst, to increase the confu-
> sion, the Fire-eater undertook to drink up all the *Gas,* and throw the town into
> utter darkness; and the keeper of Toby, the Sapient Pig, volunteered to aid the
> insurgents, by binding himself that interesting animal should tell them what
> o'clock it was at any given moment, without a light. (*Insurrection* 7)

For all its humor, a wistfulness saturates Hone's treatment of the Bartholomew Fair revolutionaries. Beyond the borders of a space of deviance, their
singularity turns ineffectual, less menacing than merely entertaining. The
insurrection's failure may have literally spelled doom for the cause of radical
reform, but symbolically it signaled defeat for the transformative force of
monstrosities in liberal society, at least in Britain. Hone wrote his final account of Bartholomew Fair for the *Every-Day Book* in 1826, fully aware that
its days were numbered: "it is going out like the lottery, by force of public
opinion" (2: 1196). The Cockney Carnival was no place for the proper body.
But its elimination meant the eradication of a social space that affirmed the
transformative force of monstrosities, not in spite but because of their physi-

cal otherness. As fairs give way to freak shows, the proper body consolidates its claims to corporeality.

HIDEOUS PROGENY

But the possibility of insurrection lives on at least imaginatively. When the hideous monster of Mary Shelley's *Frankenstein* fully comprehends his physical difference from human beings, he swears vengeance: "from that moment I declared everlasting war against the species, and, more than all, against him who had formed me, and sent me forth to this insupportable misery" (133). The monster's response to the regulatory force of the norm of the proper body is to murderously fight back. Psychological readings of his ordeal are too clever for their own good, since they read right through the material fact of his physical deformity. But the monster never forgets it, even if his critics do. His own words tell the tale not only of his personal embodiment but also of its social valuation. He derides his "odious and loathsome person" as a "filthy type" of humanity; he acknowledges himself a "monster so hideous" that all including his creator must turn away "in disgust" (126). The violence he breeds only objectifies the implied violence of his breeding, the devaluative force of the proper body, which measures and eliminates physical singularity from full participation in social life.

That his creator is an anatomist makes perfect sense, given the role of medical science in building the proper body.[17] Victor Frankenstein's youthful interest in Agrippa and Paracelsus is quaint in comparison with what medical science teaches him. From the ancients he acquired ideal longing, from the moderns, disciplined knowledge. He learns the secret of imparting life from the latter, specifically from the knowledge of contemporary physiology. In describing his pursuit of the "ability to give life to an animal as complex and wonderful as man," Frankenstein speaks in the very language of John Hunter: "Where, I often asked myself, did the principle of life proceed?" (48, 46). Hunter found it in an organism's particulate matter and coordinative function of parts. According to his own testimony Frankenstein follows that lead: "I . . . determined thenceforth to apply myself more particularly to those branches of natural philosophy which relate to physiology" (46). He studies the "cause and progress" of "the natural decay and corruption of the human body" and prepares a bodily frame "with all its intricacies of fibres, muscles, and veins" (47, 46, 48). In doing so, he proceeds in a manner similar to Hunter's, as described by Everard Home: "many parts of the human body being so complex, that their structure could not be understood, nor their use ascertained, Mr. Hunter was led to examine similar parts in other animals, in which the structure was more simple" (*Blood* v–vi). Frankenstein solves the same problem by making such parts especially huge, relying on their functional equivalence

with human anatomy to yield a functionally equivalent human: "As the minuteness of the parts formed a great hindrance to my speed, I resolved, contrary to my first intention, to make the being of a gigantic stature; that is to
say, about eight feet in height, and proportionably large" (49). Frankenstein
builds his monster's body in the image of a physiologically functional human
being, overlooking its material singularity. In his very faithfulness to modern
physiology, he creates a pathological specimen.

However functionally equivalent, the monster's material singularity deviates wildly from the cultural norm of the proper body. Recall Frankenstein's
glimpse of the disturbing form in a flash of lightning: "its gigantic stature,
and the deformity of the aspect, more hideous than belongs to humanity, instantly informed me that it was the wretch, the filthy demon to whom I had
given life" (71). Life does not in and of itself confer humanity on a human
organism. That distinction comes through its ability to participate in civil
society. The burden of the monster's early days is to prove his worthiness of
that participation. Rejected by his creator, he begins to realize the difficulty
he faces:

> I was not even of the same nature as man. I was more agile than they, and could
> subsist upon coarser diet; I bore the extremes of heat and cold with less injury
> to my frame; my stature far exceed their's. When I looked around, I saw and
> heard none like me. Was I then a monster, a blot upon the earth, from which all
> men fled, and whom all men disowned? (115–16)

For all its functionality, the monster's body has no human equivalent. Its life
exceeds that which the proper body deems legitimate. Living the fate of deviant flesh, the monster relates to others not as a free individual so much as "a
filthy mass that moved and talked" (143).

His initial response to this fate is to believe in the liberal dream of abstract equivalence. He resolves reasonably to overcome his apparent disability by asserting his essential humanity. Longing to participate in the loving
relations of the De Lacey family, he imagines their warm reception could
he just convince them that monstrosity is only skin deep: "I persuaded myself that when they should become acquainted with my admiration of their
virtues, they would compassionate me, and overlook my personal deformity.
Could they turn from their door one, however monstrous, who solicited their
compassion and friendship?" (126). Indeed they could, as the monster soon
discovers. The De Laceys' virtues, for all their humanity, cannot accommodate physical deformity, even where it affirms their authority. In attempting
to join a human community, the monster feels the true force of its humanity:
"in a transport of fury [Felix De Lacey] dashed me to the ground, and struck
me violently with a stick" (131).

The normative force of the proper body sparks violence where it touches
deviant flesh. The monster's murderous reprisals begin when he confronts an

image of that norm that awakens a full awareness of its function. Although Frankenstein's little brother William abuses the monster at first sight ("'ugly wretch! you wish to eat me, and tear me to pieces'" [139]), that is not why the child must die. The monster turns bloodthirsty only after noticing William's pendant:

> As I fixed my eyes on the child, I saw something glittering on his breast. I took it; it was a portrait of a most lovely woman. In spite of my malignity, it softened and attracted me. For a few moments I gazed with delight on her dark eyes, fringed by deep lashes, and her lovely lips; but presently my rage returned: I remembered that I was for ever deprived of the delights that such beautiful creatures could bestow; and that she whose resemblance I contemplated would, in regarding me, have changed that air of divine benignity to one expressive of disgust and affright. (139)

A feminized image of the proper body provokes the monster to murder little William, an image that deploys a particular ideology of gender to secure the devaluation of defiant flesh. The normative force of the proper lady guarantees the monster's exclusion from domestic affection.[18] That such images produce violent effects is one of the points of Shelley's narrative.

In its murderous deviance, the monster haunts the proper body, assaulting the social practices that enforce its legitimacy.[19] He becomes their destructive double, linking medical science to carnage, threatening family with obliteration, shadowing the politics of propriety with the violence of underclass hatred. Fiendishly stalking Frankenstein, he serves as the grim conscience of a knowledge that turns deviant flesh into a specimen valued only according to a functional norm. As first William, then Justine, then Clerval, and finally Elizabeth end up dead, monstrosity takes its vengeance on the bodies that the norm so invisibly advantages. It is the monster who is the true anatomist, ravaging flesh to secure knowledge, power, and even freedom: "'mine shall not be the submission of abject slavery. I will revenge my injuries: if I cannot inspire love, I will cause fear; and chiefly towards you my arch-enemy, because my creator, do I swear inextinguishable hatred. Have a care: I will work at your destruction, nor finish until I desolate your heart, so that you curse the hour of your birth'" (141). Haunting medical science with material evidence of its social effects, the monster incarnates a malice that returns to menace its perpetrators. This prodigious being, "gigantic in stature, yet uncouth and distorted in its proportions," this tall man, comes to avenge the bones of Charles Byrne (216). The monster tests functional norms against singular bodies, producing a bounty of corpses to verify the principle of life. As deaths multiply around Frankenstein, Hunter's heir becomes the hunted.

But monstrosities incarnate an even greater threat. The monster's vengeance turns habitual only after Frankenstein rescinds the possibility of progeny. The most horrible prospect the monster materializes is that of a posthuman body. Frankenstein originally anticipated that possibility with enthusiasm, as his thoughts while building his creature's body indicate: "A new species would bless me as its creator and source; many happy and excellent natures would owe their being to me. No father could claim the gratitude of his child so completely as I should deserve their's" (49). But a hideous progeny might not succumb so easily to control. The behavior of the monster suggests that autonomy and freedom might not mean the same for deviant flesh as for the proper body. That's why he demands that Frankenstein create for him a female companion "of the same species" and with "the same defects" (140). When his creator breaks his promise to do so, it is because the progeny that might result become too horrible to contemplate: "I saw continually about me a multitude of filthy animals inflicting on me incessant torture, that often extorted screams and bitter groans" (145). The hideous progeny of monsters presents too lurid a prospect to endure. Frankenstein dismembers the monster female to defend the proper body against her fecundity.

Part of the force, then, of that cultural norm is to guard against the futures such progeny make possible. It violently arrests the transformative effects of monstrosities, to assert instead the health and wholeness of what is human. Destroyed in the process is the singular life of a posthuman body, one that lives beyond the limits of the proper—which is not to say that such possibilities are a thing of the past. That monstrosities have a life of their own is the true moral of Shelley's tale, one understood best by those deemed unfit, on the basis of physical difference, for full participation in liberal society. The monster speaks violently on their behalf, demanding companionship by virtue of monstrosity. He knows viscerally that posthuman bodies incarnate new possibilities. But terror is his final solution. A better politics of monstrosity would work to create a new sociability that acknowledges all that is abject and disreputable in the life of deviant flesh.

CHAPTER 3

POSSESSING BEAUTY

> And what was I? Of my creation and creator I was absolutely ignorant; but I
> knew that I possessed no money, no friends, no kind of property. I was, besides,
> endowed with a figure hideously deformed and loathsome. I was not even of the
> same nature as man. (115–16)

The words belong to Frankenstein's monster, but they could as easily belong
to an African slave. Although ostensible freedom came in 1837, it remains a
troubling fact of British history that the project of abolition coincides with
the emergence of raciology, the scientific classification of humans into distinct racial and national categories. It may be tempting to argue that the
British traded iron for mind-forged manacles (there were, alas, still plenty
of chains to go around), but that would be to misconstrue the relationship
between human rights and raciology in an age of revolution. Instructively,
Robin D. G. Kelly insists on that relationship: "the expansion of slavery and
genocidal wars against non-European peoples took place alongside, and by
some accounts made possible, bourgeois democratic revolutions that gave
birth (in the West) to the concept that liberty and freedom are inalienable rights" (107). Raciology fought those wars on the battlefield of human
anatomy, strategically measuring black bodies against the prevailing norm of
proper embodiment, making it possible to apportion inalienable rights on a
bodily basis.

To put the point more bluntly, the proper body is white. By its measure
black bodies turn monstrous and live beyond the pale of liberal society, without money, friends, or property. Increasing attention has been paid recently
to the operation of this logic of embodiment, most famously around the case
of Saartjie Baartman, known as "the Hottentot Venus," whose remarkable
buttocks and genitalia came to identify deviant sexuality with blackness.[1]
To the eye of Enlightenment science, race becomes the repository of all that

is deviant about flesh, the impossibility of its purity, the dubiousness of its desires. Although associations between blackness and evil have a long and sinister history, what is new to the discourse of raciology is the materiality of its claims. Black bodies don't just *represent* deviation from a norm of truth and beauty, they also *embody* it. The norm of the proper body enforces an ideal they materially transgress, making it possible to affirm universal human rights while denying their applicability to deviant flesh. Bodies, and not rational minds alone, must first qualify for those rights, proper bodies that measure up to the standards of raciology. It takes an ensemble of practices to make such judgments possible, and what follows will focus on the relationship between late-eighteenth-century aesthetics and medicine in making race a property of bodies. Possessing beauty, it turns out, involves more than just having a pretty face.

BODILY PROPERTIES

Among the more dubious and most destructive legacies of the Enlightenment is the corporeal category of race. A host of recent cultural critics, from David Theo Goldberg to Paul Gilroy to Richard Dyer, have argued that by the late eighteenth century race becomes a dominant logic of embodiment in European culture.[2] Goldberg, in his commanding examination of the cultural politics of race, *Racist Culture,* links its emergence to the concept of the modern: "race is one of the central conceptual inventions of modernity" (3). But he takes care to identify its institutionalization as a dominant logic with Enlightenment culture, arguing that "the scientific catalog of racial otherness, the variety of racial alien, was a principle product of this period" (*Racist Culture* 29). Raciology participates in a larger constellation of practices whose aim is to subdue, since "Subjection perhaps properly defines the order of the Enlightenment: subjection of nature by human intellect, colonial control through physical and cultural domination, and economic superiority through mastery of the laws of the market" (*Racist Culture* 29). Race proves a powerful weapon in the arsenal of Enlightenment thinking, one deployed against bodies otherwise refractory to the rule of reason.

But something interesting occurs during the course of this subjection. Bodies that acquire the property of race can become property themselves, and as such are deprived of the one possession liberalism attributes to any man: property in his own person. Being raced erases property in person only to refigure it in relation to another, as slave to master. The proper body—that laboring, trading, able-bodied Brit—incorporates a norm of whiteness, which is to say that for all its nationality it has no race at all, at least in a positive sense. Race, in other words, marks the constitutive exclusion through which the proper body promotes whiteness. To be racially marked is to deviate from the norm of proper embodiment. Raciology amounts, then, to a scientific study of deviant flesh that materializes race by measuring its properties, producing bodies subject to possession.

That the menace of such subjection was from its inception a problem for liberal political theory is the lesson of the famous first sentence of Locke's *Two Treatises on Government*: "Slavery is so vile and miserable an Estate of Man, and so directly opposite to the generous Temper and Courage of our Nation; that 'tis hardly to be conceived, that an *Englishman,* much less a *Gentleman,* should plead for it" (159). The estate of Man may possess no slaves, but plenty of English estates in America and the West Indies did. When Locke nationalizes the temper of resistance he raises the possibility that other nations, or maybe races, might not find slavery so vile or miserable a condition. Implicit in Locke's denunciation of slavery, and ultimately his theory of civil society, is the identification, so close as to go unnoticed, of whiteness with the estate of Man. It is not merely that Locke's post as secretary to the Carolina Proprietors commits him to the policy of subjection so clearly stated in *The Fundamental Constitutions of Carolina* of 1669 that he helped write: that a freeman "shall have absolute power and authority over his negro slaves" (302, n24). Locke justifies that authority with the argument that slaves, by being captured, had forfeited their lives during the course of a just war and "cannot in that state be considered as any part of *Civil Society*; the chief end whereof is the preservation of Property" (341).

Rather such slaves *become* the property that civil society preserves. And yet their difference from the individuals who possess them involves more than their just defeat. Locke's epistemology shows how race marks their deviation from a proper norm. Discussing the irreducibility of essences to verbal propositions in his *Essay Concerning Human Understanding,* Locke shows how color comes to be associated with the complex idea of Man:

> a child, having framed the *idea* of a *man,* it is probable that his *idea* is just like that picture which the painter makes of the visible appearances joined together; and such a complication of *ideas* together in his understanding makes up the single complex *idea* which he calls *man;* whereof white or flesh-colour in *England* being one, the child can demonstrate to you that *a negro is not a man,* because white colour was one of the constant simple *ideas* of the complex *idea* he calls *man;* and therefore he can demonstrate, by the principle *It is possible for the same thing to be and not to be,* that *a negro is not a man.* (2: 206–07)

Locke is of course criticizing the child for confusing simple and complex ideas, but he nonetheless demonstrates quite powerfully how conventional associations become nominal essential properties that in turn reinforce a norm of embodiment. The English child innocently reproduces a norm that cannot accommodate the Negro, calling his humanity into question. The property of color lends epistemological force to the Negro's possession as property.

There is at work here an aesthetics of racial representation that marks the black man as deviant *and leaves the white man unmarked*. Such is the operation of the logic of whiteness, which as Dyer describes it "reproduces itself regardless of intention . . . because it is not seen as whiteness, but as normal" (10). And what is particularly interesting about Locke's description of the child's reproduction of this norm is that the epistemological practice that reduces the Negro to a simple property is that of painting. The child paints visible appearances and in the process reproduces a national norm of embodiment. Apparently the painter does too. In both cases the perceiving subject can only represent difference as deviation, identifying black bodies with a property that puts their humanity into question. On this description painting functions to reproduce, circulate, and even materialize a corporeal norm that marks deviant bodies as subject to possession. So while it is true enough, as Goldberg indicates, that "empiricism encouraged the tabulation of perceivable differences between peoples and from this it deduced their natural differences" (*Racist Culture* 28), it is important to notice how Locke's epistemology enlists other practices toward those ends. An aesthetics of racial representation implicates the visual arts in the emergence of raciology, rendering black bodies an occasion for reproducing a norm of whiteness. Paintings make visible the bodily properties that become subject to aesthetic judgment.

WHITE ROMANTICISM

Nor is empiricism the only discourse so to race the proper body. Locke's philosophical heir and adversary, Immanuel Kant, makes a transcendental case for the racial implications of aesthetic representation. Kant's openly racist remarks are well enough known, though tucked away in his little-read early treatise *Observations on the Feeling of the Beautiful and the Sublime* (1763). He approvingly recites Hume's challenge to find a Negro of distinction: "although many of them have even been set free, still not a single one was ever found who presented anything great in art or science or any other praiseworthy quality" (111). That art or science serves as the yardstick for greatness shows how such achievements might serve culturally to advance subjection. The rationality they evince may be human, but it isn't black. Dismissing the connubial wisdom of a Negro carpenter ("'You whites are indeed fools, for first you make great concessions to your wives, and afterward you complain they drive you mad'"), Kant simply notes that "this fellow was quite black from head to foot, a clear proof that what he said was stupid" (113). Kant proves in Locke's sense an able painter, representing properties that disprove the human.

It is not as artist but as aesthetician, however, that Kant most transcendentally advances the cause of raciology. His later critical philosophy makes representation itself a means of marking and maintaining racial division. David Lloyd argues forcefully that aesthetic judgment as Kant theorizes it, most obviously in his *Critique of Judgment,* proves constitutive of a liberal polity whose racial bias still prevails today. Kant transcendentalizes the proper body of liberalism by disembodying it altogether. Its abstract exchangeability, so important to free-market economics, becomes the condition of a subjectivity as communicable as it is universal. The subject of aesthetic judgment, especially in matters of taste, approaches this universality only formally, through identification with a common sense, a public interest. Lloyd calls this disinterested subject the "Subject without properties" and shows how the formal universality of its judgments structures a liberal polity inimical to deviant flesh.

For the Subject without properties achieves that distinction only through a powerful pedagogy of the senses. Lloyd details the way aesthetic judgment gives a form to common sense that devalues its material content. In what he calls a "developmental narrative," the operation of aesthetic judgment reproduces a movement away from the matter of any given object and toward the form of the judging subject, a movement from, in Kant's words, "the charm of sense to habitual moral interest." That's how common sense arises, through the narrative development of a sensing subject toward formal—and moral—universality. In the process it becomes dispossessed of material properties—both its own and the object's. The end result of this narrative of development is to educate the senses in their own inadequacy, submitting their perceptions to the formal propriety of aesthetic judgment. The Subject without properties links individual to public interest, producing the universally communicable common sense that provides the conceptual basis of civilized society. As Lloyd puts it, "the same development that produces in each individual a capacity for subjectively universal judgments of taste produces in human societies the civilized form of the public sphere" (67). Where this development is lacking or incomplete—and Kant's examples variously include the Iroquois, the Carib, and the African—neither individuals nor the races they belong to can achieve the capacity for universal communicability that defines civilization. Lloyd draws the inevitable conclusion: "racism is structured in the first place by the cultural determination of a public sphere and of the subject formation that is its condition of existence" (68). The Subject without properties disembodies subjectivity, rendering bodies in their materiality subject to aesthetic judgment.

It is worth noting the formal homology between this Subject without properties and the slave, who, being property herself, can possess none of her own. Kant's aesthetics formally legitimates subjection in the absence of the developmental narrative that defines civilization. That is why it seems problematic, to say the least, to acquiesce readily to Kant's most powerful contributions to aesthetic theory, the analytic of the sublime. If Lloyd's assessment is correct, and aesthetic judgment serves culturally to advance the cause of domination, then the sublime becomes a potent means toward that end. No wonder it found some of its most potent—and terrifying—political applications in the theater of fascism that would captivate the public in the twentieth century. When Kant argues that, for all its terror, the sublime "pleases immediately by reason of its opposition to sense" (*Judgment* 118), or that it will "employ itself upon ideas involving a higher finality" (92), he deploys the developmental narrative that turns subjects transcendental and bodies into properties. A Romanticism that takes the sublime for one of its defining features risks recapitulating its logic of (dis)embodiment and reproducing a public sphere structured in advance to devalue black bodies. That would be a white Romanticism, the critical and historical romance of the proper body. What, one should ask now that the sublime has run its questionable course, might a criticism of Romanticism do to vindicate bodies that actually matter?

MAKING THE GRADE

It might examine the way the discourse of aesthetics interacts with other practices to promote a norm of proper embodiment that reinforces racial difference. The relationship between aesthetics and medicine in the late eighteenth century promotes exactly this effect. What aesthetics theorizes medicine materializes: a developmental narrative that distinguishes bodies on the basis of racial difference. Nowhere is this effect clearer than in the work of Charles White, a highly respected physician from Manchester known for his writings on midwifery. The work for which he is best remembered, however, *An Account of the Regular Gradation in Man* (1799), stands today as a grim classic of raciology. In it White provides material evidence for what he calls "the beautiful gradation that exists among human beings" (iii). As his choice of adjectives indicates, White's argument is both physical and aesthetic. He advances a theory of corporeal gradation that is at the same time a theory of beauty. Aesthetics confirms what nature displays: that a developmental narrative links different bodies together in a scale of incrementally increasing value—and humanity.

And who better to inspire such speculations than that master anatomist, John Hunter? According to White,

> The hint that suggested this investigation, was taken ... from Mr *John Hunter,* who had a number of skulls, which he placed upon a table in a regular series, first shewing the human skull, with its varieties, in the European, the Asiatic,

the American, the African; then proceeding to the skull of a monkey, and so on to that of a dog. . . . On viewing this range, the steps were so exceedingly gradual and regular, that it could not be said that the first differed from the second more than the second from the third, and so on to the end. Upon considering what Mr. *Hunter* thus demonstrated respecting skulls, it occurred to me that Nature would not employ gradation in one instance only, but would adopt it as a general principle. (41)

Hunter's physiology of normal function, exemplified in the anatomical series, provides White with a scientific precedent for approaching material life from the perspective of a developmental narrative. Like Kant, he sees through appearances to the general principle—gradation—that structures them. In doing so he manages to coordinate the operations of nature with those of aesthetic judgment. Both move from material to moral orders of sensation and value. The developmental narrative of regular gradation thus recapitulates in flesh, bone, and beauty the foundational gesture of Kant's common sense. As anatomist and aesthetician, White practices a natural history of liberalism.

Which explains his raciological agenda. Ever the physician, White is not content to accept so fuzzy a distinction as subjectivity to mark racial difference. He seeks it in the bones. He incorporates race. Measurement becomes his favored means of materializing racial difference because it subjects different kinds of bones to a universal standard: "I had observed that the arms were longer, and the feet flatter in apes than in the human species; and, having the skeleton of a Negro amongst others in my museum, I measured the radius and ulna, and found them nearly an inch longer than in the European skeleton of the same stature" (41–42). White recapitulates the innocence of Locke's English child when he refuses to identify deviant measurements with a European standard. In this he adheres closely to conventions of perception that Paul Gilroy associates with "the scale of comparative anatomy," a medicalized strategy of observation characterized by "specific ways of looking, enumerating, dissecting, and evaluating" (36). White looks, enumerates, dissects, and evaluates, to build a proper body that is white. He rehearses all the usual racial stereotypes, but always according to the developmental narrative of regular gradation. Thus the skin of a Negro is thicker than a European's but thinner than an ape's. Or the fulsome catamenia of white women is less in Negroes, even lesser in monkeys. Regular gradation racializes as it materializes the developmental narrative of aesthetic judgment, becoming a means to scientific knowledge of the most intimate sort:

That the Penis of an African is larger than that of an European, has, I believe, been shewn in every anatomical school in London. Preparations of them are preserved in most anatomical museums; and I have one in mine. I have examined several living Negroes, and found it invariably to be the case. A surgeon of reputation informs me, that about forty years ago, when he was a pupil to

the late *William Bromfield,* Esq. he assisted at the dissection of a Negro, whose
penis was *ad longitudinem pollicum duodecim.* It was preserved and deposited
in Mr. *Bromfield's* museum. (61)

Medical science has so much to teach! The racist implications of such museum pieces (the reduction of black bodies to the spectacular matter of reproduction) may be obvious, but for White that is exactly the point. African
bodies deviate materially from the proper norm of whiteness: "wherever deviations . . . are found to take place, they are generally in the line of gradation
from the European man down to the ape" (56).

The conclusion is obvious too: gradations mark not just divergent but
distinct kinds of people. As White puts it, "it cannot be doubted, that, from
whatever cause it may arise, there actually subsists a characteristic difference in the body system, betwixt the European and the African" (55). White's
developmental narrative goes public with the formal presentments of aesthetic judgment. Anatomy confirms what judgment asserts, that different
bodies warrant different valuations. It falls to medical science to discrimi-
nate among them: "Different species of man being once admitted, it will become a proper object of physiological enquiry to determine their number and
distinction, with the merits, excellencies and defects of each" (133). Regular
gradation leads ever upward, however, for "ascending the line of gradation,
we come at last to the white European; who being most removed from the
brute creation, may, on that account be considered as the most beautiful of
the human race" (133).

Beauty converges with civility to race the proper body. That is why White
can tout the cause of abolition in the very midst of his raciological discourse.
Bodies that deviate from the norm of whiteness may be materially different,
yet for that very reason they deserve liberal treatment:

> the Author had not the Slave Trade at all in view in this Enquiry; his object was
> simply to investigate a proposition in natural history. He is fully persuaded the
> Slave Trade is indefensible on any hypothesis, and he would rejoice in its aboli-
> tion. The Negroes are, at least, equal to thousands of Europeans, in capacity and
> responsibility; and ought, therefore, to be equally entitled to freedom and pro-
> tection. Laws ought not to allow greater freedom to a *Shakespeare* or a *Milton,*
> a *Locke* or a *Newton,* than to men of inferior capacities; nor shew more respect
> to a General *Johnstone,* or a Duchess of *Argyle,* than the most unshapely and ill
> formed. (137)

Deviant flesh deserves equal treatment not in and of itself but because it
bears relation to the norm of the proper body. Although of a different species,
Negroes merit comparison with whites of inferior capacities. White's overt
racism solves the problem of slavery by making black bodies the occasion for
common sense and the operations of aesthetic judgment that make liberal

society possible. Beauty proves a body's worth, while raciology determines its proper standing on the graded scale of humankind.

THE FACE OF BEAUTY

But does beauty have a face? If so, who possesses it? Questions, perhaps, for artists, whose task it is to find and feign the beautiful. Would that there were standards for such things. The artist's task would be less daunting if he had in his possession a model to imitate, a pattern to follow, a formula for the beautiful face. The legacy of the antique might do. Greek sculpture, in its formal purity, could serve as such a model. If ever a face were beautiful, it would be that of the Apollo Belvedere, or the Venus de Medici. Everyday faces pale in comparison. Given the existence of these perfect patterns, and their accessibility in plaster and print, the artist would do well to take them for the standard against which to measure the beauty of other faces.

This, or something like it, was the reasoning of Petrus Camper, renowned comparative anatomist and enthusiastic student of the art of drawing. Enchanted by the beauty of Greek sculpture, and steeped in the details of human anatomy, Camper sought to explain the difference between them, why the one was always beautiful, the other so often not. In 1774 he published the lectures he had given on the subject in Brussels, which in 1794 were translated into English under the title *The Connexion between the Science of Anatomy and the Arts of Drawing, Painting, Statuary, Etc., Etc.* In his introduction, Camper confesses first becoming aware of this difference as a student: "Whenever I copied after the best models of the ancient Greeks,—drew the head of a Pythian Apollo, a Venus de Medicis, a Hercules of Farnese, . . . I observed a very great difference between the faces of these and our own. I perceived also that they were much more pleasing" (n.p.). To this observation Camper adds another: that modern painters routinely misrepresent national and racial differences. He noticed this when copying a painting by Van Temple. In it, says Camper, "there was the figure of a Moor, that by no means pleased me. In his colour he was Black; but his features were European. As I could neither please myself nor gain any proper directions, I desisted from the undertaking" (n.p.). The pleasure Camper takes in the face of Apollo turns to displeasure at the confusion of a Moor's face with a European's. An ideal requires careful discrimination of its inferior gradations. Modern painters fail to recognize and to represent such differences.

Faced with this confusion, the anatomist turns aesthetician. Drawing on his extensive experience dissecting cadavers and his intimate knowledge of comparative anatomy, Camper brings science to bear on art, proposing "rules more conducive to facility, grace, and accuracy, than any hitherto offered."

Such is the truth of anatomy that, given the Greek ideal, it can determine the degrees of beauty between different faces. Hence Camper's confidence

that National differences may be reduced to rules; . . . that these directions and inclinations are always accompanied by correspondent form of size, and position of other parts of the cranium, the knowledge of which will prevent the artist from blending the features of different nations in the same individual. (n.p.)

To keep painting pure and to guarantee the representation of national differences, Camper advances an aesthetics of intelligibility that discovers beauty written in the bones, those specifically of the skull. Such beauty is a little more than skin deep, and recognizing it requires the trained eye of the anatomist.[3]

With Camper's help, the artist can acquire that eye. All that is needed is the acceptance of what Camper with pride called his greatest discovery: that the beauty of the face derives from its prognathism, the angle that it slopes away from the perpendicular. Camper describes his discovery as follows:

I observed that a line, drawn along the forehead and upper lip, indicated this difference in national physiognomy; and also pointed out the degree of similarity between a Negro and an ape. By sketching some of these features upon a horizontal plane, I obtained the lines which mark the countenance, with their different angles. When I made these lines to incline forwards, I obtained the face of an antique; backwards, of a negroe; still more backwards, the lines which mark an ape, a dog, a snipe, etc.—This discovery formed the basis of my edifice. (9)

This discovery would be easy to discountenance if it remained a matter of geometry alone. But Camper supports it scientifically by appealing to the geometry of actual skulls. Their measurement confirms what geometrical connivance implies, that differences in national beauty derive from differences in facial angle, and that those differences form a developmental narrative leading from the brute through determinate stages of the human to the Greek ideal. Their comparative arrangement thus proves most revealing:

It is amusing to contemplate an arrangement of [skulls], placed in a regular succession: apes, orangs, Negroes, the skull of an Hottentot, Madagascar, Celebese, Chinese, Monguller, Calmuck, and diverse Europeans. It was in this manner that I arranged them upon a shelf in my cabinet, in order that those differences might become more obvious. (50)

Camper's aesthetics of intelligibility turns any given face into a national type, then locates it on an abstract continuum that translates type into biologically determined race. Represented visually, the result is a grand march of beauty from brute to divinity, with intervening races clearly designated by measurable differences in facial angle (Figure 15). The Greek ideal sets the maximum of about 100 degrees, while the lesser angle of the European ranges from 80 degrees to 90, and that of the Negro can dip as low as 70 (Figure 16). Below 65 degrees is all the beasts': the orangutan, the chimpanzee, the dog. Camper's is quite literally a highbrow aesthetics, rendering racial differences intelligible according to a standard as universally valid as it is scientific.[4]

In this sense, Camper's aesthetics of intelligibility is an instrument of possession. By its means the artist comes fully to possess, not merely the criterion

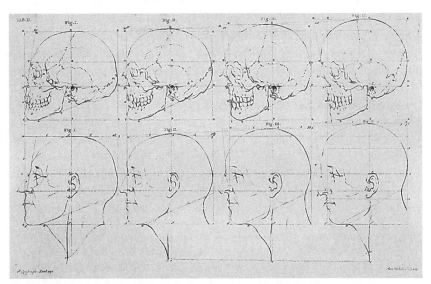

Figure 15. Petrus Camper, *The Connexion between the Science of Anatomy and The Arts of Drawing, Painting, Statuary, Etc., Etc.* (1794). Tab. 2. The Wellcome Library, London.

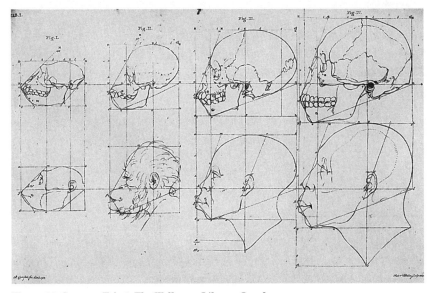

Figure 16. Camper, Tab. 1. The Wellcome Library, London.

of facial beauty, but also the faces that it measures, classifies, and thereby masters. The human face may be the object of measurement and therefore cognition, but not the singular face. By subordinating singularity to general, geometrical rule, an aesthetics of intelligibility turns faces into formulas, refers them, in all their difference, to a proper norm (Figure 17). "The foreign being," to put the point in Emmanuel Levinas's terms, "instead of maintaining itself in the inexpugnable fortress of its singularity, instead of facing, becomes a theme and an object" (50). Who then possesses a beautiful face? He who, like Camper, renders it intelligible, recognizable. For "cognition," says Levinas, "consists in grasping the individual, which alone exists, not in its singularity which does not count, but in its generality, of which alone there is science" (50). Camper's science of facial beauty and the aesthetics of intelligibility it underwrites, for all its claims to guarantee difference, assimilates the singular to the same.

But rendering the beauty of the human face intelligible requires a prior defacement, a fact too terminally apparent in Camper's illustrations, a pageantry of skulls. Camper's beautiful faces have no face, have been de-faced for the purposes of accurate measurement. Something of the violence implied in this procedure lingers on in Camper's method of obtaining a perfect profile:

> in a word, the bones of the cranium are simply covered with skin and a dipose membrane; and these are no impediments to our taking the cranium as the truest basis of the intended portrait. It was in this manner that I obtained the profile of the modern face, in the first figure of the second plate. This was very similar to many other fine heads that have been dissected by me, in my professional

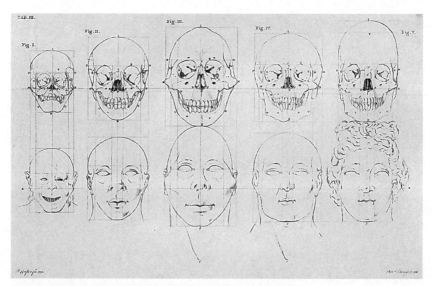

Figure 17. Camper, Tab. 3. The Wellcome Library, London.

character, and were afterwards sawn through the middle perpendicularly, that I
might be able to obtain a perfect profile. (96)

If death for Camper is the mother of beauty, violence is its father, stripping
flesh and sawing bone to reveal the beauty of the defaced face. An aesthetics
of intelligibility, grounded in the science of anatomy, takes full, fatal possession of the faces whose beauty it measures.

It's easy to dismiss Camper now as a racist crank, benighted stooge of
Enlightenment prejudice. But his aesthetics had enormous influence. Witness in this regard the work of another anatomist turned artist, Sir Charles
Bell, who would go on to make medical history by discovering the true character and operation of the nerves. In 1806, soon after arriving in London
from his native Edinburgh, Bell published a book that was well received
and widely read: *The Anatomy and Philosophy of Expression as Related to
the Fine Arts*. In it he doesn't so much reject as modify Camper's aesthetics
of intelligibility. Quibbling with the way Camper determined his measurements, questioning his negligence of the relation between face and jaw,
Bell nevertheless endorses the authority of the facial angle as a measure of
human beauty. But he adds a "new principle," which only states openly what
Camper's aesthetics of intelligibility concluded de facto: that "in the face
there is a character of nobleness observable depending on the development
of certain organs which indicate the prevalence of the higher qualities allied
to thought, and therefore human" (30). Is it any surprise that the development of such organs accounts for the remarkable proximity of European
facial angles to the perpendicular? Bell's revised manner of measuring them
shows that Camper was, if anything, too generous, "the difference being much
greater between the European and African skull" (30) than the earlier method demonstrated.

Bell's prejudice determines his measurements—or mismeasurements—
and not vice versa. His too is an aesthetics of intelligibility, rife with the
violence and fatality of Camper's. It differs, however, in the way it explains
differences in prognathism. If the European's derives from a hypertrophy of
the brain, the African's results from a hypertrophy of the jaw (Figure 18). For
Bell the facial angle measures not just beauty but also embodiment. Its incline toward the perpendicular for Europeans indicates their greater mastery
of the body. Hence the following confession, in almost whispered tones:

In our secret thoughts the form has a reference to the function. If the function
be allied to intellect, or is connected with mind (as the eye especially is), then
there is no incompatibility with the human countenance, though the organ
should bear resemblance to the same part in a brute; but, if it has a relation
to the meaner necessities of animal life, as the jaws, or the teeth, the effect is
incompatible, and altogether at variance with human physiognomy. (43)

Because the inordinate heaviness of the jaw also causes the facial angle to decrease, and not merely as Camper believed the slope of the forehead, those faces that have this feature remain their bodies' slaves. They are something less than human, ever in thrall to animal necessities. And because the true master of this condition is he who masters the body, Bell's aesthetics of intelligibility justifies possession of those whose faces fail to measure up. If, as Levinas again suggests, "To possess is . . . to maintain the reality of this other one possessed, but to do so while suspending its independence" (50), then another defacement occurs here, one that strips beauty and with it humanity from the human face. Such are the effects of an aesthetics of intelligibility. Singularity succumbs to beauty, whose measurement enslaves. Lest we presume superiority to such violence and fatality, or that prognathism is a thing of the past, we might ponder images such as Figure 19, taken from a reputable text on drawing first published in 1951 and reissued as recently as 1990.

A DIFFERENT FACE

Fortunately for the art of painting, Camper's was not the only answer to the question of the beautiful face. His contemporary Joshua Reynolds formulated an aesthetics that countenanced the possibility of beauty irreducible to intelligibility. In his Seventh Discourse, delivered to the Royal Academy of Art

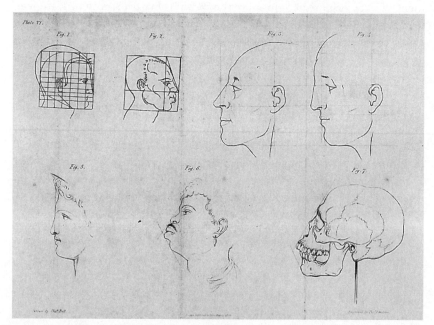

Figure 18. Sir Charles Bell, *The Anatomy and Philosophy of Expression as Related to the Fine Arts* (1806). The Wellcome Library, London.

just two years after the original publication of Camper's lectures, Reynolds criticizes those who would subject art to science, requiring of the former the sort of intelligibility that the latter characteristically yields. "It may be observed," he says, "that many wise and learned men, who have accustomed their minds to admit nothing for truth but what can be proved by mathematical demonstration, have seldom any relish for those arts which address themselves to the fancy, the rectitude and truth of which is known by another

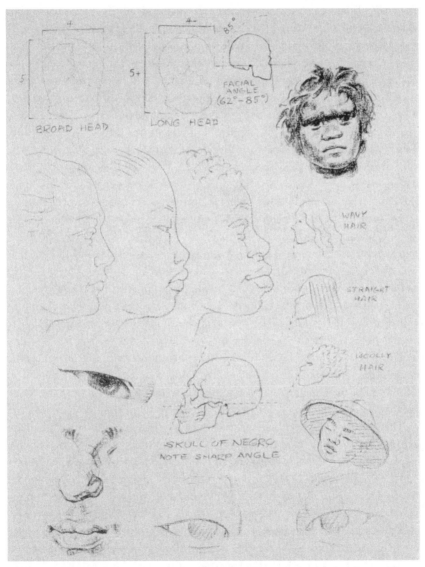

Figure 19. *Atlas of Human Anatomy for the Artist*, by Stephen Rogers Peck. Copyright 1951 by Oxford University Press, Inc. Reprinted by permission of Oxford University Press, Inc.

kind of proof" (*Discourses* 116). In his example as both painter and Academy president, Reynolds sought to inculcate an aesthetics whose specific truth "requires as much circumspection and sagacity, as is necessary to attain those truths which are more capable of demonstration" (116). Whatever we may think of Reynolds's example, its debt to rank or lucre, it provided an institutionally approved alternative to the aesthetics of the anatomists Camper and Bell.

While all maintain that beauty is an ideal toward which art must aspire, Reynolds differs from the anatomist in locating it, not beyond nature, but within it. Where for Camper beauty approaches the ideal only after it exceeds natural form (a facial angle of 90 degrees for the human face), for Reynolds it does so only by bringing that form to its fullness. Beauty is not a standard of measure so much as an instance of fulfillment. Nature and beauty appear together. They mutually accord. When Reynolds speaks of nature's "general idea" or beauty's "fixed form" he is not appealing to an abstract standard to provide grounds for intelligibility. Rather he is stating his belief that beauty occurs naturally and that nature therefore includes it, as the following passage from his Seventh Discourse suggests: "the terms beauty, or nature, which are general ideas, are but different modes of expressing the same thing, whether we apply these terms to statues, poetry, or picture. Deformity is not nature, but an accidental deviation from her accustomed practice. This general idea ought to be called Nature, and nothing else, correctly speaking, has a right to that name" (112). For Reynolds, beauty is the norm of nature, not, as for Camper and Bell, an ideal deviation from it. Only by means of natural forms and appearances can the painter represent true beauty.

In theory and in practice, Reynolds advances an aesthetics of appearance rather than intelligibility. The appearance of nature's forms, and not their measurement, sets the terms for beauty. Reynolds describes his position most clearly in a brief letter to *The Idler* that appeared in 1759, where he claims that "perfect beauty is oftener produced by nature than deformity" (*Works* 237). Because members of a given species share a distinct form, the ideal of beauty appears more frequently among them than deviations from it. This does not, however, mean that beauty is reducible to rule. What appears in nature to be beautiful does so on the basis of both form and custom. Reynolds comes close to a cultural relativism in his aesthetics of appearance. For if natural form sets the terms for beauty, such terms only acquire value relative to specific customs. To those like Camper who refer beauty to a prior standard of intelligibility, Reynolds shows little forbearance: "whoever . . . endeavors to fix a general criterion of beauty respecting different species, or to show why one species is more beautiful than another, it will be required from him first to prove that one species is really more beautiful than another. That we prefer one to the other, and with very good reason, will be readily granted; but it does not follow from thence that we think it a more beautiful form; for we have no criterion of form by which to determine our judgment" (*Works* 238–39). Appearances precede the measurement of appearances. All attempts at intelligibility come ex post facto.

The beautiful is thus for Reynolds always the beautiful "for us." Our preference for some forms over others derives, not from abstract standards, but from habit and custom, cultural norms such as that of the proper body. The difference between beauty and deformity is a function of familiarity, even prejudice: "As we are then more accustomed to beauty than deformity, we may conclude that to be the reason why we approve and admire it, as we approve and admire customs and fashions of dress for no other reason than that we are used to them; so that habit and custom cannot be said to be the cause of beauty, it is certainly the cause of our liking it" (*Works* 238). Given the force of habit in aesthetic judgments, it proves folly to standardize them, deceit to regulate them. That is why Reynolds's aesthetics of appearance remains open to relative judgments. Regarding national differences, Reynolds has this to say:

> We, indeed say, that the form and colour of the European is preferable to that of the Ethiopian; but I know of no other reason we have for it, but that we are more accustomed to it. . . . the black and white nations must, in respect of beauty, be considered as of different kinds, at least a different species of the same kind; from one of which to the other, . . . no inference can be drawn. (*Works* 241)

Where Camper standardizes in the interest of intelligibility, Reynolds relativizes in the interest of difference.[5] Where Camper measures and masters deviant flesh, Reynolds affirms its different beauty. His aesthetics of appearance lets beauty be, in its natural form and customary judgments. When near the end of his Twelfth Discourse he concludes that *"the art of seeing Nature . . . is in reality the great object, the point to which all our studies are directed"* (217), he directs students of the Royal Academy to look beauty in the face, to see its ideal features in nature's forms.

This aim grows complex when nature takes the form of the human face. Reynolds made his name and fortune as a painter of noble portraits.[6] He may have urged his students to the higher calling of history painting, but his own forte was the individual face. To paint a portrait, as Ronald Paulson suggests, was in the eighteenth century a kind of face-off: "if the sitter, his works, his life, and his times make up one side of the portrait, the painter as 'artist' and as man, as he relates to—perhaps tries to control or exploit—his subject is the Other" (278). In a portrait, the artist remains other, and therefore invisible, to the face he paints. But the act of painting can become a struggle to possess the representation it produces; in the face he paints, the painter can leave the trace of his own otherness. Face painting on this account involves a closed and agonistic relationship between the painter, patron, and subject. The addition of money paid for the finished portrait only complicates a relationship that can become, as Morris Eaves describes it, "a closed, private cycle of sen-sual or emotional need and gratification" (30). However lucrative, it appears, portraiture is not without its problems.

What would happen, one might wonder, if not the painter but the face he painted were the Other? Reynolds's aesthetics of appearance at least allows for this possibility. Nothing prevents the representation, according to one set of customs, of beauty commonly associated with another. Reynold's unfinished portrait *A Young Black* (c. 1770) enacts an agon of a different sort than that Paulson associates with portraiture (Figure 20). For here the painter is the

Figure 20. Joshua Reynolds, *A Young Black* (c. 1770). The Menil Collection, Houston.

patron, paying himself for his own labor. And here the face he paints is the
Other, nationally and for some even naturally speaking. Reynolds's aesthetics of appearance opens a space for images outside the purview of prejudice.
So although the identity of Reynolds's sitter remains questionable, as if beyond the certainties of portraiture, his beauty most manifestly does not.[7] It
comes to trouble custom. Putting the face of a young black man in a portrait's
honorific place, Reynolds upsets abstract standards grounded in degrees of
beauty. This face, for all its difference, does not play the role of servant. It is
not cast into the background. It does not possess the look of being possessed,
physically or aesthetically. Its beauty is not a measure of its prognathism;
rather it remains beyond measure altogether.

Or better yet, it measures those who face its otherness, its beautiful difference. Says Levinas, "In his face the other appears to me not as an obstacle,
nor as a menace I evaluate, but as what measures me" (58). Reynolds's portrait measures complicity in portraiture as a struggle for possession. For a
moment one sees not beauty but the way one sees beauty, the agon of possession that shapes art's highest values. "A face," as Levinas would have it, "is
pure experience, conceptless experience. The conception according to which
the data of our senses are put together in the ego ends, before the other,
with the de-ception, the dispossession which characterizes all our attempts
to encompass this real" (59). Reynolds's portrait dispossesses portraiture of
its possessing effects. Might it also raise the question, the ethical question,
of human possession? A question as unanswerable as this young black man's
face is disembodied. By leaving this portrait unfinished Reynolds forces the
issue of the Other's embodiment. It remains for those who come after to
complete the picture. That as many as ten copies of this portrait exist testifies to this necessity. Remaining in Reynolds's possession until his death, the
portrait served as a study for a generation of students. The question it raised
in the face of beauty lifts the art of portraiture above habit and custom. With
Reynolds's aesthetics of appearance appears the possibility of radical art.

DISTURBING BEAUTY

William Blake took full advantage of this possibility, as his engravings of African bodies indicate.[8] The common view of Blake's attitude toward Reynolds,
quite rightly, stresses scorn. Blake loaded his margins of Reynolds's *Discourses*
with indignation. Eaves has recently done much to justify Blake in his wrath.
As arbiter of the taste for and even the practice of painting, Reynolds ensured
that Blake's work would remain unintelligible. Hence Blake's marginal
blast, "A Polishd Villain who Robs & Murders," and his hostile commentary,
"I always consider'd True Art & True Artists to be particularly Insulted
& Degraded by the Reputation of these Discourses As much as they were

Degraded by the Reputation of Reynolds's Paintings" (657, 642). Blake's main theoretical complaint concerns the place in painting of minute particulars, which he charges Reynolds with neglecting in his devotion to "general form" and "fixed ideas." It would seem wrong, then, to claim that Blake gained much from the older and more fashionable painter's example. But Aileen Ward has suggested that Blake's years at the Royal Academy made a more lasting impression than some have been ready to allow.[9] Indeed, if anything, Blake faults Reynolds for not being faithful enough to his own aesthetics of appearance. For all his fulmination against nature as a source of inspiration, Blake assimilated Reynolds's aesthetic, putting it to much different, more disturbing use.

Blake radicalizes it. Not content to represent the form of beauty, however particular, Blake emphasizes as well the element of custom in its appearance. Like Reynolds in *A Young Black,* but much more trenchantly and purposefully, Blake includes in such appearances the prejudices that make them possible. In this he becomes a kind of genealogist of beauty and the proper body, revealing the customs and the prejudices that underwrite their value. This radicalized aesthetics of appearance shows that such values have a history, that they are not given from on high but wrought of curse and cudgel. Blake is most explicit as genealogist in work most explicitly about Africans, as in the plates he engraved for Captain John Stedman's *Narrative of a Five Years' Expedition, against the Revolted Negroes of Surinam,* published in 1796. There he troubles the beauty of appearances in such a way as to reveal its presumption. Consider in this regard the engraving that bears the title *Family of Negro Slaves* (Figure 21). The contrast between the man and woman is as strange as it is stark. He's so statuesque, so heroically posed, she's so slovenly and uncivilized. Once it occurs, however, that the man, for all his blackness, appears quite literally in the form of an Apollo, Blake's purpose becomes clearer (Figure 22). By putting this slave in the posture of a Greek god, the acclaimed the ideal of physical beauty, Blake reveals beauty to be a value grounded in and productive of the exclusion of bodily difference: in terms both of race and gender. If a slave can possess the beauty of a god, then how can his possession be justified? Only if beauty itself somehow legitimates it. As with statues, apparently, so with slaves: beauty increases their value as possessions. And appearances beyond their measure, as those of the barbarous female slave and her pickaninny kids, seem deviant in comparison, beneath the dignity of aesthetic judgment. Blake's radicalized aesthetics disturbs the beauty of such appearances.

And it does so nowhere more harrowingly than in the gruesome plate titled *A Negro hung alive by the Ribs to a Gallows* (Figure 23). A kind of pseudocrucifixion, it troubles too many ideals to be described, in any easy way, as beautiful. But it's the face of the condemned criminal that first fixes the attention. With its upward gaze and its lofty look, it is strangely beatific—and strangely familiar. It seems appropriate to take it for an echo of Reynolds's portrait, which every student of the Royal Academy would have known.[10] To do so is to notice how Blake completes Reynolds's picture, adds the body that

Figure 21. William Blake, *Family of Negro Slaves*. From John Stedman, *Narrative of a Five Years' Expedition, against the Revolted Negroes of Surinam* (1796). James Ford Bell Library, University of Minnesota.

Figure 22. William Blake's Apollo Belvedere, engraved for *The Cyclopaedia; or, Universal Dictionary of Arts, Sciences and Literature* by Abraham Rees (1815). Collection of Robert N. Essick.

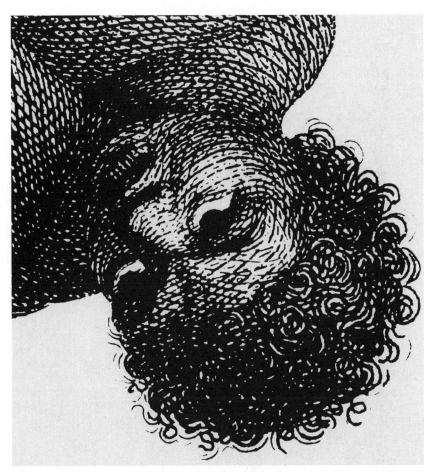

Figure 23. William Blake, *A Negro hung alive by the Ribs to a Gallows* (detail). James Ford Bell Library, University of Minnesota.

it failed to finish (Figure 24). And what a body. Contorted beyond human possibility, beautifully muscled but horribly bent, it hangs suspended between heaven and earth, bloody meat on a hook. The beauty of the face and even of the torso is utterly contradicted by the brutality of its treatment. Is this the bodily equivalent of possession, the tortured form beneath the beauty of appearance? Blake forces one to face the force of custom, the brutality that beauty both enforces and conceals. His graphic genealogy of beauty shows how, as an aesthetic value, it is implicated in enslavement, the subjection of different bodies to the horrors of possession.

Here is an ideal of beauty every bit as unjust in its effects as Camper's—with this difference, that its representation conjures an awareness of injustice. Blake's aesthetics of appearance is radical in provoking this revelation. It fulfills the possibility that the face of the Other, the beautiful face,

Figure 24. William Blake, *A Negro hung alive by the Ribs to a Gallows*. James Ford Bell Library, University of Minnesota.

presents. Levinas claims for the face the measure of infinity: "The other's face is the revelation not of the arbitrariness of the will, but its injustice. Consciousness of my injustice is produced when I incline myself not before the facts, but before the other. . . . For me to feel myself to be unjust I must measure myself against infinity" (57–58). Blake provokes the consciousness of injustice, registered on the body of this hanging slave, by forcing an encounter with a beautiful, but infinitely other, face. The only defacement here is the viewer's, measured against an irreducible infinity. Blake maximizes the ethical consciousness that Reynolds's aesthetics of appearance makes possible. By restoring to the infinity of the beautiful face the body of its customary treatment, Blake calls beauty into question and measures its admirers accordingly. If, as Levinas suggests, "the face of the other would be the starting point of philosophy" (59), then Blake is a philosopher of beauty and an artist of infinity. His aesthetics troubles custom, measuring beauty by means, not of the intelligibility of an abstract standard, but the appearance of the Other's face.

It should be clear enough by now that aesthetics in the late eighteenth century was no one thing, no unitary discourse. Camper, Bell, Reynolds, and Blake sketched and painted according to different customs, and to different ends. Blake's ways may be preferable, not because they are inherently more beautiful, or more just, but because they force one to face up to the infinite claims of a different face. Perhaps Blake owes his aesthetic habits to his own sense of difference. "Why was I born," he writes in a letter, "with a different Face, / Why was I not born like the rest of my race" (733). Ethical consciousness begins when the face of the Other forces one to see oneself differently, not as a free, rational agent, but as other even to oneself. Blake's answer to the question of beauty is not to measure it but to multiply it, as in one of his best-loved engravings, where beauty wears not one face but three (Figure 25). Who possesses the face of beauty? Are you too born with a different face?

BLACK BRITON?

If such faces could speak, what stories would they tell? The painted or engraved face possesses its subject in a definitive sense: it seals its silence. Of the representations of black faces mentioned so far, all have been produced by white artists. Were they to speak they could do so only on behalf of the black bodies they represent. While it is difficult to locate in the late eighteenth century representations of blacks produced by blacks, in at least one instance an unusual conjunction takes place between the image and the words of an African. *The Interesting Narrative of the Life of Olaudah Equiano,* published in the auspicious year of 1789, represents from the perspective of a kidnapped African and former slave the experience of one black body in liberal society. The engraving that fronts the volume depicts Equiano dressed in British finery, gazing directly at the reader while holding a book, obviously the Bible, opened to Acts 5, verse 12: "and they were all with one accord in Solomon's porch." This image meets his reader face to face, avoiding the problem of prognathism. And Equiano speaks in his own voice in the narrative that follows, which tells of a man born African and black who labors to become British. The real question Equiano poses is whether he can do so with success,

Figure 25. William Blake, *Europe Supported by Africa and America*. James Ford Bell Library, University of Minnesota.

whether a cultural norm of proper embodiment can accommodate properties that deviate from a national or natural standard.

It has often been noted that Equiano's title page demonstrates the precariousness of black identity in the cultural context of British slavery. As names pile up, identity turns nominal, perhaps no more substantive than a pronoun:

"Olaudah Equiano," "Gustavus Vassa," "The African," and finally "Himself."
He acquires yet other names as his narrative proceeds that identify him as
living property. Epitomized by the force of naming, language secures subjection and circulates power. But so too does the art of painting, a lesson Equiano
learns during a brief stint as a field slave in Virginia. Directed to fan his
sleeping master, down with a bout of sickness, Equiano experiences a series
of scares that educate him in the ways of Western representation. The first
comes through a female kitchen slave, who in spite of her condition delivers
a lecture on the powers of language, for "the poor creature was cruelly loaded
with various kinds of iron machines; she had one particularly on her head,
which locked her mouth so fast that she could scarcely speak" (63). The next
scare comes from a watch hung on the chimney in his master's room: "I was
quite surprised at the noise it made, and was afraid it would tell the gentleman any thing I did amiss." Then finally comes an encounter with a painting
that instills an even greater terror: "when I immediately after observed a
picture hanging in the room, which appeared constantly to look at me, I was
still more affrighted" (63). Equiano becomes subject in that bedroom to the
regime of Western representation, and it fills him with fear. It is not merely
that he sees how language occasions the use of force. His terror registers his
subjection to the cognitive conditions of representation as Kant describes
them: time and space. The watch and the painting set the representational
terms for his life among Europeans, and both observe his every move. He
comes to realize that they are no mere objects but technologies of observation
that function to manage bodily agency. The panopticon as easily takes the
form of a painting as a prison. In either case its effect is to produce, through
the affective experience of being observed, a subject that observes itself and
behaves accordingly. Proper embodiment proceeds through such technologies
of observation and the discipline they incorporate. As slave, Equiano both
understands their logic and feels their force.

But Equiano's response is one of the things that makes his narrative so
interesting. Rather than capitulate to the overt conditions of his enslavement,
he cunningly exploits its representational terms. Having been hailed as a subject, Equiano sets about to become British, which involves mobilizing on his
own behalf the discourses and practices constitutive of proper embodiment.
He lives to embody the developmental narrative that underwrites liberal society, a test case for the possibility that an African body can acquire British
identity. Can the Briton incorporate the black? Equiano devotes his life to that
prospect. The first step would be to acquire that one possession liberal political theory attributes to all men: property in person. As a slave, Equiano by
definition lacks it, succumbing in his capture (according to Locke's argument)
to the dictates of a just war. But as the slave of an able trader he learns something important about that apparently original property. As Sonia Hofkosh
suggests, Equiano comes to see in his slavery that "the economic structure

of property and power underwrites the very possibility of personal freedom" (335). Property in person is not original but derived, precisely from the economic system that identifies the subject with its possessions.

Equiano's pursuit of a proper body must begin, then, with the purchase of his own person. Trying his luck as a "commerce merchant" (116), he earns a little, then a little more, until through the economic perspicacity that Macpherson associates with the possessive individual, he not only prevails on his owner to set contractual terms for his freedom, he actually meets them, to his owner's chagrin: "'What!' said he, 'give you your freedom? Why, where did you get the money; have you got forty pounds sterling?' 'Yes, sir,' I answered. 'How did you get it'; replied he; I told him, 'Very honestly.'" (135). As property Equiano understands the economic conditions of proper embodiment. In the very odd economic moment when he purchases his body he finally acquires the property in his own person that is liberalism's condition of free agency. Equiano buys his manumission and with it the awareness of a new autonomy: "before night, I who had been a slave in the morning, trembling at the will of another, now became my own master, and completely free" (137).

It remains only for Equiano to reap the rewards of freedom. With its purchase he initiates the developmental narrative that structures liberal society. The movement from slave to free man reenacts the rise from mere sensation to moral judgment that is the condition of the social formation as Kant theorizes it in his aesthetics. Having acquired the first qualification for a proper body, however, Equiano still labors under the burden of bodily difference. His interesting narrative tests its own developmental aspirations against the cultural politics of embodiment. For a black man in the West Indies, for instance, freedom was without the cultural institutions that could enforce it. Equiano reached the conclusion that so many others have reached since: "Hitherto I had thought only slavery dreadful; but the state of a free negro appeared to me now equally so at least, and in some respects even worse, for they live in constant alarm for their liberty, which is but nominal, for they are universally insulted and plundered without redress; for such is the equity of West Indian laws, that no free Negro's evidence will be admitted in their courts of justice" (122). Equiano's solution to the problem of colonial injustice is to seek freedom where its meanings might be more than merely nominal, across the seas in "Old England," the one true territory of liberty. To become fully free, in other words, for Equiano means to acquire a national identity, to be embodied as a true Briton equivalent to all others. That Equiano associates that identity with a geographic territory shows how liberalism, economics, and nationalism interact to embody the proper Brit. England was the land without slavery, the Somerset decision of 1762 having rescinded the claims of masters on slaves on English soil. For the nominally free former slave, becoming British means acquiring material freedoms.

But Equiano's narrative documents the social obstacles to this moral ideal, the cultural politics that precludes the attribution of British identity to black bodies. When he finally gets to England, Equiano discovers that his economic freedoms prove limited. Possessing property in his own person, he qualifies to participate in economic relations, but his body sets the terms of exchange. Equiano lives physically the contradiction at the heart of free-market economics between the interchangeability of laboring bodies and their material singularity. The only jobs available to him as a black Briton are those associated with lower orders: positions as servant, hairdresser, sailor, laborer. And although England may have banished slavery, Equiano discovers to his chagrin that the legal system enforcing the freedoms of black Britons works with such selectivity and insouciance as to leave them ever open to renewed subjection. In the particularly tragic instance of an acquaintance who was kidnapped and returned to slavery in St. Kitts, eventually to die there, Equiano learns what is required to pursue justice for black bodies. Scheming to apprehend the perpetrators of this crime, he stoops to cunning: "My being known to them obliged me to use the following deception: I whitened my face, that they might not know me, and this had the desired effect" (180). The pursuit of justice by—and for—a black man requires putting on a white face. Could there be a more telling proof of the racial bias of liberal society and its institutional practices? Equiano eventually loses his advantage through the greed and incompetence of his white attorney, but the point here is simply to note how agency accrues primarily to bodies that go unmarked, unraced, unnoticed. To advance the cause of justice, this black Briton puts on whiteface.

Which is to say that in becoming British Equiano undertakes the task of becoming white. The developmental narrative that moves from mere sensation to moral judgment to legitimate liberalism moves from blackness to whiteness in good raciological fashion. Does that make Equiano's interesting narrative the literary equivalent of whiteface? In submitting to representation as a condition of identity and even embodiment is Equiano masking his black body? Equiano never recants his commitment to becoming British and in the end even advances economic arguments for the abolition of slavery, as in his closing "Query.—How many millions doth Africa contain? Supposing the Africans, collectively and individually, to expend 5£ a head in raiment and furniture yearly when civilized, &c. an immensity beyond the reach of imagination!" (234–35). But the true lesson of his interesting narrative yields quite different conclusions. The first is that black bodies never can become proper British bodies, at least in late-eighteenth-century England. So transparent and yet pervasive are the raciological assumptions of liberalism that national identity remains for Equiano a matter of proper (read white) embodiment. Seeking a freer and more lucrative life than the one Old England offers, Equiano takes again to the sea, eventually charting an array of voyages coextensive with the furthest reaches of empire: the Middle East, the West Indies, even the North Pole.

This amazing mobility leads to the second lesson of Equiano's narrative. Not its development so much as its dispersion proves most instructive. Trafficking so widely among the seas and nations Equiano enacts something other than the British identity he so desires. This African man writing in English about his encounters with Turks, Jamaicans, Americans, and Mosquito Indians wildly multiplies the possibilities for identification beyond the boundaries of being British, practicing a counteraesthetics to the one that circulates through the possessing beauties of liberal sociey. Equiano performs the possibility of the diasporic identity that Gilroy believes can disrupt "the fundamental power of territory to determine identity by breaking the simple sequence of explanatory links between place, location, and consciousness" (123). Equiano may at times want to forge such links, but his narrative more frequently breaks them, producing instead a hybridized complex of identifications. In trying to become British Equiano transgresses the limits of national identity, corrupting its integrity, confusing its racial propriety. "Here, at least," as Gilroy says, "identity must be divorced from purity" (117). A norm of embodiment that excludes the African obstructs the transcultural possibilities of diasporic identities. Equiano's interesting narrative demonstrates that black bodies matter after all. Possessing beauties of their own they materialize new, transnational freedoms.

Part II
HABITUATIONS

CHAPTER 4

BAD HABITS

. . . only by forgetting that he is an
artistically creating *subject, does man live*
with any repose, security, and consistency.
—*Nietzsche, "On Truth and Lying in an Extra-Moral Sense"*

I n April 1816, Samuel Taylor Coleridge placed himself voluntarily in
the care of a doctor, the benevolent James Gillman. Coleridge had for
years been desperate to break his opium habit, trying various cures, but to
no avail. The time had come for strict measures, and he resolved "to submit
himself to any regimen, however severe. With this in view," wrote Dr. Joseph
Adams, who had been treating him, "he wishes to fix himself in the house
of some medical gentleman, who will have the courage to refuse him any
laudanum, and under whose assistance, should he be the worse for it, he
may be relieved" (Gillman 271). After an initial interview that left Gillman,
like Coleridge's Wedding Guest, "almost spell-bound, without the desire of
release," the poet committed himself to the doctor's care for a period of one
month. He remained eighteen years (273).

During that time it fell to Gillman not so much to cure Coleridge as to
control his habit, watching over the sometime poet and philosopher to secure
some semblance of health. Coleridge predicted it would be difficult. In a letter
accepting the offer of asylum he promised to cooperate in every way that he
could:

> My ever wakeful reason, and the keenness of my moral feelings, will secure
> you from all unpleasant circumstances connected with me save only one, viz.
> the evasion of a specific madness. You will never *hear* any thing but truth from
> me:—prior habits render it out of my power to tell an untruth, but unless care-
> fully observed, I dare not promise that I should not, with regard to this detested

poison, be capable of acting one. No sixty hours have yet passed without my having taken laudanum. (*Letters* 4: 630)

Although Coleridge cannot tell a lie, he can act one. His "specific madness" splits speech and agency, saying and doing, leaving him subject to an abject habit that compels behavior he cannot control. The therapeutic aim of his benign confinement is therefore to institute that control, to enforce the norm of the proper body, specifically through a regime of surveillance that can regulate not only his opium habit but also its characteristic madness. Coleridge finds comfort, if no full cure, in this personal asylum. With it comes renewed vitality as philosopher and moralist—as if asylum and philosophy are somehow allied. Indeed, Coleridge's turn in his later years toward philosophy and morals involves a turn away, not merely from opium and the monstrosity of habituation, but from poetry, too, and the truth of excess. What, one might ask, has been lost in the interminable task of rehabilitating Coleridge?

"*JUNKIE*"

Coleridge was an opium eater for well over half of his life.[1] By his own effusive testimony this bad habit was the bane of his existence. "Conceive a miserable wretch," he wrote to his friend Josiah Wade, "who for many years has been attempting to beat off pain, by a constant recurrence to the vice that produces it" (*Letters* 3: 511). This cycle of medication and withdrawal yielded a drug-dependent Coleridge, a self-medicating subject whose life and writing testified to the ill effects of his habit. To his contemporaries he presented an appearance of promise unfulfilled. Writing in 1824 William Hazlitt regretted that so prodigious a talent should produce so little: "All that he has done of moment, he had done twenty years ago: since then, he may be said to have lived on the sound of his own voice" (234). Thomas Carlyle advanced similar conclusions about Coleridge's career: "To the man himself Nature had given, in high measure, the seeds of a noble endowment; and to unfold it had been forbidden him" (quoted in Lefebure 30). Then there is Robert Southey, who set the standard for a whole tradition in criticism with his claim that "every person who had witnessed his habits, knows that for the greater—infinitely the greater part—inclination and indulgence are the motives" (quoted in Cottle 373). Such judgments do not openly attribute Coleridge's apparent failure to his habit of eating opium. Other public figures—William Wilberforce, Clive of India, James Mackintosh, Thomas De Quincey—were after all known to be drug dependent without disastrous personal effect. But the habit of pathologizing Coleridge as somehow failed, broken, beaten—deviant—set in early and still shapes the way he is read, celebrated, or dismissed.[2]

The justification for this othering, particularly in our own time, has come routinely to involve his use of opium. Thus Elizabeth Schneider, while admitting Coleridge was a habitual user, saves "Kubla Khan" from all unseemly pharmacological taint, concluding that the poem's "special character was not determined or materially influenced by opium" (17). Coleridge may have had a drug problem, but his poetry manifestly does not. Alethea Hayter is not so sure, suggesting that at least something in that poetry "emerged from a rare condition produced in him by opium," a special kind of reverie in which the external senses slept while the internal became hyperaware. She nonetheless views opium eating as deviant behavior, the affliction particularly of those "who long for relief from tension, from the failures and disappointments of their everyday life, who yearn for something which will annihilate the gap between their idea of themselves and their actual selves"—a psychological type she labels "The Inadequate Personality" (40). Coleridge, one is left to conclude, was in some deviant way inadequate. This opinion reaches its epitome in Molly Lefebure's biography, *Samuel Taylor Coleridge,* blithely subtitled *A Bondage of Opium*. It is here that Coleridge finally, after a century of moralizing criticism, achieves the stature of master addict. Lefebure dares to declare aloud what Coleridge's friends would only confide in whispers, that Coleridge's life and labors were a failure and that demon opium was the cause: "his predicament was not simply a matter of a sapped will. Samuel Taylor Coleridge's imaginative powers and concentration were literally destroyed by the drug: his intellectual capacity was fearfully eroded: his sense of truth hopelessly distorted (one of the major effects of morphine addiction)." This conclusion is of a piece with Lefebure's claim of intellectual honesty for her biography, which attempts for the first time "to present Samuel Taylor Coleridge as it seems that he really was—a junkie" (14).

Before we accept the moral, mental, and emotional deviance implied in that tag, however, we might notice a thing or two about Coleridge. For all the accusation of indolence, much of it admittedly his own, he seems able to have kept producing at a pace that would make any dean of humanities proud. The Bollingen edition of his works runs now to fourteen volumes and contains an astonishing variety of writing: essays, lectures, journalism, plays, poems, a philosophical treatise (or what was to become one), and marginalia. If Coleridge failed as a writer, he failed prolifically. Six thick volumes of letters and four annotated volumes of notebook entries only further prove the obvious point: the charge of indolence and its ill effects bears more on Coleridge's reputation as a "junkie" than his achievement as a writer. Perhaps criticism and not Coleridge has been inadequate. Perhaps the junkie needs rehabilitation, not so much to confirm as to comprehend his monstrosity. What, one might ask, is the truth of habituation, the wisdom of the junkie? The alternative to such questions is the soporific confidence of conventional, normalizing criticism.

*F*IX

For Coleridge the truth of an opium habit begins in pain. According to one pharmagraphical confession, opium came to him "like a charm, a miracle," relieving a painful swelling in his knees that had left him "almost bed-ridden for many months" (*Letters* 3: 476). On the basis of such testimony, and there is plenty of it in his letters and notebooks, Coleridge's life appears to have been a long if broken litany of pain. A weak constitution left him prone to sickness as a child. A desperate ague weakened him further as a schoolboy. Rheumatic fever laid him low for six months at seventeen, preparing the way for the joint pain that would hound him as an adult. Then come the various and extravagant symptoms that require self-medication: toothache, gum infection, migraine, inscrutable pains in limbs, chest, and bowels, the latter often accompanied by diarrhea or constipation of Herculean magnitude. "What I suffer in mere *pain* is almost incredible," Coleridge wrote to Tom Poole in 1801 (*Letters* 2: 721). Opium, at least initially, was a grand panacea, an all-purpose palliative that made the body, for a time anyway, bearable.

Although it is hard for us in retrospect to dispel the purple haze that hovers around it, for Coleridge and his contemporaries opium was an extremely effective and dependable pain reliever.[3] In the words of its best historians, "At the opening of the nineteenth century . . . doctors and others still thought of opium not as dangerous or threatening, but as central to medicine, a medicament of surpassing usefulness which undoubtedly found its way into every home" (Berridge and Edwards xxv). Indeed, the hugely popular medical handbook, William Buchan's *Domestic Medicine,* recommends the use of opium in cases ranging from gout to rheumatism to migraine, pronouncing it "a valuable medicine when taken in proper quantity" (342). Coleridge himself maintained to his acquaintances that he had been "seduced into the use of narcotics" (Gillman 223) by such claims during his bout with swollen knees: "in a medical Journal I unhappily met with an account of a cure performed in a similar case (or what to me appeared so) by rubbing in of Laudanum, at the same time taking a given dose internally—It acted like a charm, a miracle!" (*Letters* 3: 476).

That "medical Journal" was most likely John Brown's *Elements of Medicine,* edited by Coleridge's friend Thomas Beddoes. In it Brown extols opium's power as a pain reliever. "The virtue of opium is great," he maintains, primarily because it excites torpid flesh: "The pains, that opium is calculated to remove, are all those, that depend upon general asthenic affection," among which Brown includes the pains of gout, chronic rheumatism, sore throat, headache, and gunshot wounds (1: 245n). Using laudanum to treat rheumatic pains was meant to stimulate the body, producing a sweat that would excite the whole system: "In order to render the sweat universal and of sufficient duration, it should be excited by Dover's powder, or laudanum, . . . and kept up for twelve hours in full flow" (2: 168). Opium superinduces the bodily activity whose omission occasions pain—a precociously Freudian account of hypercathexis. Such are the exciting effects of opium.

But it also works as a dependable euphoriant. In Brown's considered opinion, opium "banishes melancholy, begets confidence, converts fear into boldness, makes the silent eloquent, and dastards brave. Nobody, in desperate circumstances, and sinking under a disrelish for life, ever laid violent hands on himself after taking a dose of opium, or ever will" (1: 285). Brown was only lending contemporary medical support to traditional pharmaceutical wisdom. In that wondrous farrago of fact and fantasy, *The Mysteries of Opium Revealed,* Dr. John Jones attests that "it is good and useful in all *Pain* and *grievous Sensations*" because "it takes off all Frets and turbulent Passions of the sensitive Soul, as . . . Melancholy Madness, or such as proceed from grievous thoughts or apprehensions, Losses, Crosses, Despair, Fears, Terrors, or the like" (328, 267). The reason: it induces "a pleasant *Ovation of the Spirits*" whose effect "has been compar'd (not without good cause) to a permanent gentle *Degree* of that Pleasure, which Modesty forbids the naming of" (20). Opium spiritualizes sexual pleasure permanently (for as long as its virtue lasts). Melancholia passes into a euphoria that is "like a most delicious and extraordinary *Refreshment* of the Spirits upon a very *good News,* or any other great cause of *Joy*" (20), though not without possible somatic side effects, since opium "is of great use to excite to Venery, cause Erections, to actuate a dull *Semen*" (357).

If Dr. Jones is a trustworthy authority in these matters (and his own extensive use of the drug at least merits respect), by the eighteenth century opium was the drug of choice whenever the melancholy fit should fall. When trained physicians add their medical imprimatur, as does George Young in *A Treatise on Opium,* a questionable narcotic acquires the cachet of a potent panacea. Coleridge may complain to Cottle of "a depression too dreadful to be described" (*Letters* 1: 319), but a time-honored remedy stood close at hand. Opium both reduced pain and produced euphoria—a lovely fix indeed. Hence John Murray's belief, recorded in his *System of Materia Medica and Pharmacy,* that "as a palliative and anodyne, it is indeed the most valuable article of the materia medica, and its place could scarcely be supplied by any other" (quoted in Berridge and Edwards 63).

HABIT

Such medicine could be habit forming, as indeed it was for Coleridge. He complains throughout his letters of the enervating effects of taking opium, as in the following confession, directed to his friend J. J. Morgan in 1814: "By the long Habit of the accursed Poison my Volition (by which I mean the faculty *instrumental* to the Will, and by which alone the Will can realize itself—it's *[sic]* Hands, Legs, & Feet, as it were) was completely deranged, at times frenzied, dissevered itself from the Will, & became an independent faculty" (*Letters* 3: 489). Here again Coleridge describes his "specific madness," which on this account splits volition from will, producing compulsive behavior ungoverned by conscious intention. Apparently an opium habit has nothing to do with will. It produces a body that prevailing norms cannot accommodate.

Before dismissing this explanation as the sophistical trick of a junkie, one might ponder more closely Coleridge's understanding of habit. In a curious notebook meditation, Coleridge interrogates its strange agency: "Is not *Habit* the Desire of a Desire?—As Desire to Fruition, may not the faint, to the consciousness *erased,* Pencil-mark-*memorials* or relicts of Desire be to Desire itself in its full prominence?" (*Notebooks* 1: 1421). In the metaphor that Derrida has since made famous, Coleridge likens habit to writing, the nonconscious, material anteriority of speech. Habit is to desire as written script to its meaning. Where for Derrida, writing designates a constituent absence in the emergence of meaning, for Coleridge it bespeaks a constituent loss in the emergence of desire.

For habit, like writing, re-presents what is *not* present—in this instance desire, as in the similar case of Rousseau's quaint little compulsion.[4] It does so by consolidating traces of desire, "Pencil-mark-*memorials* or relicts," as Coleridge calls them. These traces, "to the consciousness *erased,*" memorialize the "full prominence" of a desire not fully present within them. They remember, so to speak, a constitutive loss in the emergence of desire. Habit, then, is best understood as a mode of somatic memory. It memorializes desire in behaviors that demonstrate desire's loss, so forcefully in fact that habit itself can come to substitute for "Fruition": "May not the Desirelet, a, so correspond to the Desire, A, that the latter being excited may revert wholly or in great part to its exciting cause, *a,* instead of sallying out of itself toward an external Object, B?" (*Notebooks* 1: 1421). In a reversal worthy of Derrida, Coleridge wonders whether desire might realize fruition in the habit that produces it. Cause and effect would merge in a logical loop wherein the loss of desire is a condition of its emergence. Habit represents a strange presence indeed, if it somatically remembers what is interminably lost. But that seems to be Coleridge's conclusion, which may explain his heartrending desire for a world without habit, without loss, without opium:

> If I could secure you full Independence, if I could give too all my original Self healed & renovated from all infirm Habits; & if by all the forms in my power I could bind myself more effectively even in relation to Law, than the Form out of my power would effect—then, *then,* would you be the remover of my Loneliness, my perpetual Companion? (*Notebooks* 1: 1421)

Coleridge looks here to law to rehabilitate a will enervated by infirm habits, a prospect that will appear increasingly attractive over the years. But for the moment one might examine the habit he finds so debilitating. For if habit is a mode of memory, and if opium is habit forming, then what, one might wonder, does an opium habit remember? Might Coleridge's abject habit memorialize more than just "inclination and indulgence"?

RUSH

Either under the influence of the narcotic draught, of which the songs of all primitive men and peoples speak, or with the potent coming of spring that penetrates all nature with joy, these Dionysian emotions awake, and as they grow in intensity everything subjective vanishes into complete self-forgetfulness. (Nietzsche, *Tragedy* 36)

So writes Nietzsche in *The Birth of Tragedy* of the excessive pathos that the Greeks associated with the approach of their god Dionysus. With Dionysus comes great terror, and yet ecstasy too. That is why the closest familiar analogy to these Dionysian emotions is intoxication. Nietzsche's word is "Rausch," the disruptive force of which lingers in the colloquial use in English of "rush" to describe overwhelming occurrences, particularly of a pharmaceutical sort. What a rush.

But one must listen closely to catch the undertone of Nietzsche's words. For the Dionysian is not a supernatural power that seizes the human in times of intoxication. Nietzsche describes it, along with its incommensurable counterpart the Apollonian, as a play of "artistic energies which burst forth from nature herself" (38). Nothing apart from nature appears, then, in the rush of Dionysus. On the contrary, in the Dionysian, nature plays the artist, to the terror and the ecstasy of humankind:

Schopenhauer has depicted for us the tremendous *terror* which seizes man when . . . suddenly dumfounded by the cognitive form of phenomena because the principle of sufficient reason, in some one of its manifestations, seems to suffer an exception. If we add to this terror the blissful ecstasy that wells from the innermost depths of man, indeed of nature, at this collapse of the *principium individuationis,* we steal a glimpse into the nature of the *Dionysian,* which is brought home to us most intimately by the analogy of intoxication. (36)

The Dionysian is a double hit, at once bane and bliss. It comes to disrupt and to incite. It stirs feelings of terror *and* ecstasy. You would have to type these words one over the other to represent their simultaneity in the Dionysian. So much for the proper body. Allied to intoxication, this pathos disturbs its regulatory effects.

The coming of Dionysus challenges the propriety, exchangeability, and able-bodied agency of the proper body. Recall that Coleridge observed in his abject

habit a disseverence of will and volition. The latter acquired a haunting life
of its own ungovernable by the individual called Coleridge. For himself and
his many detractors this dissolution of autonomous agency bespeaks a total
collapse of moral force: "inclination and indulgence." But as Nietzsche says,

> there are some who, from obtuseness or lack of experience, turn away from such
> phenomena as from "folk diseases," with contempt or pity born of the conscious-
> ness of their own "Healthy-mindedness." But of course such poor wretches have
> no idea how corpselike and ghostly their so-called "healthy-mindedness" looks
> when the glowing life of the Dionysian revelers roars past them. (37)

Could it be that Coleridge's habit, as somatic memory, recalls this "glowing
life"? Perhaps the contempt and pity heaped on the opium eater registers the
terrible ecstasy of the Dionysian, not to mention the relative ghostliness of
normal healthy-mindedness.

Habit as memory; opium habit as Dionysian memory: these are the possibilities that Coleridge the junkie confronts. Nietzsche's interest in the Dionysian, as one of "nature's art-impulses" (38), centers in its occurrence, not
merely as intoxication, but as nonimagistic art. Born of the collapse of the
Apollonian *principium individuationis,* a Dionysian art exceeds the image, allowing something to sound for which we otherwise lack ears:

> The wisdom of Silenus cried "Woe! Woe!" to the serene Olympians. The indi-
> vidual, with all his restraint and proportion, succumbed to the self-oblivion of
> the Dionysian states, forgetting the precepts of Apollo. *Excess* revealed itself
> as truth. Contradiction, the bliss born of pain, spoke out from the very heart of
> nature. And so, wherever the Dionysian prevailed, the Apollonian was checked
> and destroyed. (47)

The truth of excess that attends the Dionysian must of necessity exceed images and norms. It disrupts the regulatory force of the proper body and its
proprietary agency. Hence the self-oblivion of the individual, whose *loss* of
identity and proper embodiment best figures the truth of excess. Only a nonimagistic art can convey this loss, which is why music is for Nietzsche the pur-
est example of Dionysian art. Music, like memory, occurs as strange presence.
It can be heard only as it passes away; loss is the medium of its occurrence.
And in its interminable loss of presence whispers a bliss born of pain.

Loss

This is the real hallmark of the coming of Dionysus: the pathos of contradiction, the simultaneity of bliss and pain. As Nietzsche describes it,

> only the curious blending and duality in the emotions of the Dionysian revelers
> remind us—as medicines remind us of deadly poisons—of the phenomenon that

pain begets joy, that ecstasy may wring sounds of agony from us. At the very climax of joy there sounds a cry of horror or a yearning lamentation for an irretrievable loss. (40)

When the Dionysian occurs, it awakens a memory, the lost memory of loss in the midst of deepest joy. When the Dionysian occurs as art, this memory becomes a force that sustains rather than simply destroys—sustains *as* it destroys. That is why Nietzsche can declare that "it is only as an *aesthetic phenomenon* that existence and the world are eternally *justified*" (52): life, which like music occurs only as it passes away, which deforms even as it produces all that is beautiful, valuable, or true, this life of loss can only be justified—eternally—through affirmation.[5] Dionysian art affirms life by remembering its irretrievable loss while making that memory the means of its further occurrence. It is crucial to distinguish here between "loss" in this affirmative, productive sense and "lack" in a privative and originary sense. The latter descends from Hegel as the engine that drives dialectic. However dialectical Nietzsche's polemic may appear in *The Birth of Tragedy*, its turn toward the Dionysian does not arise as antithesis to the thesis of the Apollonian. Rather it describes an incommensurable art impulse whose productivity occurs as loss, even as dying organisms beget new life.[6] It is in this sense that life becomes an "aesthetic phenomenon": old forms beget new as loss articulates excess. "All perform their tragic play, / . . . / Gaiety transfiguring all that dread" (Yeats 159). Art might thus become a means of rehabilitating a life of loss through affirmation.

Such medicines must at times remind one of poisons. The loss they remember will from some perspectives appear deadly. If it seems right to approach Coleridge's opium habit as Dionysian memory, then it should come as no surprise that through it excess reveals itself as, if not quite truth, then perhaps life. That abject habit may memorialize an irretrievable loss his poetry also remembers—and affirms. This possibility would, however, require a rehabilitation of the conventional image of Coleridge. He would turn from weak victim of "inclination and indulgence" into a creature of excess and strange delay, a belated votary of Dionysus, whose coming destroys the proper body along with its will:

> In this sense the Dionysian man resembles Hamlet: both have once looked truly into the essence of things, they have *gained knowledge,* and nausea inhibits action; for their action could not change anything in the eternal nature of things; they feel it to be ridiculous or humiliating that they should be asked to set right a world that is out of joint. Knowledge kills action; action requires veils of illusion: that is the doctrine of Hamlet, and not the cheap wisdom of Jack the Dreamer. (Nietzsche, *Tragedy* 60)

Coleridge the Dionysian: that is the way he ought to be remembered. This great Hamlet of a writer languished out of knowledge, not "inclination and indulgence." For a time art came to him, as Nietzsche suggests it must, "as a saving sorceress, expert at healing. She alone knows how to turn these nauseous thoughts about the horror or absurdity of existence into notions with which one can live" (60). If art heals Dionysian man, poetry was Coleridge's best medicine, better far than opium, turning a knowledge of excess—"the essence of things"—toward an affirmation of the life of loss. For a time.

HONEYDEW

Ultimately Coleridge submitted to a new control, but not before composing some astonishing lyrics. Among them the most notorious remains "Kubla Khan: or a Vision in a Dream. A Fragment."[7] Although in the apology that prefaces the poem he admits to publishing it "rather as a psychological curiosity, than on the ground of any supposed *poetic* merits" (*Poetical Works* 1: 295), few would accept his judgment. "Kubla Khan" haunts modern writing like a monster, inspiring endless articles and even books with just fifty-four magical lines. This lost dream of loss has been amazingly productive, and contrary to the healthy-minded claims of so much of that criticism, the poem begins in opium. Coleridge confesses in the text that intervenes between the title and the poem that "Kubla Khan" came to him in a reverie—"a profound sleep, at least of the external senses." And he is frank if disingenuous about what produced it: "an anodyne" that had been "prescribed . . . in consequence of a slight indisposition." Coleridge forces one to approach his "vision in a dream" as an occurrence that opium made possible; whether it really happened that way or not is beside the point. Unless the poem is printed without its preface, one only enters Xanadu under the influence of opium.

And the reason should be obvious by now. "Kubla Khan," like Coleridge's opium habit, memorializes the Dionysian. Coleridge comes close to admitting as much in the poem's concluding description of the enraptured poet: "he on honeydew hath fed / And drunk the milk of Paradise" (*Poetical Works* 1: 295, hereafter cited by line). The lines recall Socrates' description in *Ion* of lyric poets in the act of composition: "they are seized with the Bacchic transport, and are possessed—as the bacchants, when possessed, draw milk and honey from the rivers, but not when in their senses. So the spirit of the lyric poet works" (Plato 220). Socrates associates the lyric poet in the state of composing with Dionysian states. So does Coleridge. And so does Nietzsche. For the latter, lyric as opposed to epic poetry announces the Dionysian. The ancients knew why: "they took for granted *the union,* indeed the *identity,* of the *lyrist with the musician*" (49). This union of music and poetry gives the lyric its peculiar force. Language works differently in the lyric than in other kinds of discourse. It refers, not to things, but to music itself: "in the poetry of the folk song, language is strained to its utmost that it may *imitate music* . . . the word, the image, the concept here seeks an expression analogous to music and now feels in itself the power of music" (53, 54). If music, as strange presence, passes away as it occurs, and if the language of the lyric strains to imitate such music, then the lyric memorializes the loss of its own occurrence. It occurs as a loss that announces excess. Hence the double structure of lyrical *mimesis*: the lyric imitates the occurrence (in language) of its occurrence (as music), a mimesis not merely of its own form, but of its formation and deformation. The lyric, in the music of its evanescence, remembers the Dionysian.

DULCIMER

It is a truism, though not quite an empty one, to say that "Kubla Khan" is the most musical of poems. But its music is no mere ornament of a beguiling little lyric. It indicates the operation of this lyrical mimesis. Coleridge himself describes the double structure of such mimesis when he relates the manner of the poem's composing, "if that indeed can be called composition in which all the images rose up before him as *things*, with a parallel production of the correspondent expressions, without any sensation or consciousness of effort" (*Poetical Works* 1: 95). The composition of "Kubla Khan" occurs exactly as Nietzsche suggests it should, since "the lyric genius is conscious of a world of images and symbols—growing out of his state of mystical self-abnegation and oneness" (50). Images arise as things with a parallel production of correspondent expression, without consciousness of effort. This double structure of occurrence involves two components: images and expressions. Take the former for language and the latter for music and "Kubla Khan" turns Dionysian. The question to ask of its language then becomes, not what are the texts in which it originates, but how does it imitate its occurrence as music? What is the manner of its passing away?[8]

Loss—and its productivity—is the preoccupation of Coleridge's preface and poem alike. The legendary tale of the man from Porlock is a parable of loss. Disrupted from his reverie, the poet returns an hour later to find that

> though he still retained some vague and dim recollection of the general purport of the vision, yet, with the exception of some eight or ten scattered lines and images, all the rest had passed away like images on the surface of a stream into which a stone has been cast, but, alas, without the after restoration of the latter. (*Poetical Works* 1: 296)

Not the vision but the vision's loss is what Coleridge undertakes to imitate, and as he does so he doubles, triples, even quadruples his account: with first the story itself of the distracting businessman, then a self-quotation that misrepresents loss by promising an impossible restoration, then a resolution (in Greek) to sing a sweeter song, originally "Today" but changed mercifully in 1834 to "tomorrow." Finally comes the poem itself, that sweet musical remembrance of Kubla's miraculous pleasure dome. These multiple accounts of Reverie Lost imitate the occurrence of music, making loss constitutive of the poem's emergence. That is why its language and imagery, when finally they come, imitate their passing. Kubla's dome, for all its rare device, appears first doomed (by "Ancestral voices prophesying war!"[30]), then dimmed to nothing (vanishing in the abyss between stanzas). And when a poet steps in at the end to revive it, his only access comes through a music that is always already gone:

> Could I revive within me
> Her symphony and song,
> To such a deep delight 'twould win me,
> That with music loud and long,
> I would build that dome in air,
> That sunny dome! Those caves of ice! (42–47)

A poetry built of music passes instantly away. But in "Kubla Khan," with its apology and its preface, its self-quotation and its sublime imagery, loss turns productive. Its musical occurrence, like the somatic memory of opium eating, announces excess. In this manner, a Dionysian art affirms the life of loss: it multiplies the memorials of its occurrence. Sweet music indeed.

Loon

But such music is as difficult to endure as it is to create. Among the hazards of the Dionysian is a loss of interest in life. Hamlet is the great exemplar because the knowledge of excess that comes in the horrific image of his father's ghost renders all the world absurd: "now no comfort avails any more; longing transcends a world after death, even the gods; existence is negated along with its glittering reflection in the gods or in an immortal beyond" (*Tragedy* 60). A Dionysian art intervenes to exhaust these feelings of nausea and absurdity, producing plays within plays, poems within poems. But a danger persists that the loss constitutive of such art will receive, out of fear or grief or weariness, a transcendental interpretation, a normalizing critique.[9] Excess succumbs to intelligibility, effecting a loss of loss. The ecstatic agonies of the Dionysian, those pains of opium's dubious pleasures, can just as easily receive transcendental as lyrical treatment.

Something of the sort occurs to Coleridge as Dionysian artist: he turns from the lyric, with its musical excess, toward the more certain world of philosophy and the proper body. Habits of opium and poetry become rehabilitated through transcendence and the norm of embodiment it enforces. And in this Coleridge resembles his own most powerful creation, the Ancient Mariner,

whose strange, excessive tale bespeaks a loss so complete that it requires
transcendental interpretation:

> O Wedding Guest! this soul hath been
> Alone on a wide wide sea:
> So lonely 'twas , that God himself
> Scarce seemed there to be.
> (*Poetical Works* 1: 208, hereafter cited by line)

Like "Kubla Khan," "The Rime of the Ancient Mariner" makes the occurrence
of loss constitutive of its narration, but unlike that more musical poem it in-
terprets that occurrence transcendentally. "The Rime of the Ancient Mariner"
rehabilitates the Dionysian by rendering its ecstatic agonies intelligible. This
baleful poem prophesies Coleridge's turn away from poetry.[10]

"Hold off! unhand me, grey-beard loon!'" (11). The Wedding Guest sees a
glint of madness in the Mariner's basilisk eye. Beyond the pale of the quo-
tidian, on the very threshold of a wedding feast, the Mariner tells an agonizing
tale of loss and recovery that arises compulsively out of the simple question:
"'What manner of man art thou?'" (577). If the tale's answer is Dionysian man,
then its teller must indeed be crazed, lost in the occurrence of the memory of
excess. Coleridge takes great care to document the madness of the Mariner.
The extravagance not only of his tale's content but also of its sheer length indicts him. In a profusion of words and images it speaks of a loss of speech:

> And every tongue, through utter drought,
> Was withered at the root;
> We could not speak, no more than if
> We had been choked with soot. (135–38)

In so excessively speaking the loss of speech the Mariner makes loss constitutive of the tale he tells. He is an artist in the Dionysian mode, narrating
loss as a means to narration.

But he is mad too—medically speaking. In its excess, the Mariner's speech
is painfully consistent with medical descriptions of melancholia, that traditional pathology of loss. Writing originally in Latin in *A Methodical System
of Nosology* (1808), William Cullen places melancholia in the class of diseases
called Neuroses ("sense and notion injured, without an original fever, and
without any local disorder"), under the order of mental illness called Vesaniae
("a disorder of function of the judging faculty of the mind, without fever or
sleepiness"), and defines it thus: "a partial insanity without dyspepsia," where
"partial insanity" involves the perception "of false relations of things so as
to excite unreasonable passions and actions," and where dyspepsia would
indicate hypochondriasis (140). Melancholia begins in false perception and
produces deviant behavior. William Pargeter, owner of a private lunatic asylum, published a treatise titled *Observations on Maniacal Disorders* (1792)

in which he claims that in melancholia "the error of the intellectual power
is confined principally, often entirely, to one subject" (6). In *Observations on
the Nature, Kinds, Causes, and Prevention of Insanity* (2d ed., 1806), Thomas
Arnold, M.D., concurs, defining melancholia as "a permanent delirium, without fury or fever, in which the mind is dejected, and timorous, and usually
employed about one object" (16). Because delirium without observable bodily
ailment appears almost exclusively in language, aberrant speech becomes
the main symptom of melancholia in the medical discourse of Coleridge's day.
Speaking obsessively about a single subject, the melancholiac disrupts the
linguistic norms that constitute and confirm health for the physician. The
result is the loss of social relations. "'God save thee, ancient Mariner! / From
the fiends, that plague thee thus!'" (79–80): no wonder the Wedding Guest
fears the Mariner. He is mad; his speech proclaims it in the idiom of its own
excess.

STRANGE POWER OF SPEECH

And yet talk is the Mariner's therapy too. The loss that is constitutive of
his narration brings his identity to presence, makes him visible and audible
to both the Wedding Guest and ourselves. Speech has the strange power
of recovering what was lost. But bear in mind the double movement of
re-covery—at once to uncover, and cover again; to recover is as much to lose
as to possess. Every time the Mariner tells his tale he loses anew the identity it presents. Hence his painfully compulsive narration, born in agony and
chanted in passion:

> Since then, at an uncertain hour,
> That agony returns;
> And till my ghastly tale is told,
> This heart within me burns. (582–85)

Speech meliorates an agony otherwise without image, but only temporarily.
The Mariner's identity, re-covered in the tale, is lost in its telling. The whole
strange story of the Albatross and the water snakes occurs in compulsive
response to that astonished interrogative (What manner of man . . . ?), and
the manner of the Mariner disappears in its appearance. That is why he
frequently repeats his performance. Loss is constitutive of its coming to presence, the characteristic manner of the Dionysian. Doomed compulsively to
repeat a tale that unmakes him, the Mariner announces excess.

But he does not do so in a mode of affirmation. One of the effects of his disturbing tale, in spite of its manner, is to assert a transcendental and therefore
normative interpretation of its constitutive loss. Its strange power of speech
produces, in its excess, an authoritative speech of power. It becomes possible

therefore to interpret the "The Rime of the Ancient Mariner" in metaphysical rather than Dionysian terms, an interpretation advanced by its famous marginal gloss, which reaches the conclusion that Mariner must "teach, by his own example, love and reverence to all things that God made and loveth" (*Poetical Works* 1: 209). Perhaps this explains Coleridge's remark to Anna Laetitia Barbauld regarding the moral of his poem: "in my own judgment the poem had too much" (*Table Talk* 87). Too much morality will assure the loss of loss. The Mariner can easily be interpreted—he does so himself—as beholden to a higher power. His identity comes to be defined once and for all by a discourse of moral reference and evaluation. And the loss constitutive of his narration receives a transcendental interpretation. This time it is for good.

Then there's the fate of the Albatross. Its death is nothing in itself, a mere event in an eventful world. But interpretation of that event is everything, at least to the Mariner. When the Albatross ceases to be a just bird and becomes as well a signifier in a moral discourse, it serves to regulate the strange speech that produces the Mariner's identity: "Instead of the cross, the Albatross / About my neck was hung" (141–42). A new morality naturalizes the old in this appropriation, substituting for the sign of the cross that of the Albatross, which signifies by another substitution the Mariner himself. The identity that this moral discourse produces is apparently more natural but no less responsible than its earlier Christian avatar. When the Mariner blesses the water snakes he legitimates this discourse. Even though the act itself might as easily affirm the beauty of a life of loss, its interpretation privileges a higher power: "Surely my kind saint took pity on me, / And I blessed them unaware. / The selfsame moment I could pray" (286–88). The Mariner's strange speech produces in him an identity that, however menacing, ultimately depends on a higher power. Melancholia receives transcendental treatment as prayer rehabilitates delirium. Thereafter the Mariner can be interpreted as a morally responsible, self-disciplining man.[11]

ABSTRUSE RESEARCH

Coleridge struggled against opium to become that kind of man. It is a commonplace of criticism that Coleridge turns from poetry to philosophy and morals about the time he tries finally to kick his "accursed Habit" (*Letters* 3: 476). Transcendental philosophy rehabilitates a melancholy Coleridge, treating the life of loss with abstruse truth. One might say with Nietzsche that "here philosophic thought overgrows art and compels it to cling close to the trunk of dialectic" (*Tragedy* 91). Nietzsche is speaking of the Platonic dialogues but the point applies to Coleridge: his writing turns away from lyric and toward philosophy, away from the truth of excess and toward the power of law and proper embodiment. Dionysian man yields to the type Nietzsche associates with Socrates, the theoretical man, who "with his faith that the nature of things can be fathomed, ascribes to knowledge and insight the power of a panacea" (97). Not opium, not poetry, but philosophy finally becomes for Coleridge the elixir of life. As early as 1802 Coleridge attests to its therapeutic powers:

> And haply by abstruse research to steal
> From my own nature all the natural man—
> This was my sole resource, my only plan:
> Till that which suits a part infects the whole,
> And now is almost grown the habit of my soul.
> (*Poetical Works* 1: 367)

Philosophy, too, can be habit forming. A Truth habit is much more acceptable than a drug habit. Coleridge's turn to philosophy is a turn away from—and forgetting of—the Dionysian, which so invigorated his earlier poetry. His philosophical alternative institutes assimilation to moral discourse as the condition of health and happiness—as indeed it was for Coleridge himself in his desperate efforts to abandon opium: "In the one crime of OPIUM, what crime have I not made myself guilty of!" (*Letters* 3: 511). By finally fulfilling his long-standing resolution to place himself "in the House, and under the constant eye of some medical man" (*Letters* 3: 398), Coleridge erects a material structure of moral law and discipline, a private asylum that, internalized, would ameliorate his "specific madness" and produce lasting recovery.[12] That this asylum so obviously resembles the structure of the late-eighteenth-century asylums for the insane shows how such practices coordinate private and public agencies.[13] There is something of the asylum about Coleridge's later philosophical writings, a tendency to reproduce its relations of power as the condition not only of personal and political health but even of artistic freedom.

ASYLUM

For the great French physician and psychiatrist Philippe Pinel, humane reformer of the asylum, the treatment of mental illness was primarily a moral matter. Quoting the *Encyclopaedia Britannica,* he describes his approach as follows: "'In the moral treatment of insanity, lunatics are not to be considered as absolutely devoid of reason, i.e. as inaccessible by motives of fear and hope, and sentiments of honour. . . . In the first instance it is proper to gain an ascendancy over them, and afterwards to encourage them'" (103). It would be easy but ill-advised to overlook the institutional framework in which Pinel's treatment occurs. Although it aims at producing a morally responsible, self-disciplining individual, it does so in the confines of an asylum whose structure it works to internalize. According to Pinel, cure depends less on the inmates themselves than on the character and behavior of its primary moral agent and exemplar, the governor. Successful treatment becomes possible only "at a well regulated asylum . . . subject to the management of a governor, in every respect qualified to exercise over [the inmates] an irresistible controul" (59–60). The power granted to this governor is a direct corollary to the fundamental "laws" of the asylum:

> to allow . . . all the latitude of personal liberty consistent with safety; to proportion the degree of coercion to the demands upon it from his extravagance of behaviour; to use mildness of manners or firmness as occasion may require,—the bland arts of conciliation, or the tone of irresistible authority pronouncing an irreversible mandate. (83)

The "enlightened maxims of humanity" that guide Pinel's moral treatment produce an individual whose autonomy is an afterimage of institutional power and its proper embodiment (68). When an inmate internalizes the governor and regulates speech accordingly he or she is pronounced cured.

For all its humanity, then, Pinel's moral treatment of insanity privately incarnates institutional power. It produces the truth of recovery by erecting an asylum within, an internalized site of self-discipline. Foucault describes the effects of such therapeutics as the instantiation of "a sort of invisible tribunal in permanent session" (*Discipline and Punish* 265). The great achievement of Pinel's asylum as a social institution is to have made possible this private tribunal: "The asylum in the age of positivism, which it is Pinel's glory to have founded, is not a free realm of observation, diagnosis, and therapeutics; it is a juridical space where one is accused, judged, and condemned, and from which one is never released except by the version of this trial in psychological depth—that is, by remorse" (269). If the asylum becomes that institutional space that produces the truth of recovery, then Coleridge is one of its finest achievements. That his was a domestic and not institutional arrangement only exaggerates the force of its example. By submitting to the care of a physician in order to control his opium habit, Coleridge not only becomes the first celebrity to enter rehab, he also becomes a living testimonial to the power of this juridical space and the effects of its internalization in the psychodrama of remorse, recovery, and relapse. Through his example is born a legion of recovering habitués. But something dies, too, or at least falls silent: the life of excess as somatic memory. Coleridge's recovery is as much a matter of forgetting as self-discipline. Lost to memory is the life of loss and the monstrous force of Dionysian art. Knowledge comes increasingly to take its place, a knowledge that reproduces institutional relations of power as a condition of proper embodiment and human health. Transcendental philosophy thus fits neatly into the juridical space of the asylum. Both institute bodily control over bad habits by appealing to higher power. Poetry is all but forgotten.

IMAGINATION

Dionysian poet turns transcendental philosopher. Even Coleridge's aesthetic
theory betrays a trace of the asylum. Witness the influential theoretical statement Coleridge made in *Biographia Literaria* (1815–17) concerning the "es-
emplastic power" of Imagination. It's a peculiar statement, since to define
this creative faculty Coleridge immediately divides it in two:

> The Imagination, then, I consider either as primary, or secondary. The pri-
> mary Imagination I hold to be the living Power and prime Agent of all human
> Perception, and as a repetition in the finite mind of the eternal act of creation
> in the infinite I Am. The secondary Imagination I consider as an echo of the for-
> mer, co-existing with the conscious will, yet still as identical with the primary in
> the *kind* of its agency, and differing only in *degree,* and in the *mode* of its opera-
> tion. (*Works* 7:1: 304)

Although typically taken to establish the divine agency of imagination, this
statement also betrays its institutional origins. For the double structure of
imagination reproduces at the origin of the work of art the power relations
of the asylum. However "eternal" the "act of creation in the infinite I Am,"
the individual creative act is but the echo of an imperious moral authority. It
is regulated by a power that, although identified with God, resembles in its
agency that of Law as Coleridge describes it in *The Friend,* no. 7, "Essay IV:
On the Principles of Political Philosophy." Both regulate the visual: imagination as "the living Power and prime Agent of all human Perception," law as an
"awful power . . . acting on natures pre-configured to its influences." And both
legislate the verbal, assimilating the acceptable in art and politics to an authoritative moral discourse: "This is the Spirit of Law! the Lute of Amphion,
the Harp of Orpheus! This is the true necessity, which compels man into the
social State, now and always, by a still-beginning, never-ceasing force of
moral Cohesion" (*Works* 4:2: 100–01). Coleridge finds in such necessity a cure
for his "specific madness," a reunion of will and volition in the operation of
"an *invisible* power . . . a Power, which was therefore irresistible, because it
took away the very Will of resisting . . . acting on natures preconfigured to
its influence" (100). Law is such a power and Imagination is another. For all
its transcendental pretensions, Coleridge's Imagination has social origins.
Like Pinel's governor, like "the awful power of Law," it preconfigures the artist to respond to its influence. Hence the moral authority of its products. The
modern Imagination, at least as Coleridge defines it, works in the juridical
space of an invisible asylum, which may be why the art of the insane inspires
such fascination: the dangers of the Dionysian ever menace the moralized
Imagination.

But it is not Imagination alone that regulates this space and the bodies it
masters. That task requires another institution, the character and function of

which becomes the subject of Coleridge's late tract, *On the Constitution of the Church and State, According to the Idea of Each* (1830). The turn away from bad habits and toward the proper body fulfills itself in Coleridge's advocacy of religion as the institutional means of producing it. A healthy body politic requires pervasive assimilation among its members to a regulatory moral discourse. Institutionally, that task falls to the church, "inasmuch as the morality which the state requires in its citizens for its own well-being and ideal immortality, and without reference to their spiritual interest as individuals, can only exist for the people in the form of religion" (*Works* 10: 69). Religion thus conceived is a more political than spiritual institution, reproducing a moral unanimity that regulates national identity. The kind of identity that arises in Coleridge's poetry as a means of meliorating the life of loss becomes the foundational unit of a self-disciplining body politic, at least in that social order whose history and tradition coincide with England's: "in regard of the grounds and principles of action and conduct, the State has a right to demand of the National Church, that its instructions should be fitted to diffuse throughout the people *legality*, that is, the obligations of a well-calculated self-interest, under conditions of a common interest under common laws" (*Works* 10: 54). To the established church Coleridge assigns the task of spreading this identity throughout the nation. State religion reproduces and regulates the health of the proper body in liberal society. The politics of the conservative sage of Highgate are in part the prejudices of a reformed opium habitué, dependent no longer on drugs but on ideas and institutions that promote bodily health and happiness. Religion truly is the opiate of the masses.

CODA: OF TRUTH AND EXCESS

Pondering his life from a posthumous perspective, Coleridge anticipates its value as exemplary narrative: "After my death, I earnestly entreat, that a full and unqualified narration of my wretchedness, and of its guilty cause, may be made public, that at least some little good may be effected by the direful example!" (*Letters* 3: 511). As case study and moral fable Coleridge's narco-narrative might represent something true. This link between truth and excess warrants further treatment. Coleridge begins his life as artist in the manner of the Dionysian. He ends up a philosopher, preferring morality to music. Lost in the interim is the abundant life of loss, the disrupting rush of excess ever deforming living forms. Coleridge may have gained discipline, security, and even health as a result, but at the cost of forgetting the creative life that his poetry remembers.

Oh, that this Socrates might longer have practiced his strange music! But for a few harrowing recoveries, the lyric was lost to Coleridge. His melancholy story is not simply that of a hapless junkie. It tells of loss that announces excess. It bespeaks an interminable disappearance. Little wonder then that the melancholy Coleridge should seek pharmaceutical or philosophical treatments "here, when the danger to his will is greatest" (*Tragedy* 60). Health requires a return to social relations, however desperate the means: "And did I not groan at my unworthiness, & be miserable at my state of Health, its effects, and effect-trebling Causes? O yes!—Me miserable! O yes!—Have mercy on me, O bring something *out* of me! For there is no *power,* (and if that *can* be, less *strength*) in aught within me! Mercy! Mercy!" (*Notebooks* 2: 2453). Is criticism capable of rehabilitating Coleridge? Of recovering the truth of excess, the wisdom of the junkie? Mercy, mercy!

CHAPTER 5

CRAZY BODY

Owing to dyspepsia afflicting my system, and the possibility
of any additional derangement of the stomach taking place,
consequences incalculably distressing would arise,
so much so indeed as to increase nervous irritation,
and prevent me from attending to matters of overwhelming
importance, if you do not remember to cut the mutton in a
diagonal rather than a longitudinal form.
—De Quincey to a cook

If you are what you eat, what is the diet of a transcendentalist? All prejudices, says Nietzsche, come from the intestines—a witty remark, considering that his word for prejudices, "Vorurtheile," gestures toward something that precedes judgment.[1] Bowels before cognition? De Quincey thinks so too. In an entry to a diary he kept in 1803, he makes a portentous claim:

> The intimate connection, which exists between the body and the mind, has never (to my knowledge) been sufficiently enlarged on in theory or insisted on in practice. To shew the ultimate cause of this would be very difficult though not (I think) impossible. But on the present occasion it would be almost superfluous; because, throughout the whole of the following system, I suppose previously that the reader admits the fundamental points on which it is grounded; and, even though he should not, I don't care a damn. (Lindop 98)

Perhaps De Quincey should have cared a damn. If critical tradition is any indication, few of his readers have shared those fundamental points. He continues to be treated as the guilty subject of private suffering, the sad penitent of substance abuse, or, more recently, the pale-mouthed prophet of imperialist dreams.[2] But if we take seriously De Quincey's hint that the intimate

109

connection between body and mind is a pervasive interest of his, then a passage like the following will acquire a peculiar force:

> *Fiat experimentum in corpore vili* is a just rule where there is any reasonable presumption of benefit to arise on a large scale. What the benefit may be will admit of a doubt, but there can be none as to the value of the body, for a more worthless body than his own, the author is free to confess, cannot be. It is his pride to believe that it is the very ideal of a base, crazy, despicable human system. (*Confessions* 103)[3]

The passage comes from the appendix De Quincey added to his *Confessions of an English Opium Eater* for its republication in book form. With characteristic jocularity, he offers his body to medical science with the proviso that it not take immediate possession. There are benefits to be had from examining a crazy body. It might lead to the conclusion, for instance, that cognition is a material process, not just a mental one. *The Confessions of an English Opium Eater,* far from representing the anguish of an alienated autobiographist, makes the mind of a transcendentalist a matter of digestion.

THE PHILOSOPHER'S BODY

Consider the implications of De Quincey's charming, purloined memoir, "The Last Days of Immanuel Kant."[4] Given the imposing reputation of its purported subject, it's an odd essay. De Quincey never mentions the intellectual achievements that made Kant's name famous.[5] That ubiquitous groupie of lettered celebrity Henry Crabb Robinson comments suggestively about the essay, "He made much of the bodily constitution of a great man, with no allusion to his mind or philosophy" (Leask, *British Romantic Writers* 178). Robinson perceives the audacity of the account De Quincey provides of Kant's senescence, illness, and death. The memoir puts the philosopher's body before his mind, testing mind's life against body's health. With this twist De Qunicey turns on England's foremost interpreter of Kant, Samuel Taylor Coleridge, whose *Biographia Literaria* pushed transcendental philosophy to pious heights: "the transcendental philosopher does not enquire, what ultimate ground of our knowledge there may lie out of our knowing, but what is the last in our knowing itself, beyond which we cannot pass" (300). Coleridge elimates materiality, including that of the body, from the philosopher's purview—at a time in his life when he was waging a private little war against opium dependency. In response, De Quincey embodies the claims of transcendental philosophy to have determined the formal conditions of cognition and therefore to have found an ideal value for human life. Kant's last days materialize those claims in the banal drama of the philosopher's demise.

According to the memoir, Kant's "was a life remarkable, not so much for its incidents as for the purity and philosophic dignity of its daily tenor" (*Collected Writings* 4: 328). The material vehicle of that daily tenor was health: virile, indomitable, beatific health. De Quincey's source, Ehregott Andreas Christoph Wasianski, reports that with the exception of a single ague and a minor contusion, Kant "had never (properly speaking) been ill" (4: 365). His constitution was hale and robust, renowned both for its freedom from disease, and more positively, for its self-sensation of health: "Kant's health was exquisite, not merely negative health, or the absence of pain, and of irritation, and also of *mal-aise* (either of which, thought not 'pain,' is often worse to bear), but a state of positive pleasurable sensation, and a conscious possession of all his vital activities." Sleep was such a state, one that Kant relished with unusual sensuality. In tender detail De Quincey recapitulates the great philosopher's preparations for bed, his private undressing and ritual "*nesting*" in his bedclothes until he was "swathed like a mummy . . . self-involved like the silk-worm in its cocoon." Kant's anticipation of the pleasure to come was positively erotic:

> When packed up for the night in the way I have described, he would often ejaculate to himself . . . "Is it possible to conceive a human being with more perfect health than myself?" In fact, such was the purity of his life, and such the happy condition of his situation, that no uneasy passion ever arose to excite him, nor care to harass, nor pain to awake him. (4: 338–39)

If Kant's intellectual powers were amazing, his bodily functions were enviable.

Far be it from the philosopher, however, to find bodily health in itself satisfying.[6] "In the judging of health," Kant writes in his *Critique of Judgment,* "we may notice this distinction. It is immediately pleasant to everyone possessing it (at least negatively, i.e. as the absence of all bodily pains). But in order to say that it is good, it must be considered by reason with reference to purposes, viz. that it is a state which makes us fit for all our business" (42). Like all things in transcendental philosophy, the body's value is a function of representation. The evaluation of health requires referring it to reason by means of the idea of purpose. Only by representing and referring health to the faculties of cognition can we determine whether it makes us fit for all our business. It may be the purpose of the *Critique of Judgment* to show that this determination results from a free, indeterminate accord of the cognitive faculties, but Kant's basic point should be obvious: the body's health requires the mind's approval. Transcendental philosophy divides the body into two parts, the material and the formal, then reconnects them through representation, subjecting the former to the latter. Hence Kant's skepticism toward simple sensation: "Only what [a person] does, without reference to enjoyment, in full freedom and independently of what nature can procure for him passively, gives an [absolute] worth to his presence [in the world] as the existence of a person" (43). For Kant, the business of human life is freedom, to which even positive bodily health is just a means.

The reason, as Gilles Deleuze shows, is simple: freedom "is the only concept (the only Idea of reason) which gives to things in themselves the sense or the guarantee of a 'fact' and which enables us really to penetrate the intelligible world" (*Kant's Critical Philosophy* 31). Securing a realm not subject to causality, the concept of freedom lifts the mind out of matter to reveal its participation in the supersensible. Things such as the body can be known only through their appearances. As Kant writes in *Anthropology from a Pragmatic Point of View,* "I know myself only as I appear to myself" (22), and when it comes to the body, such appearances are always just skin deep. In itself the body stands beyond the reach of sure knowledge, an anatomy of ambiguity to the practitioner of critique. The question of the body's health remains, therefore, unanswerable. In *The Conflict of the Faculties* Kant offers a brief critique of medical judgment that defines its limits: "we do not call a man ill unless he *feels* ill, although a disease which he does not *feel* may lie hidden in him, about to come forth. Hence if he does not feel ill, he is entitled to express his well-being only by saying that he is *apparently* in good health." The body remains the morbid creature of sensation. Critical philosophy operates to secure a higher freedom, as medicine must too: "medical science is *philosophical* when the sheer power of man's reason to master his sensuous feelings by a self-imposed principle determines his manner of living" (181–83).

Freedom comes through the disciplinary relation of the philosophical mind to the body that Kant describes with the word "regimen" ("Diatetik"), which he defines as the "art of *prolonging* life (not enjoying it)" (181). If a truly philosophical regimen deploys reason to master morbid feeling through a self-imposed principle, then representation grounds bodily health. Kant illustrates the effects of such regimen with uncharacteristically personal anecdotes: he masters a feeling of constriction by contemplating its empty mechanism; he triumphs over a rare bout of insomnia by pondering the word "Cicero." Kant's cure for bodily discomfort is to reason it away, to represent to himself a form of health that depathologizes the body until "sheer force of resolution averts an illness" (205). Such a regimen frees him for the business of freedom and the work of philosophy, "mental work [that] can set another kind of heightened vital feeling against the limitations that affect the body alone" (189).

Parting company with Kant, De Quincey advances a representation of Kant's last days that refuses the priority of representation over health. The body grounds representation and not vice versa. Hence the emphasis on the severe regularity of Kant's habits, on days that all look interminably the same: up at five, writing until one, a walk after dinner, study until ten, then lusciously to bed. In a note De Quincey offhandedly tells of "a brilliant and accomplished barrister" and relative of William Cowper's "who shot himself under no other impulse than that of pure *ennui* or *taedium vitae,* or, in fact, furious rebellion against the odious monotony of life" (4: 339n). Not Kant. "To *him* the monotony of this succession was not burdensome, and probably contributed, with the uniformity of his diet, and other habits of the same regularity, to lengthen his life" (4: 342). De Quincey seems especially fascinated by that diet, which like so much else attests to Kant's Roman discipline. For breakfast, a cup of tea and a pipe of tobacco. Kant eats nothing else until dinner, which as his *Anthropology* indicates is more an event than a meal (143–47). Guests arrive at one and are met with a hospitable spread, including "sufficient choice of dishes . . . to meet a variety of tastes" and wine in decanters placed "anacreontically on the table." After soup Kant always takes a dram of Hungarian wine or Rhenish. Because the purpose of dinner is to provide relaxation from the toils of the morning, he gives himself up with "determinate abandonment . . . to social enjoyment" (4: 331). Conversation abounds on all subjects save transcendental philosophy, and the meal becomes that "physio-intellectual thing" that De Quincey describes richly in his essay "The Casuistry of Roman Meals" (*Collected Writings* 7: 11–43; 37). Kant is for De Quincey the Philosopher Who Eats, whose meals as much as reason make him fit for all his business.

But if eating, and not representation, determines the value of health, then what becomes of cognition? De Quincey's re-presentation of Kant's last days turns into a descriptive critique of transcendental philosophy, for Kant's banishment of philosophy from the dinner table betrays a dissociation of body and mind. Kant either eats or thinks and takes care not to confuse these two different kinds of habits. In a footnote that alludes openly to the *Anthropology,* De Quincey records that Kant "disapproved of eating alone, or *solipsismus convictorii,* as he calls it, on the principle that a man would be apt, if not called off by the business and pleasure of a social party, to think too much or too closely, an exercise which he considered very injurious to the stomach during the first process of digestion" (4: 336n). Critique and digestion do not mix; their operations are mutually exclusive. As Kant himself puts it, "Thinking . . . is a scholar's food" and does not sit well with comestibles. Eating must proceed without the distractions of thought, so to attend to the body's material needs, the philosopher must adhere to "a firm resolution to go on a *diet with regard to thinking*" (*Conflict* 199). Dinner and company provide the substance of this diet, without which thinking might ravage the stomach. Transcendental philosophy requires the prior appeasement of the body, the cultivation of good digestion through a regime of reasonable eating.

The body will out, however, and neither Kant's diet nor his philosophy may be as healthful as it appears. De Quincey takes more than a little delight in repeating Kant's most striking physiological trait. He didn't sweat. Seventy-five degrees Fahrenheit was the customary temperature of his rooms, and he was never known to perspire. Elsewhere De Quincey draws him as "an old, arid, and adust metaphysician," who "could not possibly look more like a mummy when dead than he had done alive" ("On Murder Considered as One of the Fine Arts"; *Collected Writings* 13: 35). Kant's constitutional aridity suggests there is something physiologically amiss with the kind of health he values. The Philosopher Who Eats is a living mummy, a desiccated creature of linen and dust. For all his dietary discipline, for all his intellectual finesse, there is something dead about his body. Its highest life is elsewhere. As if to register the distress of such circumstances, Kant's final illness first appears as a depraved appetite. He craves English cheese, lots of it, and demands cup after cup of coffee. "As the winter of 1802–3 approached," De Quincey relates, "he complained more than ever of an affection of the stomach, which no medical man had been able to mitigate, or even to explain" (4: 357). After a lifetime of subordination to the claims of cognition, the philosopher's body demands its due.

And the mind suffers accordingly. Kant's "morbid affection of the stomach" conjures phantasmata for the transcendentalist. "His dreams became continually more appalling: single scenes, or passages in these dreams, were sufficient to compose the whole course of mighty tragedies, the impression from which was so profound as to stretch far into his waking hours" (4: 359). Indigestion troubles cognition, changing its movements, frustrating its modes. Time, one of its a priori principles, dilates beyond the reach of reason, blending consciousness with sleep. Under such bodily circumstances, Kant comes to resemble De Quincey, who in a gesture of fellow-feeling suggests in a footnote that "for Kant's particular complaint . . . a quarter grain of opium, every eight hours, would have been the best remedy, perhaps a perfect remedy" (4: 359n). Indeed, as we shall see, a change of diet would have made all the difference. Kant's last days testify against the value—for life—of transcendental philosophy. For all its dry durability, Kant's kind of health may not be to the body's benefit, at least not every body's. Hence the pathos of Kant's final, vital act: "at intervals he pushed away the bedclothes, and exposed his person" (4: 376).

THE FATE OF EATING

"The Last Days of Immanuel Kant" poses a difficult question to Kant's heirs, asked best by David Krell: "What if, from the point of view of the harmonious interplay of the creative faculties, robust good health were in fact the genuine pathogenic disturbance?" (*Infectious Nietzsche* 202). As Nietzsche might say, How now? Are there pathologies of health? A question for critical physiologists—among whom De Quincey seems to be one of the first. His antipathy for things Kantian rings less clear in "Last Days" than elsewhere. In "German Studies and Kant in Particular" it reaches a recantatory crescendo

(*Collected Writings* 2: 81–109). There De Quincey confesses his early faith that Kant's thought held "the keys to a new and creative philosophy," a faith dashed by his discovery that where it promised the heavens, it delivered only pretty pictures and cardboard props: "I had found [it] to be a philosophy of destruction, and scarcely in any one chapter so much as *tending* to a philosophy of reconstruction. It destroys by wholesale, and it substitutes nothing" (2: 86). It was bad enough that this discovery tinged De Quincey's originally benign temper with "cynical disgust" (2: 107). But it threatened as well a more material corruption: "for man was an abject animal if the limitations which Kant assigned to the motions of his speculative reason were as absolute and hopeless as, under *his* scheme of the understanding and *his* genesis of its powers, too evidently they were. I belonged to a reptile race" (2: 89). Transcendental philosophy or, rather, the disillusion it induces threatens De Quincey with bestiality, a becoming reptile that might effect the materialization of cognition. Kant turns out to be, as De Quincey later styles him, "a disenchanter the most profound" (2: 108).

It is worth bearing this opinion in mind while reading the book that made De Quincey famous. The *Confessions of an English Opium Eater* is his first and darkest riposte to Kant's philosophy. With a literalness that has escaped generations of readers, De Quincey anticipates the question put descriptively in "The Last Days of Immanuel Kant": what if eating rather than representation determines the value of health? Or, to ask the question a little differently, what if incorporation instead of sensation sets the terms for valuing life? Not philosophy but physiology might best administer the test of living. That De Quincey came to think so quite early seems the point of an epistolary description (c. 1802) of life at Manchester Grammar School:

> As to health, I may say very fairly that I have not passed one quarter of the time I have been at this school in health . . . for there are three things at Mr Lawson's which murder health. The first is want of exercise. [. . .] The second is the badness of the air. [. . .] The third is the short time one has to eat one's dinner in; I have rarely time to push it down, and as to chewing it, that is out of the question. (Lindop 61)

Higher education can be hazardous to your health if it subordinates body to mind. De Quincey wants a little exercise, a little air, and a little time to chew and eat. For him incorporation rather than representation is the condition of cognition.

Viewing his education from a physiological perspective, De Quincey perceives its bias against the body. The kind of cognition it promotes and the kind of life it affirms seem physiologically gratuitous. But what if eating mattered as much as thinking? What if what he swallows is as important as what he perceives? Such questions become De Quincey's bread and butter, and they bespeak an unprecedented attention to the fate of eating. What he incorporates and how it affects him are the stuff of critical knowledge. Learning, in the words of Grevel Lindop, "to accept ill health as his normal condition" (326), he turns his attention to his diet. Although he subsists abstemiously for most of his life on rice broth, minced collops, boiled potatoes, and that ritually flayed mutton, the constitutive element of his daily aliment is opium. Habitual opium eating forces De Quincey to see life physiologically, unencumbered by the ruse of representation and the larger claims of critical philosophy.[7]

That insight dawns with De Quincey's first, desperate ingestion of opium, to treat rheumatic pains in his head and face:

> I was necessarily ignorant of the whole art and mystery of opium-taking; and what I took, I took under every disadvantage. But I took it; and in an hour—oh heavens! What a revulsion! What an upheaving, from its lowest depths, of the inner spirit! What an apocalypse of the world within me! That my pains had vanished was now a trifle in my eyes; this negative effect was swallowed up in the immensity of those positive effects which had opened before me in the abyss of divine enjoyment thus suddenly revealed. (*Confessions* 60–61)

If transcendental philosophy is a destroyer, opium is an agent of reconstruction—and in terms not merely cognitive but radically, irreducibly physiological. When representation cedes to eating as the means of evaluating health, the body becomes the material ground of the various operations Kant called cognition. With the apocalypse of the world within, De Quincey suspends the old opposition of body and mind. Cognition occurs materially for him, the effect as much of incorporation as sensation.

De Quincey wittily illustrates later in the *Confessions* the way transcendental philosophy treats the body. In the urbane depiction of happiness that concludes his account of an "intercalary year" of pleasure under opium's divine influence, he commands a painter—a German one, no doubt—to paint him a picture of a room in the dead of winter containing books, tea, and a female companion, a decanter:

> Into this you may put a quart of ruby-colored laudanum; that and a book of German metaphysics placed by its side will sufficiently attest my being in the neighborhood; but as to myself, there I demur. I admit that, naturally, I ought to occupy the foreground of the picture, that being the hero of the piece, or (if you choose) the criminal at the bar, my body should be had into court.

But De Quincey's body cannot, by means of representation, be had. The painter works like the transcendental philosopher to make a form available for judgment. This goal, however, requires the form's material destruction. So De Quincey invites the painter to invent a suitable substitute: "No; paint me, if at all, according to your own fancy; and, as a painter's fancy should teem with beautiful creations, I cannot fail, in that way, to be a gainer" (83). This picture of De Quincey's body bears no necessary relation to the thing itself—and never can bear any, if as Kant insists, representation traffics only in appearances.[8]

Contrast with this tableau an earlier encounter in which De Quincey must assert the material terms of embodiment. He has recently come to London on the futile whim to borrow money against his expectations. In opening negotiations with moneylenders, he finds to his chagrin that he has to prove formally who he is materially: "It was strange to me to find my own self, *materialiter* considered (so I expressed it, for I doted on logical accuracy of distinctions), accused, or at least suspected, of counterfeiting my own self, *formaliter* considered. However, to satisfy their scruples, I took the only course in my power" (47). De Quincey produces corroborating evidence of his material existence. Formal representation in this instance does not transcend and cannot be dissociated from its materializations. By documenting his embodiment De Quincey affirms his situatedness in the complex web of material relations that are his body. Whereas the philosopher destroys body to privilege representation, the moneylenders refuse this opposition. Both bodies and signs are material, social artifacts. By relating them, De Quincey simply lives, without reference to anything beyond his embodiment.

Which is not to say that he lives easily. De Quincey's *Confessions* amounts to the personal memoir of a hunger artist. His documentation of life, *materialiter* considered, inspires an intimate awareness of its digestive conditions. If eating is his alternative to representation, the stomach is his faculty of judgment, the primary means whereby De Quincey relates himself to a material manifold. Laying the physical foundations for later dietary habits, he describes his sojourn in London as one long, unmitigated hunger, characterized by bodily anguish little known in the annals of confessional literature: "now began the latter and fiercer stage of my long sufferings; without using a disproportionate expression, I might say, of my agony. For I now suffered, for upwards of sixteen weeks, the physical anguish of hunger in various degrees of intensity, but as bitter, perhaps, as ever any human being can have suffered who has survived it" (37–38). This gnawing hunger bespeaks neither simple physical privation nor existential malaise but a mode of agency that evaluates life by incorporation. It is in this sense that De Quincey will later declare that "not the opium-eater, but the opium, is the true hero of the tale, and the legitimate center on which the interest revolves." Opium affirms life materially, corporally, and hence has a "marvelous agency" (100). Opium eating does not so much satisfy hunger as revalue it, put it to work.

For the problem with being homeless and hungry in London is that it goes nowhere, produces nothing. De Quincey sleeps and dreams, only "to wake in captivity to the pangs of hunger" (56). Eating becomes a health hazard, as when De Quincey breakfasts unexpectedly with the perversely named earl of Desart, an event that conjures the memory of an earlier dietary debacle: "my appetite was quite sunk, and I became sick before I had eaten half of what I

had bought. This effect, from eating what approached to a meal, I continued
to feel for weeks; or, when I did not experience any nausea, part of what I ate
was rejected, sometimes with acidity, sometimes immediately and without
any acidity" (54). De Quincey's preternatural hunger requires something
other than food to assuage it, some direct physical stimulus to concentrate
its agency, like the glass of port and spices, procured by the angelic Anne,
that acts on his "empty stomach (which at that time would have rejected all
solid food) with an instantaneous power of restoration" (44). Forced by hunger to ponder the fate of eating, De Quincey becomes the first philosopher
of bad digestion. His daily diet of opium arises as much out of its material
agency as its psychotropic effects, not merely to assuage but to turn productive, in his words, "a state of unutterable irritation of stomach (which surely
is not much like dejection), accompanied by intense perspirations and feelings such as I shall not attempt to describe" (85). Physiology and not subjectivity is the true subject of the *Confessions*.

KANTRADICTIONS

We have clearly come some distance from Kant's careful, Roman regimen. De
Quincey aches intestinally and he sweats profusely, two conditions unknown
to the robust idealist. His critical attention to such bodily functions makes
his *Confessions* a dietetic parody of the *Critique of Judgment*. The overt cor-
respondences between them show De Quincey to be having a little fun at the
expense of the great disenchanter. He insists throughout that the rewards of
opium eating involve no gross sensuality but, on the contrary, the most exquisite intellectual satisfactions. Not beauty, as Kant would have it, but opium
produces the highest pleasures of cognition, for it

> introduces amongst [the mental faculties] the most exquisite order, legislation,
> and harmony. . . . [It] communicates serenity and equipoise to all the faculties,
> active or passive; and, with respect to the temper and moral feelings in general,
> it gives simply that sort of vital warmth which would always accompany a bodily
> constitution of primeval or antediluvian health. (62–63)

De Quincey openly parodies the formulas of Kant's idealism to reveal its—for
lack of a better word—idealism. The accord of the mental faculties attests, as
Kant suggests, to the possibility of a supersensible order, harmony, and even
legislation. But that accord is hardly free and indeterminate, having been
produced by opium. The order, harmony, and legislation to which it attests
are material through and through. De Quincey shows Kant's transcendental
philosophy to be a stupid if understandable mistake for good digestion. The
opium eater knows better. Bodily anguish has taught him to view the mind's
life materially. His postprandial pleasures do not signify the supersensible.

The notion that they might emerges only bodily as the afterimage of an antediluvian health.

And Kant aside, human health tends not to be dependably antediluvian.
De Quincey's *Confessions* systematically exposes the digestive innocence of
transcendental philosophy. Where Kant's analytics of the beautiful and the
sublime in the *Critique of Judgment* mount a transcendental critique of the
cognitive faculties, De Quincey's descriptions of the pleasures and pains of
opium materialize their operation. Aesthetics proves more visceral than Kant
had ever imagined, if the beautiful is a function more of good digestion than
of apparent purposiveness and universal communicability of its representations. The opium eater knows all its pleasures without having recourse to the
supersensible to legitimate them. Music, for instance, provides pleasures that
are no less material for being intellectual: "opium, by greatly increasing the
activity of the mind, generally increases, of necessity, that particular mode of
its activity by which we are able to construct out of the raw material of organic sound an elaborate intellectual pleasure" (67). Such is the agency of opium
that its incorporation inspires aesthetic pleasure whose disinterestedness
and communicability are functions not of harmony among cognitive faculties,
but of bodily processes. Contra Kant, De Quincey refuses to take pleasure
as a representation for cognitive harmony. On the contrary, even intellectual
pleasure is a bodily condition that can be as easily elucidated by opium as by
transcendental critique. Perhaps this is why De Quincey's aesthetics is peri-
patetic, at least in its pleasurable phase: the materiality of intellectual pleasure requires not cognitive but bodily movement—to the opera, around the
marketplace, among the dark and labyrinthine streets of midnight London.
Even De Quincey's sedentary pleasures, as when he gazes through a window
on Liverpool "from sunset to sunrise, motionless, and without wishing to
move," are materially situated and physically embodied. De Quincey resists
reaching beyond his body to affirm the life, the pleasurable life, of the mind.

"I shall be charged with mysticism, Behmenism, quietism, etc.," De Quincey
continues, and he might have added imperialism to the list (70–71). But his
work is progressive where it turns away from critical philosophy and toward
a physiological aesthetics. If "the pleasures of opium" materialize the beautiful, "the pains of opium" embody the sublime. And if those pleasures are part
and parcel of good digestion, those pains relate similarly to bad. The pains
begin with an attack "by a most appalling irritation of the stomach, in all
respects the same as that which had caused . . . so much suffering in youth,
and accompanied by a revival of all the old dreams" (74). De Quincey's sublime arises out of an embodied logic more intestinal than representational.
Like Kant's, it occurs in images that strain perception to its limits, terrible
dreams that overwhelm cognition in their multiplicity and their magnitude.
But De Quincey's dreams are not representations in any traditional sense.
They partake of what he describes as a "physical economy" that assimilates a

perceived image to the body of the perceiver, as when De Quincey, describing his fear of dropsy, suspects that "the brain might thus be making itself (to use a metaphysical word) *objective,* and the sentient organ *project* itself as its own object" (89, 94). So it is not some bodily beyond that he intuits in the pains of opium but the beyond of his own body, its material sublime. The pain of Kant's sublime, characteristically, represents the rule of the supersensible, albeit negatively. De Quincey's does not represent so much as incorporate the beyond of the body, in the body. It is as if the opium swallows the eater to turn him inside out. Hence the tyranny of the human face, or the "endless growth and self-reproduction" of a carceral architecture enclosing "engines and machinery, wheels, cables, pulleys, levers, catapults, etc." (93). These are objectivities of sentient organs, the materializations of a perceptivity as extensive and complex as human physiology. De Quincey's response to their terrible occurrence recapitulates indigestion: the dreams "always filled me with such amazement at the monstrous scenery that horror seemed absorbed, for awhile, in sheer astonishment. Sooner or later came a reflux of feeling that swallowed up the astonishment" (96). Kant's dialectic of the sublime cedes in De Quincey's account to a physico-intellectual peristalsis. The pains of opium assimilate cognition to the material demands of digestion.

The overall effect of De Quincey's *Confessions,* then, is to materialize cognition. But what does it mean to think, not about things, but things—in themselves? It would mean transgressing Kant's sacred limit of representation, the formal boundary that divides phenomena from noumena. As preposterous as it sounds, something of the sort occurs, or is at least attempted, in De Quincey's account of his most painful horrors, his Oriental dreams. They elaborate vast, fearsome tableaux vivants including all "the exuberant and riotous prodigality of life" (97). And they do so without resorting either to the ideal or a representation that would privilege it. Consider the following, famous passage:

> All before had been moral and spiritual terrors. But here the main agents were ugly birds, or snakes, or crocodiles, especially the last. The cursed crocodile became to me the object of more horror than almost all the rest. I was compelled to live with him, and (as was always the case, almost, in my dreams) for centuries. I escaped sometimes and found myself in Chinese houses with cane tables, etc. All the feet of the tables, sofas, etc., soon became instinct with life; the abominable head of the crocodile and his leering eyes looked out at me, multiplied into a thousand repetitions; and I stood loathing and fascinated. And so often did this hideous reptile haunt my dreams that many times the very same dream was broken up in the very same way: I heard gentle voices speaking to me (I hear everything when I am sleeping), and instantly I awoke: it was broad noon, and my children were standing, hand in hand, at my bedside, come to show me their colored shoes, or new frocks, or to let me see them dressed for going out. (96)

De Quincey contrasts two regimes of life in this looming passage, one grounded in the difference between family reality and oneiric illusion, and another, crueler dispensation arrogant of such distinctions and implacably, prodigally material. Such is the life of the reptile race to which De Quincey, in his disillusion with Kant, confessed he belonged. It is the life of things, which De Quincey here thinks materially without recourse to mere appearances. In passages such as this he approaches the sort of experience Gilles Deleuze and Félix Guattari describe as schizophrenic, the "experience of intensive quantities in their pure state, to a point that is almost unbearable. . . . Nothing here is representative; rather, it is all life and lived experience" (18, 19). Such might be the material alternative to cognition that De Quincey advances in his *Confessions*. It records the appalling intensities of digestion in the movements of cognition. That carnivorous crocodile as lived intensity: the becoming reptile of De Quincey's stomach.[9]

HEALTHY HYGIENE

Think of De Quincey's *Confessions* as a record less of psychological examination than intestinal hygiene. As such it crosses purposes not only with critical philosophy but also medicine, the discipline that most scrupulously values life in material terms. If the early years of the nineteenth century saw the emergence of public hygiene as a means of maintaining and managing a healthy body politic, the *Confessions* registers a complaint against that endeavor's salubrious assumptions. *Being an Extract from the Life of a Scholar*: the work's subtitle signals its medical agenda. "Extract," as any good physician would have known, denotes "something drawn or taken out of a thing"—"the substance extracted." The *OED* takes the word to be "a pharmaceutical term applied to the tough or viscid matter obtained by treating any substance with solvents." That makes De Quincey's *Confessions* a physiological substance, the extract of a scholar's body. Opium goes in this body and the viscid matter of confession comes out. But just how healthy is this extract? By associating his *Confessions* with the physiological effects of opium eating, De Quincey affirms a kind of health irreducible to public hygiene, one more physiologically astute and materially conditioned than even medicine can endorse.

The need for a pervasive morality of public health was the driving force behind the work of Bristol physician Thomas Beddoes, Coleridge's friend and the father of the poet Thomas Lovell Beddoes. In 1802 he published *Hygiea,* a four-volume examination of common ailments and preventions that aimed at cultivating public commitment to "the most important object in mortal life—Habitual Well Being" (1: 16). Beddoes is as devoted to the value of health as Kant is to that of reason. If medicine can be described as a bodily riposte to

metaphysics, then an advocacy of public hygiene can be viewed as an attempt
to affirm the value of health without reliance on transcendentals. Beddoes's
project of public health is an explicitly moral one. Taking for granted the fact
that "our moral organization is pretty much what it is made to be," Beddoes
sets out to build a better body politic (1: 68). In this he participates in the general political agenda of an increasingly professionalized medicine.[10] The normative force of the concept of public hygiene appears openly in the subtitle of
*Hygiea: Essays Moral and Medical on the Causes Affecting the Personal State
of Our Middling and Affluent Classes.* Beddoes's hygiene is tailor-made for
liberal society. The lower orders are exempt from his attention because they
lack the education and moral discipline to make much of it, and the upper
classes—well, their decadence speaks for itself. Public hygiene is a trickle-
down morality best practiced on the bodies of those most prone to consider
practical medical knowledge authoritative and to acquire it.

So a commitment to reason characterizes *Hygiea,* reason professionally
and not transcendentally determined. And how does medical knowledge make
those who have it healthy? Here is Beddoes on its operation and effects:

> Seasonable care should be taken to provide each individual with a set of ideas,
> exhibiting the precise relation in which his system, and the several organs of
> which it is compounded, stand to external agents, particularly to those with
> which he is likely to come most in contact;—that these sets of ideas be so placed
> in his head, that he may refer to them with as little difficulty as to the watch he
> wears in his pocket;—and that as by the one he adjusts his business to his time,
> so by the other he may be always able to accommodate his actions to his powers.
> (1: 20–21)

Medicine may be physically grounded, but for Beddoes health is the effect
of a set of regulative ideas. They determine the relation between the body
and extrinsic "agents" rather than ideas and extrinsic things, but their basic
function bears striking resemblance to Kant's conceptual categories. Perhaps
medicine for the middle class is the transcendentalism of the body politic,
physical in its applications but disciplinary in its regulative force. The dual
metaphor that concludes the quotation is instructive in this regard: if hygiene is a watch and living is the business it regulates, then a healthy public
is a bourgeois public, one that lives by its timepiece.

The political bias of public hygiene appears as well in Beddoes's discussion of the importance of good digestion to habitual well-being, and in this
Hygiea establishes the dietary norm from which De Quincey's *Confessions*
noticeably deviates. So fundamental is digestion to what Beddoes calls "the
physical power of enjoyment" that he describes the stomach and alimentary
canal generally as a "faculty of pleasurable sensation." The capacity to feel
pleasure—and therefore to enjoy living—depends on the smooth operation of
this faculty. Health begins in good digestion, which arises most predictably

out of a practical knowledge of the digestive process. Enter the physician. Beddoes describes that process with a metaphor that reveals where the material body stands in the eyes of hygiene:

> The succession of steps may be compared to a very complicated manufactory, where the material, before it can attain the necessary perfection, passes through the hands of a multitude of artisans, each of whom, in his department, must do justice to the fabric; or else the whole labor will be as good as lost. (2: 20)

Digestion is a complicated process involving the labor of multitudes. The bowels are a health factory the perfection of whose products depends on coordination among diverse operations and communication among distinct departments. Any disruption of the process, caused by poor materials, for instance, or refractory laborers, could be disastrous for a healthy economy. Best keep things moving smoothly, and how better than through oversight by trained professionals? By describing human digestion in such terms Beddoes associates the body with a class—working artisans—that falls outside of the purview of *Hygiea,* at least as stated in its subtitle. Hygienically considered, the human body still requires guidance from above, from medical rather than conceptual a priori categories. Public hygiene regulates the labor of material life in a way that makes physicians rather than philosophers the captains of the body industry.

And according to Beddoes a healthy diet is one that keeps the body working effortlessly and continuously. This business is tricky, because the essence of eating is change: the transformation of food from one form to another. Digestion drives this process and diet provides the fuel. The gastric factory runs on organic matter, which is "distinguished from inorganic bodies by [its] susceptibility of change" (21–22). Hence the importance of the set of ideas that regulates this process: it determines the course of material change in a manner most conducive to public health. Those ideas serve to insulate the body against the transformative process that takes place within it, maintaining and reproducing a human organism congenial to the norm of medicine. Digestion might otherwise open the body to the sort of material transformation that happens to food: "some of the elements, after undergoing new combinations, shall be given out in the form of air; some in a liquid state; and the remainder shall be unlike any thing the body contained at first" (2: 21–22). As a kind of sustained organic alchemy, digestion must occur in such a way that only food changes materially. Its products may be various, but its ultimate effect must be uniform: health, the higher ideal of public hygiene. The human manufactory needs a managing authority that comprehends its operations and directs their transformative force toward that salubrious end.

That is why intoxicants pose a threat to digestion. They change its capacity for change, to the body's detriment. Beddoes takes pains to demonstrate that liquor and opium disrupt digestion by obstructing its transformative

effects on food. The addition of either to the diet puts the manufactory on
strike, suspending its normal operation and therefore the production of health.
Disregarding the regulative ideas of good hygiene, the opium eater runs a business that will not produce. The ultimate—and for Beddoes disastrous—effect
of bad diet is to change the body, until "indigestion establishes itself by degree in full form. It is attended by loathing, rejection of food, by constantly
distressing flatulency, tremors, comfortless nights, emaciation, and decay of
intellectual faculties" (2: 53). Such is the fate of those who make opium a
regular part of their diets. Indigestion transforms the opium eater's body—
much to the mortification of the intellectual faculties—from the manufactory
of human health into a cadaverous infirmary. And because responsibility for
this change rests entirely with the opium eater, Beddoes's *Hygiea* makes the
private subject the foundation of public health.

THE DAILY DOSE

De Quincey's view of such matters, not surprisingly, differs significantly. In
his appendix to the *Confessions,* De Quincey tells of consulting a doctor about
his interminable intestinal pains. Queried whether indigestion might be
the cause, the doctor provides a provocative diagnosis: "His answer was no;
on the contrary, he thought that the suffering was caused by digestion itself,
which should naturally go on below the consciousness but which, from the
unnatural state of the stomach, vitiated by so long a use of opium, was become distinctly perceptible" (106). Eating opium has materially changed the
way the body operates. When digestion enters consciousness, cognition turns
material. Thanks to the ability to perceive digestion, to think the stomach,
eating becomes a mode of cognition. The manufactory thinks itself and thinks
for itself, without recourse to the set of regulative ideas that produce health.
So much for public hygiene. De Quincey eats dangerously.

A steady diet of opium has crazed his body. That this fate was not without
its burdens is the lesson of the persistent attention De Quincey pays to his
intestines. The manufactory operated unpredictably at best, and its products
were below standard. As early as 1814 Mary Wordsworth remarked in a letter to her sister-in-law, Dorothy, that De Quincey had been "confined almost
to his bed for a week. Mr. S. says he has a diar[rhoea], such a one no doubt
as C[oleridge]'s—and from the same cause" (Lindop 203, first interpolation
Lindop's). That naughty cause transformed digestion from a means of living
to its own end. De Quincey's largely liquid diet was an attempt to appease
his bowels. "I have in the course of my misfortunes fasted for thirty years,"
he confessed near the end of his life, though his motives were hardly spiritual (Lindop 364). *Irregularity* is too generous a euphemism to describe them.
Opium slowed digestion to a crawl, but trying to quit turned it chaotic; these

effects incited a cycle of habituation and reform that had De Quincey eating opium to relieve symptoms caused by removing it from his diet. His bowels, to quote his biographer, became "a battleground between laudanum and various purgatives" (Lindop 346). If money for the latter ran short, De Quincey would appeal to his publisher for secret deliveries of Seidlitz Powders in hope of ending long days of stasis (up to ten at a stretch). On arrival, however, that end could be problematic, as shown by the dubious local celebrity he describes achieving once when living in close quarters: "In the whole system of houses, to which this house is attached, there exists but one *Templum Cloacinae*. Now imagine the fiend driving a man thither thro' 8 and 10 hours successively. Such a man becomes himself a public nuisance, and is in some danger of being removed by assassination" (Lindop 347). De Quincey's crazy body has a mind of its own that makes him a menace to public health.

It therefore seems inconsiderate of his experience to evaluate it, à la Wordsworth, by the measure of the private subject. De Quincey lives and practices an alternative to such subjectivity. He does not introspect so much as he monitors himself; he is concerned less with personal salvation than with pharmaceutical maintenance. And in place of little epiphanies to make life sweet, he has his daily dose, which ranges from 150 to 3,000 drops of laudanum but never reaches zero. In the materiality of his self-awareness De Quincey resembles the odd Viennese woman Beddoes describes who, thanks to an abdominal wound that never healed, had a remarkably intimate command of her digestive process. When oppressed by indigestion, "she had recourse to an expedient, which many a glutton might envy her, and which consisted in taking the oppressive food with her finger out at the wound" (2: 19). For the opium eater health results from a similarly material relation to his body. His daily dose produces a habitual well-being that is contingent and variable according to specific demands and purposes. He is the material artisan of a personal health impossible to reproduce in the manufactory of public hygiene, a point De Quincey illustrates when describing how his application for life insurance was refused "on the argument that [he] had used Op[ium] to excess . . . and might do so again" (Lindop 336, second interpolation Lindop's). De Quincey *practices* self consciousness—as an eater and artist of opium. His *Confessions* comes out of him as the material effect of dietary distress, not as the ruminations of an ashamed voluptuary. De Quincey's alternative to subjectivity amounts simply, terminally, to the care of his bodied self.[11] That is the extent of the opium eater's morality: a dietetic hygiene that affirms life as a matter, not of transcendence or even of health, but of daily maintenance.

It is all too easy to condescend to De Quincey morally, to stamp him an addict and judge him accordingly. The moral of his narrative he addresses to the opium eater alone: "if he is taught to fear and tremble, enough has been effected" (101). Concerning himself he refuses such judgments: "Guilt . . . I do not acknowledge" (24). Why then do we continue to indict him, in book after critical book, for felonious addiction? Perhaps because to read him from an extramoral perspective would be to open ourselves, intellectually and bodily, to the full force of his physiological aesthetics and to the kind of life it affirms. But it is worth giving De Quincey final hearing, if only to glimpse that life momentarily:

> An inhuman moralist I can no more endure, in my nervous state, than opium that has not been boiled. At any rate, he who summons me to send out a large freight of self-denial and mortification upon any cruising voyage of moral improvement must make it clear to my understanding that the concern is a hopeful one. . . . Let no man expect to frighten me by a few hard words into embarking . . . upon desperate adventures of morality. (76)

No, moral judgment will not do for De Quincey, not the least because his *Confessions* does away with its supersensible grounds. A better measure than morality might be the more material one of vitality. If Kant lived into his seventies on a steady diet of tea and transcendence, so did De Quincey on opium and dreams. Perhaps Nietzsche is the true physician of such souls: "For there is no health as such, and all attempts to define a thing that way have been wretched failures. Even the determination of what is healthy for your *body* depends on your goal, your horizon, your energies, your impulses, your errors, and above all on the ideals and phantasms of your soul. Thus there are innumerable healths of the body" (*Gay Science* 176–77). De Quincey's is the health of a confirmed and scrupulous opium eater. If productivity is any measure, his diet served him well, cultivating a different kind of health perhaps than Kant's or even Beddoes's, but one suited to the peculiar vitality of De Quincey's crazy body. Hence his strange, disturbing confidence

> That those eat now who never ate before;
> And those who always ate now eat the more. (25)

PART III
APPROPRIATIONS

CHAPTER 6

MOTHER FLESH

*Anyone who does not take after his parents is really in a way
a monstrosity, since in these cases Nature has in a way strayed
from the generic type. The first beginning of this deviation
is when a female is formed instead of a male.*
—*Aristotle,* Generation of Animals

Some say it was for money, others for love, but in 1775 Martin Van Butchell pickled his wife. She had recently died, and so aggrieved was her widower that, with the help of John Hunter's brother William, himself a master anatomist and man midwife to Queen Charlotte, he preserved her body and displayed it under glass. A letter printed in the *Morning Post* describes the process in detail:

> The bowels were first taken out. The vessels were afterwards emptied, as perfectly as possible, of the blood which they contained, and injected with the oil of turpentine. After the body was well impregnated with that powerful preservative, a large quantity of a red waxy injection was thrown into the vessels, which entering their minute cavities and distending them, gave to the face and other parts of the body a most striking appearance of life. (13 May 1775)

Although Mrs. Van Butchell had given her loving husband several children, her final impregnation required professional assistance and spawned a different kind of life. Her body was dead, but its substance lived on, creating not merely consolation for her husband but sensation about town. Clad in her wedding clothes, she presided over Van Butchell's home with such distinction that she was soon receiving a better class of visitor than ever before, "great numbers of the nobility and gentry, who soon found, that though it was quite foreign to the intentions of Mr. Van Butchell to make a shew of his deceased wife, some consideration would not be a disagreeable return for the trouble and attendance which these visits occasioned" (*Wonderful* 1: 194).

It would be indelicate to conclude that Mrs. Van Butchell was worth more to her husband dead than alive, but her posthumous fecundity at least bears pondering. Propped in that parlor, her body produced happy effects among the living: celebrity for both husband and his anatomist friend, entertainment for the toney, and for the household—ready cash. There was another effect too, less innocent perhaps but more revealing of Van Butchell's motives for immortalizing his beloved. Darkly was it rumored that "this resolution of keeping his wife unburied, was occasioned by a clause in the marriage settlement, disposing of certain property *while she remained above ground*" (*Wonderful* 1: 194). A woman's corpse makes a pleasant partner if it comes with an ample dowry. Van Butchell had the legal contract and the medical cunning to guarantee the perpetual possession of both. Maybe that explains the peculiar cheer that concludes the report in the *Morning Post*: "Upon the whole, he seems pleased with his sweet, handsome, and silent wife. What would you say if this whim should happen to strike those leaders of decorum that govern the world of fashions?"

Perhaps it already had. Martin Van Butchell's treatment of his wife's corpse reveals much about the uses of female bodies in late-eighteenth-century British culture, just as the theory of possessive individualism was taking hold. What, one should ask, becomes of those bodies under such cultural circumstances, or more precisely, what operations on them produce the autonomy of liberalism's rational subject? That's a complicated question, and only a partial answer will emerge in what follows. But Van Butchell's sweet, domestic necrophilia raises the following possibilities: first, that, culturally considered, female bodies incarnate abject matter, whose vitality can only be comprehended through medical knowledge; second, that obstetric medicine circulates such knowledge, producing and regulating the way female bodies matter in the private and public spheres; and finally, that these bodies reproduce a kind of property, the property in person that all liberal subjects possess but that females paradoxically do not. Liberal society gets built over the dead bodies of prolific women. They become, in Butler's terms, "a constitutive outside to the subject, an abjected outside" (*Bodies* 3). Understanding just how this abjection arises will require an examination of the discourses and practices that make it possible: the knowledge of sexual anatomy, the habits of obstetrics, and the precepts of female education. From the historical perspective of their interplay, the liberal feminism of Mary Wollstonecraft amounts to a great, fateful attempt to reanimate a female body that can accommodate the liberal subject. If her effort proves mistaken, it is only by virtue of its incompleteness; it remains for her daughter Mary Shelley fully to vindicate the monstrous life of mother flesh.

SEXING THE FLESH

The biological facts of sexual difference, however obvious they may appear, are of fairly recent invention. As Thomas Laqueur demonstrates in powerful detail, the traditional view of the human body in Western culture was monomorphic: the two sexes shared a single human (that is, male) anatomy. Both had the same genitals; in women they remain inside the body while in men they become extruded.[1] Thus Galen, whose sense of sexual difference became established medical fact for well over a millennium, could claim on the basis of the best anatomical evidence that women bore testes and seminal ducts internally, while men carried theirs externally in the scrotum (Laqueur, "Orgasm" 2). The reason for apparent sexual differences between men and women was less anatomical than metaphysical: men were blessed with greater vital heat than women, forcing their genitals outside their bodies and giving them a leg up on the ladder of perfection. Their bodies were basically the same as women's, only their vitality differed. This anatomical identity between the sexes provided no ground for claims of their equality, since the female frame, for all its similar equipment, lacked an ennobling quantum of vital heat. But monomorphism did affirm the importance of all aspects of the generative process, as the silent history of female orgasm shows. Conception traditionally required the complete participation of both sexes, which meant full and shivering orgasm for women as well as men. Without it the generative process failed to ignite. With it babies would be healthfully and happily conceived.[2] Small consolation, perhaps, for a legacy of sexual bondage, but the anatomical identity of male and female made the carnal pleasure of women a necessary precursor to reproduction.

All this changed by the late eighteenth century. Sexual difference acquired anatomical specificity and became incorporated in human flesh. Laqueur describes the emergence among anatomists and physicians of a new "biology of incommensurability" that made differences between the sexes a matter of—*matter*: "Writers of all sorts were determined to base what they insisted were fundamental differences between male and female sexuality, and thus between man and woman, on discoverable biological distinctions" (Laqueur, "Orgasm" 2). Such distinctions and discoveries included the size of the head, the width of the shoulders, the shape of the pelvis, and the whole system of articulated bones, ultimately yielding the first engravings of an anatomically distinct female skeleton in 1759. Nor were the bones alone the augur of sexual difference. Soft tissues enfleshed the sex, not merely in obvious secondary characteristics but more purposefully in the subtle processes of gestation. The formerly female testes acquired a new name, "ovaries," appropriate to their distinct function. That undiscovered country of the unborn, the uterus, was first measured and anatomically mapped. The clitoris came into its own as an organ unrelated in form or function to the penis, a seat of independent pleasure that may or may not accompany the acts that induce gestation. And this "discovery" effectively eliminated the variable of female orgasm from the equation of conception, rendering that process a simple mechanism that worked with or without the benediction of a woman's pleasure. By the late eighteenth century, female bodies differed materially from male bodies in the way they grew, the way they worked, the way they lived, and the way they mattered.

The new biology of incommensurability sexed the flesh to new political ends, making the bodies of women, in Laqueur's words, "the battleground for redefining the most ancient, the most intimate, the most fundamental of human relations" ("Orgasm" 18). That the battle was waged silently makes it no less pitched. Liberal political theory mounts a quiet assault on the anatomically female body, or more precisely, deploys that body against itself as a kind of secret weapon. Laqueur notices the cultural contradiction of liberalism's body politics: it presumes a "neuter body, sexed but without gender" at the very moment when human bodies are becoming biologically sexed (19). Could it be that sexing the flesh is somehow constitutive of a body "regarded simply as the bearer of the rational subject" (19)? That incorporating sexual difference guards against its politicization in liberal discourse?

These are tricky but inevitable questions for a cultural analysis that advocates corporeal freedom. The operations that incorporate sex incarcerate it too, as a look at a key moment in the history of reproductive anatomy will prove. It is in the operations of medical knowledge that power most intimately seizes flesh, subjecting it to imperatives of the proper. When Foucault claims that "power relations can materially penetrate the body in depth, without depending even on the mediation of the subject's own representations," he describes the way anatomy and medical science work: they penetrate and regulate bodies without reference to minds (*Power/Knowledge* 186). Even apparently humane disciplines such as medicine can have imperious biopolitical effects. Anatomy and obstetrics don't just investigate the female body. They open it up, see what there is to see, know what there is to know. Then they bury it—or pickle it for public display.

PHYSICIAN GENERAL

Just as bodies were being biologically sexed a medical specialty arose to manage childbirth: obstetrics. The story of how man midwives usurped this traditional province of women's wisdom has been told many times, but rarely with the awareness that obstetrics doesn't just treat pregnant women but first produces the generative body it then treats.[3] It bestows medical legitimacy on a female body peculiarly subject to geniture and thus incorporates a sexual identity particularly suited to liberal society. The great strategist of the campaign to annex pregnancy to medicine was Mr. Van Butchell's friend and fellow embalmer, William Hunter. Others before him had advanced the cause in the trenches, most notably William Smellie, whose pioneering use of the forceps gave man midwives an instrumental role to play during difficult deliveries. His tools and his tenacity opened the way to the medicalization of pregnancy. But it was William Hunter who secured for man midwifery the disciplined knowledge that made it the distinct medical specialty eventually called obstetrics.[4] Anatomy was Hunter's passion and man midwifery his profession. He was good at both, rising from modest beginnings as a medical assistant to become the first man midwife admitted to the Royal College of Physicians and eventually physician extraordinary to Her Majesty Queen Charlotte.

Largely through Hunter's influence and example the use of forceps for a time fell out of fashion. He viewed nature as the best guide during times of troubled birth.[5] But this faith in nature was more a function of comprehending than submitting to her ways. Hunter was a crack anatomist and the human body became his field of glory. In his only publication on anatomy, *Two Introductory Lectures,* he describes the physician's relationship to the body in openly martial metaphors:

> The comparison of a physician to a general, is both rational and instructive. The human body under a disease, is the country which labours under a civil war or invasion; the physician is, or should be, the dictator and general, who is to take the command, and to direct all the necessary operations. To do his duty with full advantage, a general, besides other acquirements, useful in his profession, must make himself master of the *Anatomy* and *Physiology,* as we may call it, of the country. (70)

The doctor's job is to wage a war of health against the diseased human body, and to do that successfully he must master the best weapons in his arsenal, anatomical and physiological knowledge. What is important to realize about such knowledge is that it arises, like most weapons of war, in the service of carnage. Death and not life is the condition of its production.

Hence Hunter's insistence on the necessity of dissection to the advancement of medical knowledge: "Were I to guess at the most probable future improvements in physic, I should say that they would arise from a more general, and more accurate examination of diseases after death" (73). The war of health, however, needs a ready supply of conscripts, and Hunter rues the difficulty of finding bodies fit for this second slaughter:

> The dead body cannot be too fresh for dissection; every hour that it is kept, it is losing something of its fitness for anatomical demonstrations; the blood is transuding and bringing all the parts nearer to one colour, which takes off the natural and distinct appearance; and putrefaction is advancing, which makes all the

fleshy parts tender and indistinct. . . . For these reasons we may conclude, that, except there be an avowed establishment, for a plentiful supply of dead bodies, a truely useful, and complete course of Anatomy, can only be given in a great city. Whatever pity it may be, that so few professors can have sufficient supplies of dead bodies, we should be very unreasonable to blame those who cannot have that advantage. (87)

At least Hunter is charitable toward physicians unable to procure ready cadavers. The parts and processes of bodily life become knowable only in terms of the death that awaits them and toward which they hasten in their shimmering vitality. Death stops them cold, allowing accurate observation and measurement of tissues otherwise too vital and volatile for medical knowledge. Anatomy is a death ray in the war of health, and the knowledge it yields turns motile matter into inert material, the solid stuff of medical science. Foucault provides a historical account of such knowledge and the kind of perception that makes it possible in *The Birth of the Clinic,* showing just how deep run the allegiances between life science and death: "It is from the height of death that one can see and analyze organic dependencies and pathological sequences. . . . Death is the great analyst that shows the connexions by unfolding them, and bursts open the wonders of genesis in the rigor of decomposition" (144).

GRAVID UTERUS

In 1774 William Hunter published his wondrous anatomical engravings of the pregnant womb in various stages of gestation, *The Anatomy of the Human Gravid Uterus*. It instantly displaced Smellie's *Anatomical Tables* (1761) as the definitive anatomy of the organs and operations of female reproduction: twenty-eight plates folio with indices and explanations in double columns, Latin and English.[6] And it was years in the making. Hunter describes the difficulty of compiling so meticulously faithful an anatomy in his preface, a task that may never have been his had not fortune smiled:

> in the year 1751 the author met with the first favourable opportunity of examining, in the human species, what before he had been studying in brutes. A woman died suddenly, when very near the end of her pregnancy; the body was procured before any sensible putrefaction had begun; the season of the year was favourable to dissection; the injection of the blood-vessels proved successful; a very able painter, in this way, was found; every part was examined in the most public manner, and the truth was thereby well authenticated. (n.p.)

If evidence were needed of Foucault's claims for an alliance between the truth of anatomy and death, Hunter's book provides it. Medical knowledge of the gravid human uterus was apparently stymied for a lack of pregnant cadavers. But having smiled once, fortune seems to have become Hunter's familiar. Soon "a second subject was procured," affording "a few supplemental figures." Then as luck would have it "a third subject occurred very opportunely, which cleared up some difficulties." In all eleven corpses came Hunter's way complete with fetuses at different stages of development.

His book of wombs presents them in an order of reverse generation, from full term to first trimester. In the process it pares away the surrounding female flesh like a rind. Two things are striking about Hunter's treatment of the bodies of the women he anatomizes. First, they are without history—existentially anonymous, interchangeable husks of flesh. Anatomical knowledge of the female body requires prior excision of individual womanhood to the point that what remains is a rudimentary mother flesh that all women—as women—have in common (or so Hunter would insist). Second, these bodies are not merely dead but de-composed. Foucault was right: the wonders of genesis become visible only through a rigorous decomposition. And it's not a pretty sight. The anatomist's gaze, however, directed toward the miraculous matter of generation, sees through it to a knowledge that comprehends and explains it. That this knowledge concerns *flesh,* and not as in Smellie's anatomy primarily the bones, is the lesson of the student's progress through Hunter's pages. As more and more flesh gets shaved away and the processes of reproduction become clearer and clearer, the female body dies to science and motherless fetuses float in empty space. The effect visually and culturally is to incarnate death in mother flesh, then quietly to dispose of the corpse.

The first plate of the *Gravid Uterus* (Figure 26) shows the burgeoning belly of Hunter's pregnant cadaver, stripped of its covering of skin and fat. Modesty for some reason compels a gesture of vestment, but the biologically sexed body of Laqueur's analysis is triumphantly displayed—and splayed. It's not just the burdened abdomen that announces the female here but the open thighs, distended labia, and engorged vagina. The possibility of sexual pleasure has been eliminated from this posture, however, attributing an involuntary biological necessity to the regenerative process that ballooned this woman's body. Eliminated too at least from sight are head and hands, seats respectively of reason and fine motor skill. The female body here is biologically distinct, sexually functional, but emphatically dead, anatomical testimony to a living process of which it is the occasion but not the cause.

By plate VI (Figure 27) the identification of mother flesh with death seems complete. It is not simply that this gruesome image shows the dead pregnant female to be the only bodily perspective from which to view the reproduction of human life. Now this body is something *more* than a corpse, a visceral mound of human offal. The legs have been hacked away, exposing meat that could be ham except that it's part of a woman's body. The genitals have been sliced off, creating a new mouth caught in an expression somewhere between

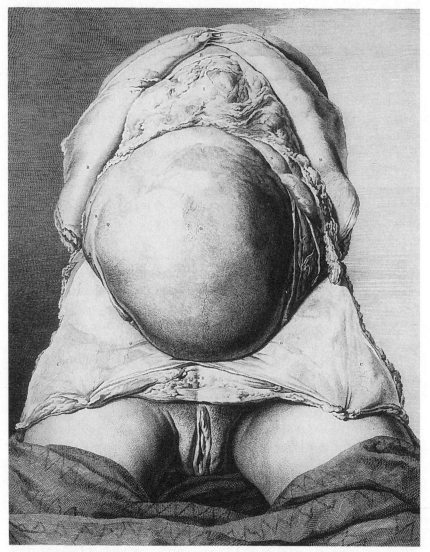

Figure 26. William Hunter, *The Anatomy of the Human Gravid Uterus* (1794). Tab. 1. The Wellcome Library, London.

horror and surprise. The walls of the uterus have been peeled back to reveal a little, beautiful body that supersedes the horror show incarnate in mother flesh. Could there be a more obvious instance of Foucault's adage that knowledge was made for cutting? L. J. Jordanova calls attention to the contrast between the butchery brought on mother flesh and the tenderness lavished on its offspring's representation, as if violence inflicted in the name of anatomy were somehow constitutive of successful geniture ("Gender" 390). Add to this effect the qualities of abjection these images associate with a pregnant

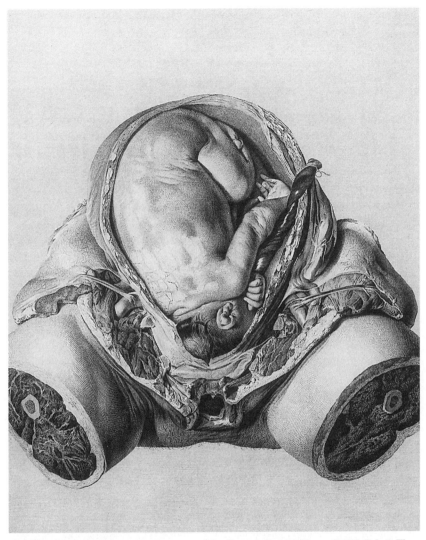

Figure 27. William Hunter, *The Anatomy of the Human Gravid Uterus* (1794). Tab. 6. The Wellcome Library, London.

corpse—its appearance as food, its status as waste, its necrotic sexuality, its morbid gestation—and it becomes all but impossible to dissociate death from the reproductive capacity of the female body. Life is all the child's, while its mother's flesh incorporates death. That is why it seems too easy to conclude with Andrea Henderson that Hunter saw in such a body "the passive site of a Nature that is wild both in the sense of being free and beastly" (109). Whatever faith Hunter had in nature's free and beastly ways arose from a prior anatomical knowledge grounded materially in the gravid uteri of eleven dead specimens. Life passes through mother flesh and lands in the knowing hands of the obstetrician.

"*. . . THIS DEFILEMENT . . .*"

Hunter's anatomy of the human gravid uterus turns the generative body into a cadaver. Viewed with the sovereign gaze of medical science, it's just a specimen, a factitious material instance of organic processes and physiological functions. But to the untrained eye—a mother's, for instance—it's a desecrated corpse. Something of the revulsion that attends such sights lingers in Hunter's clean, clinical engravings. It's important to resist for a moment the implied claim of anatomy to eschew that visceral response. If one of the effects of anatomical science is to assert an affective threshold above which disciplined knowledge holds dispassionate sway, then all that falls below becomes its Other. Anatomy needs corpses to produce knowledge but casts them aside in the process. The gravid uterus may give rise to life, but outside the operating theater it's only viscera: extraneous, abject matter. Medical science actively produces abjection but renders it unknowable by means of that affective threshold. Hence the importance of a visceral response to Hunter's triumph of anatomy: it affirms the otherness of mother flesh to its anatomical descriptions.

In a painfully obvious instance of the logic of constitutive exclusion, Hunter's anatomy of the gravid uterus both materializes abjection and excludes it from the purview of medical science. Female bodies become abject matter. But seen with the anatomist's eye, they are clean and docile corpses too, wholly subject to the knowledge of obstetric medicine. Their abjection doesn't disturb the medical gaze. It's just a fact of life. In the visceral matter of pregnancy, female bodies incarnate abjection, embodying the ambiguity of life's indebtedness to death. It takes a woman like Julia Kristeva to find words for the abjection that medicine represents without acknowledging:

> corpses *show me* what I permanently thrust aside in order to live. These body fluids, this defilement, this shit are what life withstands, hardly and with difficulty, on the part of death. There, I am at the border of my condition as a living being. My body extricates itself, as being alive, from that border. Such wastes drop so that I might live, until, from loss to loss, nothing remains in me and my entire body falls beyond the limit—*cadere,* cadaver. If dung signifies the other side of the border, the place where I am not and which permits me to be, the corpse, the most sickening of wastes, is a border that has encroached upon everything. (3)

Hunter's engravings of the gravid uterus make the pregnant female body such a border where death crosses to life through a movement of abjection:

not-life becoming life by shedding what's spent, not-I becoming I by extruding what's inert. Female bodies produce new bodies by dropping corpselike away, materializing the ambiguity of their own otherness to life.

Where Kristeva attributes this movement of abjection to primordial fecundities and archaic relations, it might be worth approaching it as the effect also of specific practices associated with anatomy. It's an obvious point, but for all their acclaimed faithfulness to nature Hunter's beautiful plates cannot present the *process* of uterogestation as anything but a series of distinct stages. The eye of anatomy sees in freeze-frame, and the effect deanimates female bodies. But even corpses have a life of their own. When Hunter admits in his preface that until his fit of fortune "few, or none of the anatomists, had met with a sufficient number of subjects, either for investigating, or for demonstrating the principal circumstances of uterogestation in the human species" (n.p.), he obliquely describes one great obstacle to definitive anatomical knowledge: bodies rot. That problem doubles when the object of knowledge is gestation. The anatomist then has to contend with the movement of flesh in two dimensions: into life and into death. Hunter's solution was to perfect the means of arresting that movement, gaining for the medical gaze precious time to do its work. In his *Two Introductory Lectures* he celebrates the latest advances in the fine art of preserving flesh:

> The modern improved methods of preserving animal bodies, or parts of them, has been of the greatest service to Anatomy; especially in saving the time and labour of the Anatomist, in the nicer dissections of the small parts of the body. For now, whatever he has prepared with care, he can preserve; and the object is ready to be seen at any time. And, in the same manner he can preserve anatomical curiosities, or rarities of every kind; such as, parts that are uncommonly formed; parts that are diseased; the parts of the pregnant uterus and its contents. (57)

Monstrosity, disease, pregnancy: the art of preserving specimens allows the anatomist to stockpile examples of each for close inspection, which, like his brother John, Hunter did with abandon. But what is lost to preservation is what escapes representation: the movements of animal flesh. The abjection that Hunter's anatomical images produce, then, is not that of the inert so much as the active corpse. True defilement invests a mother flesh irreducible to substance, flesh that leaks, gestates, burgeons, or liquefies, putrefies, slimes. Such involuntary agencies come to trouble the disciplined knowledge of anatomy, occurring beyond the affective threshold that secures its authority. Hence the force of faithful specimens, lifelike preparations, and anatomically correct images. Kristeva correctly concludes that "if someone personifies abjection without assurance of purification, it is a woman, 'any woman,' the 'woman as a whole;' as far as he is concerned, man exposes abjection by knowing it, and through that very act purifies it" (85). But such personifications and purifications have culturally specific origins and effects. By the late eighteenth century obstetric medicine served both purposes, personifying abjection in the generative female body and purifying it with the disciplined knowledge of anatomy.

GENERATIVE DEBT

"Man is born free but exists everywhere in chains": so goes Rousseau's famous summation of the contradiction of civil society. Rousseau's solution to the injustice he saw everywhere was his celebrated social contract, the voluntary subscription of a free individual's will to the general will of the community. Man is *born* free; his chains are forged voluntarily. If free men forged them for mutual benefit, then they wouldn't be chains at all but the agreeable bonds of citizenship. Although it may seem too obvious a fact to mention, to become a citizen in this sense requires first to be born. What is the status of mother flesh in the social contract that makes freedom a birthright? Carole Pateman has shown how social-contract theory, the foundation of liberal society, presumes a prior sexual contract that sanctions the possession of women's bodies by men: "The original pact is a sexual as well as a social contract: it is sexual in the sense of patriarchal—that is, the contract establishes men's political right over women—and also sexual in the sense of establishing orderly access by men to women's bodies" (2). This right of access occurs with marriage, which becomes the secret deal that seals the social contract and allows man to be born—and born free—in the first place. But how is it that female bodies, which are born just as are male ones, don't quite inherit the same freedom? What makes them subject to the sexual contract? Pateman relies largely on Rousseau's own claims for the natural inferiority of the female body in strength and manageability to explain its subjection in social contract theory. It might be instructive to consider, however, the extent to which other cultural practices articulate with liberal political discourse to produce the sexually contractable female body.

Rousseau's claims, of course, are more than a little self-indicting. They appear most explicit in *Emile: or On Education,* his manual on how best to raise up the free man of the social contract. There he imagines the perfect companion for his little Emile, the happily named Sophie, whose ways and wiles reveal all there is to know of woman. To draw her fully Rousseau comments freely on the fundamental characteristics of her sex, producing a political anatomy of the female body from a liberal perspective. In keeping with the biology of incommensurability typical of his moment, he distinguishes women from men on the grounds of material sexual difference, even where that difference may escape observation:

On the basis of comparative anatomy and even just by inspection, one finds
general differences between them that do not appear connected with sex. They
are, nevertheless, connected with sex, but by relations which we are not in a position to perceive. We do not know the extent of these relations. The only thing
we know with certainty is that everything man and woman have in common
belongs to the species, and that everything which distinguishes them belongs to
the sex. (357–58)

Anatomical discrimination between sexed bodies sets the terms for the sexual
contract. But what might be surprising is the way Rousseau argues for the
legitimacy of such relations. It is not the weakness of women's bodies that
enables conjugal right but on the contrary their overwhelming force in attracting and managing the bodies of men. An "invariable law of nature . . .
gives woman more facility to excite the desires than man to satisfy them. This
causes the latter, whether he likes it or not, to depend on the former's wish
and constrains him to seek to please her in turn, so that she will consent to
let him be the stronger" (360). The sexual contract in this description is not
an agreement struck between free and equal individuals but a truce negoti-
ated between two kinds of bodies, one productive of infinite excitement and the
other capable of only finite satisfaction. Conjugal right requires the interrup-
tion of the female body's sexual force, making consent, the enabling act of contractual relations, an effect and not a cause of the sexual contract. Women's
bodies lack volition except through such relations, circulating otherwise in a
sexual economy irreducible to a man's capacity for satisfaction.

So before the sexual contract and making it necessary occurs a prior appropriation of the generative capacity of mother flesh. Rousseau makes it clear
that the real problem women's bodies pose in civil society is their facility not
so much for making love as for making babies. Sexual desires have material effects. Pateman emphasizes the menace that geniture presents to liberal
political theory when she suggests that "physical birth symbolizes everything
that makes women incapable of entering the original contract and transforming
themselves into the civil individuals who uphold its terms" (96). But the problem of birth is more than symbolic. For Rousseau it requires the incarceration
of the female in her own regenerative flesh: "Women, you say, do not always
produce children? No, but their purpose is to produce them" (362). Identifying
women's bodies with female sex and female sex with reproduction, Rousseau
establishes a relation of obligation between the sexes that antedates either the
social or the sexual contract. The "unlimited desires" (359) of women's bodies ultimately become manageable through a sexual, material indebtedness
of mother flesh to a father's proprietary claims.

The foundational contracts of liberal politics rise out of a prior relation of
generative debt. Two apparently natural imperatives drive Rousseau's whole

economy of sexual relations. The first is the imperative to reproduce, an injunction whose necessity Rousseau establishes mathematically in a footnote:
"In order for [the human species] to be preserved, every woman must, everything considered, produce nearly four children; for nearly half of the children
who are born die before they can have others, and the two remaining ones are
needed to represent the father and the mother" (362n). Sexual reproduction
yields as much death as life, so women must not only conceive but conceive
quadruply. But the imperative to reproduce necessitates another to guarantee proper geniture in civil society. The second imperative is to remember, an
injunction that makes the sexual contract possible by insinuating the father
into mother flesh. Sexual reproduction takes time, and women's bodies are
mobile. The command to remember the father creates an obligation between
the sexes that turns a mother's body into collateral for a generative debt incurred at conception.

For Rousseau the needs that accrue to a woman during pregnancy, parturition, and parenting are wholly a function of her ability to incarnate paternity in her offspring: "She serves as the link between them and their father;
she alone makes him love them and gives him the confidence to call them his
own" (361). He can imagine no greater human calamity than befalls the family
of a woman forgetful of this generative debt:

> the unfaithful woman . . . dissolves the family and breaks all the bonds of nature.
> In giving the man children which are not his, she betrays both. She joins perfidy
> to infidelity. I have little difficulty seeing what disorders and what crimes do not
> flow from this one. If there is a frightful condition in the world, it is that of an
> unhappy father who, lacking confidence in his wife, does not dare to yield to the
> sweetest sentiments of his heart, who wonders, in embracing his child, whether
> he is embracing another's, the token of his dishonor, the plunderer of his own
> children's property. (361)

Mother flesh must remember the proprietary rights of the father. And that
means that the generative body by definition cannot possess either itself or
its productions. The womb lacks entitlement to its own operations and fruits.
The property in person liberalism attributes to each individual cannot be
generative, cannot *be* to that extent female. Even when, as in Rousseau, social relations displace material possession as the condition of civil obligation,
female bodies become the means and not the masters of voluntary contract.
Generative debt incurred at conception chains mother flesh to the proprietary claims of freeborn men.

And as with any debt, to forget repayment is to merit punishment. Rousseau's description of the unnaturing effects of female promiscuity gives some
hint of what awaits the woman who fails to combine with the imperative of
liberal political discourse to reproduce the second imperative to remember
the father. Let the bodies of unwed mothers and prostitutes testify even to

this day to the force of such punishment. That it seems somehow justified is of a piece with liberal politics. Female bodies become its site for asserting the memory of the father—through the production of pain. That, after all, is how social contracts work according to Nietzsche in *The Genealogy of Morals*. The material body ultimately plays the debtor in contractual relations, establishing an equivalence between pain and indebtedness. Break the contract and pay the price—in the coin of the flesh. Nietzsche's motto of mnemotechnics is a formula for producing relations of indebtedness: "'If something is to stay in the memory it must be burned in: only that which never ceases to hurt stays in the memory'" (61). The double imperative that liberal political theory directs toward the female body—to reproduce and to remember—burns the memory of paternity into generative mother flesh. Sexual and social contracts become possible because a generative debt regulates reproduction. Women's bodies secure those contracts by becoming the material place of their enforcement. If, as Elizabeth Grosz claims, "the injury caused by the failure to keep promises, by the failure to pay off debts, by the failure to remember to what one is committed, is rendered commensurate with the degree of pain extracted from the body," then pain extracted from regenerative bodies circulates as a currency that funds sexual and social contracts. It's birth on the installment plan: the pain of parturition repays a debt that makes men free.

NATURE'S WAY

And by all accounts birth is painful. I have looked on in numb agony as a child tore its way through mother flesh, and I was thankful for the gifts of analgesics and masculinity. Late-eighteenth-century obstetrics managed the pain of birth by understanding it, and in this served the cultural purpose of planting generative debt in the reproductive capacity of female bodies. William Hunter, whose authority in such matters was a function as much of live deliveries as dead dissections, distinguished two kinds of labor pains and taught his students how to identify and respond to each. In his lectures on the gravid uterus he advocates a knowing disregard of the laboring female's cries of most intense pain:

> there is this difference in the Pains of lying in Women, the grinding, or preparing Pains (as all extraordinary ones are of this kind) which open the Womb and are Worst of all. The Patient talks during these Pains which to her are intolerable, & complains bitterly, but she bears the forcing Pains more patiently, & says nothing. If they never had grinding pains before, they will speak in this manner, never was any body so bad & yet not die, they will beg when sometimes at the worst to be killed out of the way. In this desperate manner will they talk & rave all the time a Pain is upon them. When they keep talking thus, you may

be sure they are only grinding Pains & not forcing ones, & when it is thus, by
letting them go on, I get the Time killed, never allowing it to be Labour till the
Pains begin to be a little effectual. When the forcing Pains come on they strain
& say nothing, these should be attended to, & the Patient desired to bear down,
& be put to Bed. (*Abstract* 33)

The whole art of man midwifery is knowing when to intervene. A delivering
woman betrays a foolish tendency to identify her worst pains with the occurrence of labor. The man midwife knows better and manages those pains to best
advantage, rendering the generative body indebted to his better knowledge.

That is why Hunter's approach to the art of midwifery is so imperiously
benign. Where his precursor Smellie was always at the ready with forceps
and fillet to pluck a struggling infant from the jaws of death, Hunter could
trust wholly in the ways of a nature that man midwifery fully comprehended:
"When Labour is actually present I do little or nothing. In the time of a pain
I support the Back a little with my hand. . . . Thus I assist a little but leave
it principally to nature. Assisting much is extremely improper, tho I pretend
to be doing something, yet I do very little for them, & hardly any more than
to take off the reproach of doing nothing at all" (34). Hunter's man midwife is
a master of medical illusion, pretending to assist where nature does all the
work. One might reasonably wonder why a man midwife should attend so
natural a process as parturition at all. But Hunter's nonchalance signals a
victory in the cultural conquest of female anatomy. His respect for nature's
way has less to do with the material operations of mother flesh than its prior
indebtedness to obstetric medicine. Nature can be trusted because it empowers men midwives. As Hunter reports proudly to his London students, "Every
body who have lived in this Town a number of Years, tell me they are sensible
of the Differences of having fewer Children born Dead, & what is the Reason
of it? It is only within these 20 Years that Women have had MenMidwives
universally" (38).

What matters culturally is not just that obstetric medicine subjects women,
but that it does so by materializing a female body peculiarly suited to sexual
and social contracts. Nature works that body automatically; it makes babies
without volition. The man midwife adds a little free agency to an otherwise determinate process. Texts on midwifery from the last decades of the eighteenth
century, the great majority written by men, repeatedly emphasize the nonvoluntary nature of the female body in labor.[7] Thomas Denman, whose two-
volume *Introduction to the Practice of Midwifery* (1787) became a standard in
the field, locates the origins of midwifery in male compassion toward women
suffering "the evils attending parturition": "The supplications for assistance,
and the affections of men, would not permit them to remain unconcerned or
inactive spectators of the misery of those, to whom they were indebted for the
chief part of their happiness" (2: 117). Enter the man midwife—at first with
forceps. Denman's account of the physiology of geniture and birth makes the

female body the conduit of natural forces it cannot voluntarily control, since "all the passive changes which the parts undergo, and all the active powers exerted for producing these changes, are not only entirely independent of the will of the patient, but are full equal to the end which they were designed to accomplish without any assistance" (2: 372–73). Thus "the action of the *uterus* is totally independent of the will." Because invasive assistance "is no more wanted for the purpose of forwarding a natural labour than for any of the ordinary functions of the body," the man midwife's job is primarily to police and in the event of disturbance to regulate its nonvoluntary agency (1: 372). From the perspective of obstetric medicine, mother flesh has no will of its own.

This was a professional conviction to which Dr. John Clarke, who attended Wollstonecraft to her last, gives full credence. His *Practical Essays on the Management of Pregnancy and Labour* (1793) actively pathologizes any vestige of volition in the regenerative body. Its first line associates mother flesh with death, promising a treatise on "women who die in consequence of uterogestation" (1). The avoidance of that grim prospect comes through the fundamentally preventive medicine of midwifery, whose purpose is to see that a woman's body does not succumb to its own nonvoluntary powers. "The first object of an accoucheur," says Clarke, "should be to regulate the exertion of the woman's powers, and to prevent those inconveniences which are likely to be produced by the violence of them" (17). This regulation comes about by effectively eliminating a woman's voluntary involvement with her body's labour and vesting it in a man midwife's freer agency: "A waste of strength is to be avoided, by taking care that the woman do not employ her voluntary exertions in the course of the labour . . . because the uterus possesses of itself sufficient powers, aided by the involuntary action of the abdominal muscles, to complete the labour" (18).

So important is the suspension of volition during birth for Clarke that the mother's life often depends on prolonging it after delivery. "The patient should be laid in bed . . . and above all she should not be allowed to be in any but an horizontal posture. I have known some instances in which the woman has died immediately after delivery, from being unable to bear an erect posture of body" (27). No wonder female bodies become subject to a sexual contract that precludes agency in liberal society. The imperative to reproduce comes in a biopolitical context that divests mother flesh of volition. To remember the father under such circumstances is to dismember the generative female body, subjecting all its parts to the nonvoluntary agency of the uterus. Of such monstrous dissections are built the female beauties of the Western world, of which another man midwife, Charles White, has left so memorable a description:

> In what other quarter of the globe shall we find the blush that overspreads the soft features of the beautiful women of Europe, that emblem of modesty, of delicate feelings, and of sense? Where that nice expression of the amiable and

softer passions in the countenance; and that general elegance of features and
complexion. Where, except on the bosom of European woman, two such plump
and snowy white hemispheres, tipt with vermilion? (97)

The nonvoluntary body of obstetrics makes women the plump appendages of
natural—and even national—functions.

Placenta

The overt procedures of man midwifery, however, have ulterior premises that
trench on the flesh. Generative debt has a physiology to justify it, further natu-
ralizing the claims of liberal political theory. And the seat of this indebtedness,
the site of its incarnation in mother flesh, is that hitherto unmapped continent
of primordial nutriment, the placenta. The discovery of this new world occasioned some acrimony among its early explorers. The Hunter brothers, William
and John, both claimed credit for the event, yet another happy result of the
acquisition in the spring of 1751 of that recently deceased and fully pregnant
female body. William had some prior claim to the placenta, it is true, having
discovered and named the *decidua reflexa,* the membrane covering it and the
developing fetus. But John maintained for years even after his brother's death
in 1783 that he deserved credit for the placenta itself, since it was he who first
came to know exactly how it connected mother and child: "The facts being now
ascertained, and universally acknowledged, I consider myself as having a just
claim to the discovery of the structure of the placenta, and its communication
with the uterus" (*Observations* 130). A question of possession: who, William or
John, got there first?

Who in fact matters less than what. Both agree that the placenta is that
bodily place where the lives of mother and child meet. Thanks to an especially successful injection of different colored waxes into its veins and arter-
ies, John was able to provide the first anatomical description of how mother
flesh connects physically to that of the developing fetus: "Upon cutting into
the placenta, I discovered in many places of its substance, yellow injection; in
others red, and in many others these two colours mixed. This substance of the
placenta, now filled with injection, had nothing of the vascular appearance,
nor that of extravasation, but had a regularity in its form which showed it to
be a natural cellular structure, fitted to be a reservoir for blood" (129). What
John discovers is a physiology perfectly incorporating generative debt. For
the structure of the placenta allows communication *with no direct connection*
between mother and child. Blood circulates, but through autonomous systems,
indirectly connected by the placenta. The life that mother flesh reproduces is
not, physiologically speaking, its own.

The agency of the fetus, to put the point differently, remains independent

of the female body. The physiological process of gestation reproduces the social circumstances of parturition, doubling the agency of mother flesh with
one that is even more effective. The anatomy of the placenta proves to Hunter
that not the mother but the fetus does most of the work of generation: "from
the description now given, I think we are justified in supposing the placenta
to be formed entirely by the foetus, and the decidua to be a production of the
mother" (133). Little wonder then that in describing how the placenta works
Hunter's comparisons turn conspicuously male. Regarding the movement of
the blood through it, "a just idea may perhaps be conveyed by saying, that it
is similar, as far as we yet know, to the blood's motion through the cavernous
substance of the penis" (135). Placenta as penis—an expanding paternal presence to quicken a mother's womb? The imperative to remember the father gets
incorporated into mother flesh through the placenta. Gestation reproduces
generative debt materially as the life that swells a mother's body remains,
physiologically speaking, a free agent. In this sense human bodies are born
free, while women become trapped in the carceral anatomy of reproduction.
Hunter's discovery of the placenta establishes a physiological basis for limit-
ing the agency of female bodies. They may be fit for sexual contracts, but not
for civil rights.

That might partly explain why the placenta becomes so obsessive a concern to man midwives, more so even than the infant, who seems only to merit
attention in difficult cases. Denman sets the professional standard for such
attitudes in no uncertain terms: "on the proper management of the *placenta*
the life of the patient may depend; and it is therefore fitting and necessary
that our conduct would be guided not by prejudice, but by the dictates of reason and experience" (1: 373). Those dictates require, of course, that the man
midwife respect nature's ways and leave to its rhythms the second birth of
the placenta, even when they seem slow in coming. Arguments for its hasty
delivery Denman declares to be

> groundless, having seen many instances of its being expelled in a very putrid
> state, when the patient was in perfect health; and when the patient had a dis-
> ease, the putridity of the *placenta* seemed the consequence and not the cause of
> the disease. At all events, such less mischief may be expected from the retention
> of a putrid *placenta,* than from attempts to force it away by the medicines usu-
> ally given, or by manual assistance. (2: 329)

Separated finally from the fetus, the placenta becomes subject to the nonvoluntary agency of the uterus, which obstetric knowledge concludes must be
left to itself. In this Clarke concurs, stating that he wrote his *Practical Essays*
in part to improve the "management of the placenta" and therefore "to dep-
recate the hasty extraction of it by artificial means." Like Denman he believes that such quick delivery "must endanger the life of the woman in many
cases, particularly after tedious and lingering labours, where the uterus is

indisposed to act" (22). Both men find their model in William Hunter, whose proprietary interest in the placenta's discovery gave his opinion particular authority. To his students Hunter confided that "the hurrying away of the Placenta is just as bad as hurrying the Labour, & the forcing away the Placenta is a terrible Practice. . . . by hurrying the Placenta away, parts of it are often left behind, or mischief done to the uterus. Every now and then the Placenta will remain for a day or two" (*Abstract* 36). Recommended practice among man midwives was patience in the face of nature, subjecting the female body after birth to its own covert powers. Culturally considered, the delivery of the placenta confirms the nonvoluntary agency of female bodies. The birth of the afterbirth: in an odd sense the placenta gives birth to the abject mother.

PRIVATE PARTS

It is in the cultural context of such practices as those associated with obstetrics that the liberal feminism of Mary Wollstonecraft appears most refractory.[8] She aims at nothing less than asserting the agency of mother flesh, not in the hidden recesses of gestation where anatomy stakes its claim to know the secret all of women's bodies, but in the open habits of affection where women affirm their vitality as daughters, wives, and mothers. Pateman points to the way in which liberalism attempts to depoliticize the female body by relegating it to the private sphere of hearth and home, leaving men free to relate as agents in a public sphere where social contract spells civil right: "During the genesis of civil society, the sphere of natural subjection is separated out as a non-political sphere. . . . Sex-right or conjugal right, the original political right, then becomes completely hidden" (93–94). Where obstetric medicine makes this hiddenness biologically imperative, Wollstonecraft takes gestation public, turning sexual into social relations and making the private sphere a locus of liberal politics.

Her liberal feminism is a body politics of a particularly intellectual sort. Wollstonecraft must work the trick of vindicating the agency of women's bodies without identifying it with the material sexual difference that legitimates separation of private and public spheres. "Public spirit must be nurtured by private virtue," she writes in *A Vindication of the Rights of Woman* (1792), but that virtue cannot be a quality specific to the material difference of female sex (140). Wollstonecraft accepts the biology of incommensurability that in her day distinguishes male and female but claims for bodies of both kinds the capacity to develop independent agency. Sexual identity is anatomy but not destiny, for materially different bodies can be raised to the same virtue. Their difference may indeed be incontrovertible, since "in the government of the physical world it is observable that the female in point of strength is, in general, inferior to the male. This is the law of nature" (8). But for Wollstonecraft social conventions turn natural law from a mere condition of female embodiment into its final determination: "Men have superior strength of body; but were it not for mistaken notions of beauty, women would acquire sufficient to enable them to earn their own subsistence, the true definition of independence; and to bear those bodily inconveniencies and exertions that are requisite to strengthen the mind" (85). Women's bodies, whatever their sexual difference, are as capable of independence as men's. Limits to their virtue are socially and not materially produced—by means, for instance, of an ideology of beauty. By accepting sexual difference while rejecting its cultural destiny Wollstonecraft makes it possible to ascribe voluntary agency to mother flesh. Female bodies don't just reproduce, they reproduce intelligence—and can do so intelligently.

She therefore takes pains to distinguish herself from those commentators on education who, "considering females rather as women than human creatures, have been more anxious to make them alluring mistresses than affectionate wives and rational mothers" (7). Wollstonecraft sounds here like a good liberal humanist, redeeming motherhood through reason's magic. But claiming rationality for mothers is less an essentialist than strategic maneuver. A rational mother is a voluntary agent, capable of free associations and civil relationships. The birthright of reason that liberal political theory bequeaths on the heirs apparent of the public sphere is the product of a mother's labor, the issue of her educable flesh. Wollstonecraft repoliticizes the private sphere by making mother flesh the repository and the agent of human rationality. She exploits the metaphysical slippage of obstetric knowledge—all human bodies are born but only nonreproductive bodies are born free—to associate freedom with the process and not merely certain preferred products of human birth.

The effect is to transform the sexual contract, making it as much as its social correlative a relation of mutual obligation. Properly conceived, sex for Wollstonecraft, at least in *A Vindication of the Rights of Woman,* is not a private pleasure but a social relationship. From the start it involves an intelligence that restores agency to the sexual contract: "nature, by making the gratification of an appetite, in this respect, as well as every other, a natural and imperious law to preserve the species, exalts the appetite, and mixes a little mind and affection with a sensual gust" (138). The sexual contract that ensues becomes the ground of a rejuvenated social contract in which women participate equally with men, and do so on the basis of their mutual interest in reproduction: "The feelings of a parent mingling with an instinct merely animal, give it dignity; and the man and woman often meeting on account of the child, a mutual interest and affection is excited by the exercise of a common sympathy" (138). Wollstonecraft repoliticizes the private sphere by bringing intelligence to the sexual contract, viewing conception not as brute bodily process but an effect of free relations, mutual interest, and consent.

Mother flesh is not so thoughtless as anatomists take her to be, which is why not economic exchange or mutual assistance but infancy becomes her instance of the original social relationship. Wollstonecraft responds in a note to Rousseau's account of the passage to civil society by asserting the claims of infant life to social support: "the long and helpless state of infancy seems to point [humans] out as particularly impelled to pair, the first step towards herding" (14). If infants require society then civil relations begin, not with man contracting with man but mother contracting with father. By politicizing the sexual contract Wollstonecraft inserts the reproductive body into the sphere of citizenship, turning its private life into the domestic equivalent of public agency. Mothers as much as sons are citizens.

REMEMBERING MOTHER

For all its humanism, then, Wollstonecraft's liberal feminism reincorporates female bodies, vindicating their generative agency as a quality of free, independent women. She does more than make mothers rational. She builds a better body from the bones up, starting with conception. In a strange moment in her polemic—she's decrying the "physical degradation" of polygamy—she advances an account of conception that contradicts contemporary anatomical knowledge. "The formation of the fetus in the womb," by which she means its biological sex, arises not according to natural law, but from an "accidental physical cause" (70). Quoting from John Reinhold Forster's *Observations Made During a Voyage Round the World* (1778), Wollstonecraft suggests that female vitality as much as male determines sex at conception; witness the polygamous inhabitants of Africa, whose men,

> "accustomed to polygamy, are enervated by the use of so many women, and therefore less vigorous; the women, on the contrary, are of a hotter constitution, not only on account of their more irritable nerves, more sensible organization, and more lively fancy; but likewise because they are deprived in their matrimony of that share of physical love which, in a monogamous condition, would all be theirs; and thus, for the above reasons, the generality of children are born females." (70–71)

Forster's reasoning here relies on all the familiar racist stereotypes that secure European superiority to those savage Africans, but Wollstonecraft puts them to different if not quite laudable use by showing that the bodies of black women contribute materially to sexing the fetus at conception. Although polygamy proves them not yet participants in civil society, not really on a par with Europeans, those bodies remain free from natural subjection to some mystical male principle of vitality. Conception is the business of both parties, not just one animating force, and each contributes something to the

determination of sex. It would even be possible on the basis of Forster's example to conclude that women and not men provide the decisive impetus for
sexual identity. Whatever the case, Wollstonecraft uses his account of love on
a dark continent quietly to contest the blank, imperial assurances of obstetric
knowledge.

For if female bodies participate actively in the event of conception, then
they cannot be taken as the material ground of generative debt. Wollstonecraft challenges the silent assumption of liberalism that bodily life indebts
women to men. Although she accepts its first imperative to reproduce (that
"natural and imperious law to preserve the species"), she rescinds the second
imperative to remember the father. If mother and father participate in conception, mother and father share the responsibility of memory. Turning the
tables on paternity, Wollstonecraft charges fathers with remembering the
material effects of sexual passion: "the father of a family" must not "forget,
in obeying the call of appetite, the purpose for which it was implanted" (6).
Fathers must remember mothers and both must remember the life of the
body they conceive. Not to do so squanders love's force, subjecting the bodies
of all involved—and not just that of the female—to physical recriminations,
as "when the rich sensualist, who has rioted among women, spreading depravity and misery, when he wishes to perpetuate his name, receives from his
wife only an half-formed being that inherits both father's and mother's weakness" (139). The imperative to remember the father is no protection against
the effects of depravity, which in this case prove physiological. By distributing
generative debt to both parties of the sexual contract, Wollstonecraft once
again turns physiological effects into social relationships. Conception has material consequences that far exceed gestation. Only when fathers remember
mothers and their offspring will female bodies cease to serve socially as the
place where generative debt gets repaid—through the punishment and pain
of childbirth. That Wollstonecraft knows well the operation of this retributive
equation is the lesson of her postumously published and harrowing novel
Maria: Or, the Wrongs of Woman. It catalogs the tortures visited on the bodies of women who fail in their husbandry of generative debt. Wollstonecraft
writes to end these socially acceptable tortures in the name of the father. To
her, generative debt is not a hidden cause but the obvious effect of the sexual
contract.

Freed from sole responsibility for that debt female bodies might develop
their own strength, their own vigor. Wollstonecraft's liberal feminism aims at
embodying the virtues of free agency. She turns generative debt into parental
duty and in the process remakes motherhood, taking a passive condition of
physical reproduction and making it an active force of cultural regeneration.
The concept of duty suspends the obligation of debt by making women responsible agents of bodily processes that produce liberal society: "The being
who discharges the duties of its station is independent, and, speaking of

women at large, their first duty is to themselves as rational creatures, and next, in point of importance, as citizens, is that, which includes so many, of a mother" (145). Reason does not preclude motherhood; on the contrary it operates through mothers by way of duty, and "the care of children in their infancy is one of the grand duties annexed to the female character by nature" (151). By repoliticizing mothers Wollstonecraft makes their bodies and those they produce the living agents of liberal politics. That's why nursing becomes a mother's first responsibility to her offspring. "The discharge of this duty is equally calculated to inspire maternal and filial affection: and it is the indispensable duty of men and women to fulfill the duties which give birth to affections that are the surest preservatives against vice" (152). The duty of nursing suspends generative debt by cultivating affectionate memories between mother and father. Further, it makes a healthy body the object of liberal politics from the start, providing an infant with the liquid citizenship that assures its later independence.

For bodily independence is the material aim of Wollstonecraft's vindication of women's rights, her riposte to the dependence presumed and perpetuated by political and medical theorists alike. An independent woman is physically fit, one "whose constitution, strengthened by exercise, has allowed her body to acquire its full vigour; her mind, at the same time gradually expanding itself to comprehend the moral duties of life" (50). To this end Wollstonecraft includes body in the process of cultivating mind, for "the most perfect education . . . is such an exercise of the understanding as is best calculated to strengthen the body and form the heart" (21). A mother's agency involves nurturing that of her children, especially if they are girls, since forces abound that would entrap them in the gilt cage of female beauty. Wollstonecraft's pedagogy is thus a politics in—and of—motion, a physical commitment to bodily movement as a way to keep from being caged: "To preserve personal beauty, woman's glory! the limbs and faculties are cramped with worse than Chinese bands, and the sedentary life which they are condemned to live, whilst boys frolic in the open air, weakens the muscles and relaxes the nerves" (41). Sexually considered, boys and girls may differ, but socially considered their bodies share the same need for activity, a point Wollstonecraft substantiates by insisting on the similarity of their postnatal development toward maturity: "In youth, till twenty, the body shoots out, till thirty the solids are attaining a degree of density; and the flexible muscles, growing daily more rigid, give character to the countenance" (70). Mothers have privileged access to the bodies of children during the time they are maturing and can quite literally shape their character. The robust independence of the female body in particular becomes a matter for her special care.

As a social agency, the force of motherhood can even liberate that body from the incommensurability of its biological sex. Wollstonecraft's program for bodily independence in one instance finds fulfillment in a widow who, assuming the roles of both father and mother, "forgets her sex" altogether (50). The imperative of generative debt to remember the father falls to the social force of independent motherhood, as the widow lives "to see her children attain a strength of character sufficient to enable them to endure adversity without forgetting their mother's example" (51). The female embodiment of liberal virtue cultivates a somatic countermemory of independent motherhood that raises children to the awareness of its social productivity. As body politics, Wollstonecraft's liberal feminism makes the agency of mother flesh very much a voluntary matter.

NUMBER TWO

But even for Wollstonecraft volition has its limits. The question to put to her body politics is how far it moves free of a liberal political discourse that subjects nonvoluntary flesh to superior minds. Rational mothers are free agents, and their bodies bear the fruit of independence, but not in all of their functions. Kristeva contends that one of the effects of mothering is the embodiment, physically and socially, of a sense of propriety. Unlike a father's word, which lays down the law, "maternal authority is the trustee of that mapping of the self's clean and proper body" (72). Self, body, propriety: the mother incarnates a subject whose independence requires the elimination of filth. Kristeva means the maternal with a capital "M," an archaic force that licks matter into human shape. But her remarks apply best to the rational mother of liberal feminism, the real target of her psychoanalytic adventures. What after all is psychoanalysis but the corporal dissection of the liberal subject? Kristeva's discussion of the bodily effects of mothering exposes the biopolitics of liberal feminism, a familiar denigration of flesh that remains irreducible to voluntary agency.

It's not just that Wollstonecraft in characteristically bourgeois fashion distrusts the bulked bodies of laborers, although she certainly does, as when she distinguishes the intellectual's sound constitution from "that robust tone of nerves and vigour of muscles, which arise from bodily labour, when the mind is quiescent, or only directs the hands" (38). The best bodies are the mind's offspring, and "the mass of mankind will never vigorously pursue an intellectual object" (64). Wollstonecraft's preferred body types are strappingly middle-class. But if there's one thing she can't stand, it's a woman in the privy, such a questionable occurrence that there is only one thing worse: two women in the privy. If it weren't so impolitic, one might say she waxes a tad hysterical at the very thought. Women's bodies have about them forces subversive of human decencies, a menacing fact of mother flesh that a ladies' room only exaggerates: "Why in the name of decency are sisters, female intimates, or ladies and their waiting-women, to be so grossly familiar as to forget the respect which

one human creature owes to another?" (127). This gross familiarity encour-
ages recourse to what Wollstonecraft calls "bodily wit," a ribaldry that women
indulge "because their minds are not cultivated," with the result that "their
intimacies are of the same kind" (128). A privy becomes an unclean place,
especially if the company includes servants. Their "jokes and hoiden tricks"
threaten to sully the independent female, seeming "almost on a par with the
double meanings, which shake the convivial table when the glass has circu-
lated freely" (128). Wollstonecraft insists that women keep themselves pure,
properly bodied, and to that end she recommends frequent ablutions in soli-
tude: "by example, girls ought to be taught to wash and dress alone, without
any distinction of rank; and if custom should make them require some little
assistance, let them not require it till that part of the business is over which
ought never to be done before a fellow creature; because it is an insult to the
majesty of human nature" (127).

Human bodies shouldn't shit, apparently, at least not in front of others.
It would be glib to suggest that a woman sitting alone on a chamber pot
provides the social type of the liberal subject nurtured by rational mothers.
But Wollstonecraft betrays material fear here not merely of certain bodily
functions but more importantly of the collective knowledge they occasion and
the relationships that result. The agency she attributes to mother flesh turns
involuntary where its products are inert. And in those nether realms politics
becomes impossible and human interaction anathema. The abjection that
obstetric knowledge associates with the generative female body returns here
to establish the lower boundary of liberal feminism. Its body abjures filth—
especially its own. Shitting and pissing are its beyond. Kristeva claims that
"fecal matter signifies, as it were, what never ceases to separate from a body
in a state of permanent loss in order to become *autonomous, distinct* from
the mixtures, alterations, and decay that run through it. That is the price the
body must pay if it is to become *clean and proper*" (108). This price devalues
those processes that challenge the autonomy of the freely contracting agent
of civil society. Shitting and pissing eliminate the material remainder of the
liberal subject's becoming. As involuntary processes they contradict its purity
and propriety, opening its body to vital forces far beyond reasoned control.
Wollstonecraft fears the prospect of a carnival of this raucous body, or what
would be worse, a politics of collective embodiment that affirmed rather
than abjured those fetid facts of physical life. No double entendres for her,
no grotesque and cackling crowd of flatulent females. The appropriate—and
political—response to such behavior is disgust, which guards against the
fundamental confusion that would inevitably result: "How can *delicate*
women obtrude on notice that part of the animal oeconomy, which is so very
disgusting? And is it not very rational to conclude, that the women who have
not been taught to respect the human nature of their own sex, in these particulars, will not long respect the mere difference of sex in their husbands?"

(128). To obtrude what remains abject is as politically offensive as it is personally insolent.

But that it menaces so foundational a physical distinction as sexual difference shows how seriously Wollstonecraft takes the threat of a carnival of female bodies. Liberal feminism needs abjection to assert its borders and its authority, and as if to prove that its claims on behalf of women are not all that far out of line with prevailing political opinion, Wollstonecraft calls on masculine approval to legitimate feminine hygiene. Calling "cleanliness, neatness, and personal reserve" the first graces of female beauty, she makes men their final arbiters, venturing "to affirm that when two or three women live in the same house, the one will be most respected by the male part of the family, who reside with them, leaving love entirely out of the question, who pays this kind of habitual respect to her person" (129). That the clean and proper body of liberal women should still require the approval of men shows how snugly Wollstonecraft's feminism can be made to fit into the private sphere. For all its socially productive effects, mother flesh still remains subject to involuntary functions that compromise its freedom, its humanity. Wollstonecraft becomes a carnal kind of transcendentalist with her categorical imperative to avoid causing disgust: "There is one rule relative to behaviour that, I think, ought to regulate every other; and it is simply to cherish such an habitual respect for mankind as may prevent us from disgusting a fellow-creature for the sake of present indulgence" (137). Wollstonecraft doesn't eliminate the distinction between voluntary and involuntary bodily agency that liberal political discourse deploys against women's bodies. She relocates it in a way that wins agency for motherhood while reaffirming the abjection of the nonvoluntary functions to which female bodies tend. Mother flesh may no longer be by definition abject as with the anatomists, but nevertheless becomes so when it shits, pisses, curses, and jokes. For Wollstonecraft women's bodies must remain aloof to their more visceral, vital, involuntary processes. Her liberal feminism builds a female body capable of sexual and social contracts, but indebted still to unknowable, improper functions.

RETAINED PLACENTA

That the great advocate of rational motherhood died giving birth is an irony nothing short of tragic. Vivien Jones is right to read it as "a social and discursive event" and right too to conclude that, given the state of medical knowledge in 1797 among both female midwives and their professionalized male counterparts, nothing could have been done to prevent Wollstonecraft from succumbing to puerperal fever ten days after the birth of Mary, her second child (188).[9] Her body simply betrayed all reasonable measures to save it. That Wollstonecraft should herself have had every confidence in its strength was the lesson of her first delivery some three years earlier. Writing to her friend Ruth Barlow, she describes how it went: "nothing could be more natural or easy than my labour—still it is not smooth work— . . . this struggle of nature is rendered much more cruel by the ignorance and affectation of women" (*Letters* 255). Wollstonecraft was writing only six days after giving birth to her daughter Fanny, in France and out of wedlock. Already she had been out walking and so impressed the nurse assisting her that the latter suggested she go on making babies for the new republic. This robust English mother embodied the intellectual independence and corporal vigor worthy of a new kind of politics.

So when it came to her second lying-in, Wollstonecraft had few qualms. She knew what to expect and knew too that reason would prevail over ignorance and affectation. According to William Godwin, her tender friend, husband, and first biographer, "she was so far from being under any apprehension as to the difficulties of child-birth, as frequently to ridicule the fashion of ladies in England, who keep their chamber for one full month after delivery" (174). Wollstonecraft would have none of the enforced passivity of women who unthinkingly give up their bodies to man midwives and obstetric medicine, a conviction that may have influenced her choice of Mrs. E. Blenkensop, matron and midwife of the Westminster New Lying-In Hospital, to assist with delivery. Godwin defends the choice on less explicitly political grounds when he relates that Wollstonecraft was "influenced by ideas of decorum" when she decided "to have a woman attend her in the capacity of a midwife" (174). Such concerns may or may not have preoccupied her in the actual event of delivery, but they chime with her opinion in *Vindication* that women should study medicine, especially "midwifery, [which] decency seems to allot to them" (148). Mother flesh needs women's wisdom, which ideas of decorum sanction socially. That Wollstonecraft had confidence in her midwife and expected a routine birth is the tenor of her last written communication with her husband: "Mrs. Blenkensop tells me that I am in the most natural state, and can promise me a safe delivery—But that I must have a little patience" (*Letters* 411).

But something went wrong. Wollstonecraft went into labor at five in the morning on August thirtieth and her child was born at twenty minutes after eleven that night. The baby was fine, but her mother's body refused to give. It retained the placenta. One hour passed, then another, at which point Mrs. Blenkensop, according to Godwin, "gave her opinion for calling in a male practitioner." Godwin's is the closest thing to an eyewitness account of what happened next:

> I accordingly went for Dr. Poignand, physician and man-midwife to the same hospital, who arrived between three and four hours after the birth of the child. He immediately proceeded to the extraction of the placenta, which he brought

away in pieces, till he was satisfied that the whole was removed. In that point however afterwards appeared that he was mistaken. (176)

On the problem of the placenta hangs the balance of this woman's life, a woman who had every reason to trust, if not quite all the functions of the female body, at least the collective wisdom of those who tend it. But when Mrs. Blenkensop made the decision, with which Wollstonecraft must have concurred, to call in a male practitioner, she abdicated that wisdom and gave mother flesh up to obstetrics. What needs explaining is why Dr. Poignand proceeded immediately to remove the placenta. Godwin records no excessive bleeding, only that the placenta had not been delivered several hours after birth. As noted earlier, the most influential man midwives of the day consistently recommended against extracting it, even if that meant waiting several days for it to appear or enduring its putrefaction. Denman, Hunter, and Clarke all dismiss manual detachment as unduly damaging to the uterus.[10] Imagine then Dr. Clarke's consternation on arriving at Wollstonecraft's home a few hours later. No wonder Poignand immediately departed. He had meddled with the placenta, perhaps endangering the mother's life.

Wollstonecraft's body became a battlefield for rival obstetric practices. The adversaries were not, as conventionally described, women midwifes and male practitioners, but two kinds of male practitioner, one from a lying-in hospital that treated poorer women by the dozen (Poignand) and another whose patients were middle-class and well-heeled (Clarke). The latter had the luxury of recommending against extracting the placenta. Clarke's clients could afford the long confinement that his practice required. The former had to move female bodies efficiently in and out of a charitably funded institution. Poignand no doubt proceeded as it was usual for him to do in such cases. Clarke could not have been pleased, but by the time he entered the fray the damage was done. The battle for Wollstonecraft's body was lost by both sides. Between them, all these men could do was preside over evisceration and decay. Both knew enough to target the placenta, that viscid matter of life and death. Their rival agencies, interventionist or benign, seized on it as their proper object. Wollstonecraft's placenta became the site of the medical appropriation of her mother flesh, and to this day most accounts of her death conclude that a retained placenta was its cause.

But was it? Wollstonecraft actually died of what was then desperately called puerperal fever, a class of fatal infection that can take any number of forms and has any number of causes. If parts of the placenta were retained, they could indeed incubate such a fever. But so could the raw walls of a uterus damaged by manual detachment, or the membranes of the vagina. Puerperal fever could even result from a completely normal delivery—*because it spreads through physical contact*. Wollstonecraft contracted her fatal fever from someone who attended her, not because something went wrong after her delivery.

Preoccupation with her placenta reveals more about the priorities of obstetric medicine and liberal politics than the cause of her death. The placenta must be to blame because its management—or mismanagement—is the whole point of a specialized medicine that burdens female bodies with generative debt.

What is missing from obstetric knowledge is an understanding of such bodies, not as conjuries of dissectable, preservable parts, but as moving unities of vital processes. That Wollstonecraft's own feminism would be inadequate to the purpose of affirming these processes only proves what is wanting in liberalism: a politics equal to female corporeality. As Pateman puts it, "The body of the 'individual' is very different from women's bodies. His body is tightly enclosed within boundaries, but women's bodies are permeable, their contours change shape and they are subject to cyclical processes. All these differences are summed up in the natural bodily process of birth" (96). The death of Mary Wollstonecraft martyrs mother flesh on a tree of obstetric knowledge. Would a politics of bodily process have saved her? Who can tell, but Grosz calls for something of the sort with her reminder that women's bodies, and men's too, remain irreducible to the clean and proper agency of traditional liberalism: "Bodies themselves, in their materialities, are never self-present, given things, immediate, certain self-evidences because embodiment, corporeality, insist on alterity, both that alterity they carry within themselves . . . and that alterity that gives them their concreteness and specificity" (209). Mother flesh moves and lives among habitable alterities. What would be a politics equal to its vitality?

AFTERBIRTH

The child who survived Wollstonecraft's death lived on to write a book of astonishing power and popularity. *Frankenstein* tells the tale of one man's attempt to reproduce—alone. Along the way it chants a litany of dead mothers. To reproduce in Mary Shelley's world is in material terms to become a corpse—a hauntingly familiar assumption, given the cultural force of obstetric knowledge, which explains how "obstetrics," on Alan Bewell's account, becomes "the master-code of her aesthetics" (Bewell, "Issue" 107). Giving birth is a monstrous undertaking, as Mary Shelley's own experience would prove. But it is less as an instance of monster aesthetics than as an appeal for a feminist politics that *Frankenstein* engages the obstetric knowledge contemporary with it.[11] Frankenstein's monster confronts the misogyny of such knowlege through his body's ugliness and abjection. On the verge of his own death he describes himself in precise anatomical terms: "I, the miserable and the abandoned, am an abortion" (219). The word "abortion" did not then provoke the contention it does today. In Denman's definition, it simply describes premature birth: "we will then say that all expulsions of the *foetus*, before the termination of the sixth month of pregnancy, may be called abortions" (2: 316). On the basis of papers found in Frankenstein's coat pocket pertaining to his monster's creation, in which "the whole detail of that series of disgusting circumstances which produced it is set in view," the monster discovers that his body took four months to build (126). That makes him by obstetric definition an abortion, a premature delivery left to fend for itself long before the moment of human viability.

As such he maintains a privileged relationship to mother flesh. Born without the sustenance of a mother's body, he nonetheless incarnates its abjection. He is consistently described by others and describes himself as filthy, loathsome, disgusting, hideous. The painful irony of his premature existence is that, for all his rationality and native feeling, his abject body inspires disgust. That Frankenstein made him male shows the assumptions at play in the knowledge of anatomy. But the monster's flesh is less man's than mother's, spawning revulsion and breeding death. His relationship with his creator therefore takes the form of generative debt: "I am thy creature, and I will be mild and docile to my natural lord and king, if thou wilt also perform thy part, the which thou owest me" (95). The abject body, constitutive outside to proper embodiment, returns to haunt the rational subject by asserting a counterimperative to remember the flesh. The father owes mother flesh the acknowledgment that its life matters. The monster thus inserts a feminist variable into the equation of generative debt: "I demand a creature of another sex, but as hideous as myself" (142). The abject body excluded by liberalism demands its material due. Its politics would begin by affirming life's corporeality—in all its maternity, alterity, and abjection.

At first Frankenstein feels the force of this counterimperative to remember the flesh and promises to create his monster a female companion. It's an amazing gesture, for it would involve nothing short of constructing a material foundation for a corporeal feminism. In a sardonic touch, Mary Shelley has him travel to England to accomplish the task. Only there has natural philosophy reached the point, it appears, where the female generative body has fully yielded its secrets to anatomical knowledge, as Frankenstein himself attests: "I had heard of some discoveries having been made by an English philosopher, the knowledge of which was material to my success" (147). Could it be that Frankenstein wanted to study the generative mysteries of the placenta in the tradition of its British masters, the brothers Hunter, credited with its discovery? Perhaps the glorious plates of the *Gravid Uterus* were not available in Geneva. Whatever the case, he proceeds to England only to realize the impossibility of fulfilling his promise. Approaching the successful conclusion of his gruesome work, he has second thoughts—thoughts that challenge the propriety of breathing agency into abject flesh. A female monster might be more than humanity can handle: "she might become ten thousand times more malignant than her mate, and delight, for its own sake, in murder and wretchedness." Or she might simply ignore the terms of generative debt and "refuse to comply with a compact made before her creation." Or she might revile the abject body of her mate and "turn with disgust from him to the superior beauty of man" (163).

Incorporating a fully volitional female body capable of its own agency, its own politics, is too risky a business for Frankenstein. So he turns obstetrician, delivering his new female of the burden of life: "I thought with a sensation of madness on my promise . . . and, trembling with passion, tore to pieces the thing on which I was engaged" (164). So much for the promise of a corporeal feminism. Mary Shelley stages the dismemberment of mother flesh by the very powers that would promote its vitality. It falls to later generations to animate a material politics of female embodiment. As the monster puts it: "This being you must create" (140). Hence the appeal of Grosz's profoundly physical feminism:

> There is no one mode that is capable of representing the "human" in all its richness and variability. A plural, multiple field of possible body "types," no one of which functions as the delegate or representative of the others, must be created, a "field" of body types—young and old, black and white, male and female, animal and human, inanimate and animate—which, in being recognized in their specificity, cannot take on the coercive role of singular norm or ideals for all the others. (22)

Frankenstein registers an appeal for a fully corporeal feminism, a politics that multiplies the possibilities of embodiment instead of assimilating them to a proper, and properly human, norm.

CHAPTER 7

IMPERIAL LEGS

Still 'round him clung invisibly a chain
Which gall'd forever, fettering tho' unseen,
And heavy tho' it clanked not, worn with pain,
Which pined although it spoke not, and grew keen,
Entering with every step he took, through many a scene.
—*Byron,* Childe Harold's Pilgrimage

I have given a name to my pain and call it "dog." It is just as
faithful, just as obtrusive and shameless, just as entertaining,
just as clever as any other dog—and I can scold it and vent my
bad mood on it, as others do with their dogs, servants, and wives.
—*Nietzsche,* The Gay Science

Birth got Byron off on the wrong foot. Otherwise healthy, he suffered a congenital deformity of foot and leg that, famously, encumbered him throughout his life. It was a touchy subject. On his travels in Seville in 1809, atop the cathedral for a view of the beautiful city, Byron had just taken out his golden pencil to scribble a line or two when a small dog appeared. It went immediately for his lame leg and began to snuffle. According to the guide's account, "This put Byron into a towering rage, and imprecating curses on the little dog which he kicked away in his rage, he threw the gold pencil far away on the roof of the cathedral below" (quoted in Eisler 192). A strange scene, this mongrel Mephisto come to trouble composition, but instructive too for the way it relates the poet's deformity to a form of life that isn't human. Unlike Nietzsche, Byron doesn't view his affliction as man's best friend, but it dogs him nonetheless, forcing a continuing encounter, in his poetry and his politics, with a life that remains other to the merely human health of the proper body. That this encounter comes in the historical context of England's war against Napoleonic France makes Byron's deformity, or more precisely the prostheses he used to treat it, an occasion too for the reproduction of that norm. Thanks to that deformed foot, Byron stands somewhere uneasily in between proper British embodiment and its constitutive monstrosities.

CLUBFOOT?

But just what was Byron's deformity anyway? The tradition that it was a clubfoot has the appeal of family and medical testimony. Byron's dissolute father Jack, mostly absent on the lam from creditors, took a dim view of his son's prospects in a letter to his sister Fanny: "For my son, I am happy to hear he is well; but for his walking, 'tis impossible, for he is clubfooted" (quoted in Eisler 19). A few years later the young Byron would describe himself similarly when in the company of another lame boy: "Come and see the twa laddies with the twa clubfeet going up the Broad Street" (quoted in Eisler 25). That description probably stood on the best medical authority, since the future lord was examined as a child by a who's who of contemporary physicians. No less an expert than John Hunter was called in at Byron's birth to evaluate his deformity. Later, when Byron was living with the family of attorney John Hanson, oddly enough in Hunter's old house at Earl's Court (where Charles Byrne's giant body was rendered into bones), he came under the care of Matthew Baillie, the eminent morbid anatomist mentioned in chapter 1. The oblique testimony of Hunter and Baillie, combined with that of a Dr. Millingen who attended Byron at his death, led Leslie A. Marchand to conclude that "the nature of Byron's deformity points clearly to some form of clubfoot" (Marchand, *Byron* 1: 55, n7).

But that conclusion might be a misstep. For one thing, testimony conflicts regarding just which foot was afflicted. Tom Moore, John Galt, Lady Blessington, and Countess Albruzzi couldn't say which one it was. His mother, who should know, said it was his right. But Countess Guiccioli, who should know too, said it was his left, as did Mrs. Leigh Hunt. Stendahl stood with Hobhouse in declaring for the right. Trelawney splits the difference in the first edition of his *Recollections of Shelley and Byron* (1858). Withdrawing the shroud covering Byron's corpse, he reveals the truth: "The Great mystery was solved. Both his feet were clubbed, and withered to the knee—the form and features of an Apollo, with the feet and legs of a sylvan satyr" (149). Right, left, or both? Byron's clubfoot seems a fickle deformity, like Eyegore's wandering hump in Mel Brooks's *Young Frankenstein*. How could so singular an affliction take so many different forms?

Through the mundane miracle of prosthetics.[1] Byron used surgically designed boots at least to hide if not quite to heal his physical deformity. The two

that survive, now in the John Murray Archive in London, answer some questions while raising others (Figure 28). They prove that a mother's memory
is a thing to be trusted: both were made for the right foot, one in childhood,
and one later in life. But they cast doubt on medical diagnosis. Less boots
really than leather inserts to be worn inside them, both are padded in the
thigh, suggesting a significant withering of the muscle. Both are thick in the
sole, suggesting a slight shortening of the foot or leg. And both have perfectly
shaped foot compartments, slender to the point of dainty, suggesting nothing
to indicate the inward twist of the common clubfoot. These surgical inserts
corroborate deformity of a different sort, one that caused Byron to be lame
but still capable of the unusual, swift gait Trelawney recalls in his observation that "during his brief and brilliant career in London it was noticed by his
friends that to hide his lameness he always entered a room quickly, running
rather than walking" (quoted in *Lancet* 1923, 679). Byron's prosthetic boot
helped conceal the truth of deformity from the eyes of casual observers, intimates, and experts too, leading later doctors to the subtler diagnoses of mild
spastic paraplegia or spina bifida.[2] Whatever the case, that boot alters Byron's
stance toward others, or better yet, others it altogether, forcing him to step
beyond the norm of the proper body, making prosthesis a part of bodily life.

Here's Byron writing to his mother from Harrow in 1803: "My dear
Mother— . . . I have already wrote to you several *times* about writing to
Sheldrake. I have wrote myself to not [any] Purpose, I wish you would write
to him or Mr. Hanson to call on him, to tell him to make an instrument for
my leg immediately, as I want one, rather, I have been placed in a higher form
in this School to day" (*Letters* 1: 43). Byron wants a new boot, and *now*; his
scholastic advance somehow depends on it. But depending on a prosthesis
can be tricky business, or so Byron learns through his dealings with the unre-
sponsive Sheldrake. Timothy Sheldrake was a trussmaker of some distinction
whose practical experience in treating skeletal deformities won him the respect of several influential physicians, including Hunter and Baillie. In 1798
he published *A Practical Essay on the Club-Foot* and later became a frequent
contributor to *The Lancet*. According to Marchand, it was Sheldrake who, on
the recommendation of Baillie, made first a brace then a surgical boot for
Byron's lame foot (*Byron* 1: 58).

Not according to Sheldrake. In an article in *The Lancet* for 1828 titled
"Mr. Sheldrake on Distortions of the Feet. Lord Byron's Case," Sheldrake describes how a summons to examine the young Byron found its way into the
devious hands of an impostor Sheldrake, who "made no attempt to cure his
foot; made something that he called a leg iron, and when that was done, appeared no more" (*Lancet* 1828, 779). The deception was not discovered until
years later, when Byron called on Sheldrake to inquire after further treatment, only to realize that *this* Sheldrake, by his own account, had neither received the original summons nor supplied the original treatment. Byron had

Figure 28. Byron's surgical boots. Reprinted by permission of the John Murray Archive.

fallen prey to a dissimulating maker of simulated limbs. And it was a shame, too, for according to the real Sheldrake, had *he* been able to provide timely treatment, Byron would have experienced *real* healing. As it was, although Sheldrake felt cure was still possible, the means would be cloistering and cumbersome, curtailing Byron's social life. Byron responded as a man of his station: "he expressed bitter regret that the vile trick which had been practiced upon him in early life, had cheated him of that time which might have been, without inconvenience, employed in effecting a cure, but which he could not now engage in without the greatest injury to his future pursuits" (*Lancet* 1828, 780). Good-bye therapy. A fake Sheldrake gave fake treatment with the result that Byron requires fake boots to maintain his social standing.

However unfortunate for Byron (he now had a permanent deformity of the foot) and however fortunate for Sheldrake (he still had a perfect record of cures), this ordeal reveals something interesting about the relation between life and limb, namely that it involves a relation, or really several: between the body and the world, between physical limb and prosthetic artifice, between the organic and the inorganic, between doctors and quacks. Living with a new, prosthetic boot Byron lives without old valuations of human health and wholeness, their proprieties and truths. He steps toward another way of living, a way that involves otherness. Pondering the peculiar logic of prosthesis, materialized in his own father's artificial leg, David Wills emphasizes its articulation of incommensurables. As a formal relation, prosthesis articulates matters of two putatively distinct orders. But since it involves living bodies, it is more than a formal relation. Movement is one of its conditions, the movement of otherness to and through bodies. As Wills puts it, "from leg of flesh to leg of steel, [prosthesis] is necessarily a transfer into otherness, articulated through the radical alterity of ablation as loss of integrity" (Wills 12–13). To live with or through prosthesis is to live with or through loss—of health, of wholeness, of humanness taken essentially for granted.

Prosthesis opens bodies toward the otherness that invests their movement but that goes unnoticed in the mute euphoria of health and wholeness. Wills again, a bit more clearly perhaps:

> By means of prosthesis the relation to the other becomes precisely and necessarily a relation to otherness, the otherness, for example, of artificiality attached to or found within the natural. The relation to the other is denied the confirmation of sameness that freezes its differential effect, rigidifies the oedipal structure, and ultimately represses the feminine, the homosexual, etc. (Wills 44)

Perhaps the poet of the satanic school practiced not a demonic but a prosthetic art. Perhaps his scandalous reputation arises as much from physical as from psychological tribulation. If as Wills suggests prosthesis opens a body to otherness, then perhaps Byron's surgical boots materially occasion transgression, one that challenges the sameness that the proper body promotes. A prosthetic body might matter in ways irreducible to such a norm. Byron's prosthetic boot transforms the form it simulates, making his body matter by means, not of human health and wholeness, but of artifice, otherness, materiality, inhumanity.[3]

MERE MECHANICS

That's not necessarily the way a prosthesis works from a medical perspective. Its job is either to cure what's deformed or to complete what's missing. Medicine has a much different sense of prosthetic effect than that described by David Wills. Following Foucault, one could call that effect disciplinary if one took into account its operation according to a cultural norm of embodiment.[4] Hunter and Baillie were asked to examine a foot showing a pathological deviation from that norm. Both prescribed a surgical prosthesis whose function was to correct that pathology. The actual construction of such an apparatus would have fallen to an artisan such as Sheldrake, physicians and surgeons having higher concerns than the manufacture of stays and trusses. The medical treatment of deformity recapitulates such professional distinctions. Its application of prosthesis reinforces a norm of embodiment that prefers human health and wholeness to mere materialities.[5] Where flesh deviates from that norm, as with Byron's deformed foot, it warrants disciplined treatment, the application of a surgical apparatus to straighten it out (Figure 29). Such treatment advances the appropriation of singular bodies by a norm of health and wholeness. Deformity, like criminality, occasions the production of human values, and medicine, like law, regulates their circulation through flesh.[6]

This biopolitics of medical prosthetics appears quite openly in Sheldrake's publications, probably because as a mere artisan he's at pains to demonstrate his credentials, such as they were. "The greater part of Truss-makers," he says, "as well as those who profess to remove the deformities of children, have usually been mere mechanics" (*Spine* iii). As such they require guidance by "the directions of professional men," that is, physicians and surgeons. Sadly, however, the trussmaker's craft "has been too generally followed by *ignorant* mechanics, or presuming quacks . . . they know that machines are used to remove these deformities, they hear that some particular machine has been used with success, and therefore think themselves authorized to make use of it on every occasion" (*Spine* 39–40). The pseudo-Sheldrake who originally treated Byron was such a quack, applying a machine with no medical knowledge of its effects.

The real Sheldrake knows better and views deformity with an eye trained on the norm from which it deviates:

> Every one who sees a club-foot can tell it is a distortion, or at least a deviation from the natural state of the limb; but the anatomist, who wishes to understand the disease, will endeavour to examine, separately, the state of the bones, the ligaments, and the muscles, and when he is acquainted with the particular state of all those parts, he will consider them as combined in one whole, and by this method, will be enabled to form a more correct idea of the disease, than by any other method he can pursue. (*Club-Foot* 56)

To the anatomist's spatial sense of the material body Sheldrake adds the physiologist's temporal sense of its functional development, arriving at a norm of embodiment that unites organic form with natural growth: "There is, no doubt, a natural arrangement of parts, tending to facilitate the growth and

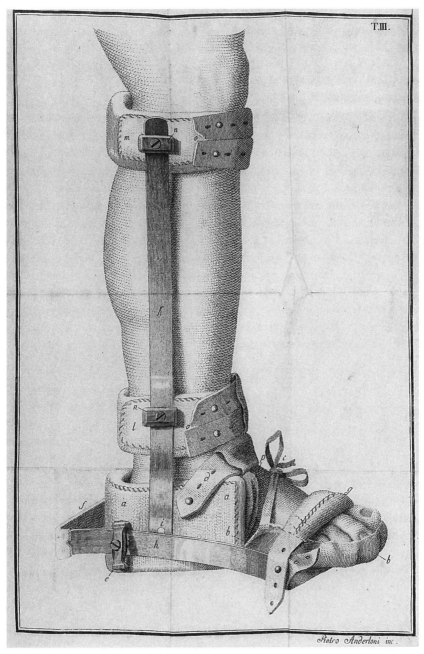

Figure 29. Foot brace. Antonia De Scarpa, *Memoria chirurgica sui piedi torti congeniti dei fanciulli . . .* (1806). The Wellcome Library, London.

progress of the bones towards their final form" (*Club-Foot* 82). Deviation from this norm means deformity, in this case clubfoot, since "by the derangements of those parts in this disease, the natural action is immediately impeded, and ... the parts ... begin to assume a new and unnatural form" (*Club-Foot* 76). Sheldrake's surgical prostheses work to return the foot to its natural shape, incarnating in the process those values of organic form and natural growth. Misshapen bones left to develop without such treatment twist away from that shape until "by negligence and time, they will at last acquire all the deformity that takes place in ... the natural club-foot" (*Club-Foot* 150). Properly applied, Sheldrake's machines impede that pathological end and restore the proper norm.

But something strange has happened to Sheldrake's language. The "new and unnatural form" of this deformity is "the natural club-foot." Apparently the unnatural is a species of the natural. It is not merely that Sheldrake is letting words run away with him. His solecism illuminates the forces at work in the medicine he's so eager to practice, making deformity not so much a deviation from a norm as an extravagant instance of it. As we have seen, John Hunter insists on this point as a cardinal principal of pathological anatomy. In his "Account of the Free Martin," published as part of *Observations on Certain Parts of the Animal Oeconomy* (2d. ed. 1786) he reminds his reader that

> Every deviation from that original form and structure which gives the distinguishing character to the productions of Nature, may not improperly be called monstrous. According to this acceptation of the term, the variety of monsters will be almost infinite. ... Neither does this appear to be a matter of mere chance; for it may be observed, that every species has a disposition to deviate from Nature in a manner peculiar to itself ... [and that] each part of each species seems to have its monstrous form originally impressed upon it. (*Observations* 75)

It turns out that expert medical authority scripts Sheldrake's strange language. Monstrosities provide a material occasion for medicine to eradicate the fact or the experience of embodied otherness. For Canguilhem this operation becomes institutionalized in medical practice as "a principle of nosologie vested with a universal authority that embraces the political order" (Canguilhem 50). One might wonder, then, how the political order recapitulates this normalizing force of medicine.

CORSICAN MONSTER

Many other forces contribute to the cultural production of the proper body. Late-eighteenth- and early-nineteenth-century Britain saw their consolidation in a task that would advance the cause of national and ultimately imperial identity: war. It has been all too easy for literary critics of British Romanticism to forget this fundamental fact of life under George III. But for twenty-two years, from 1793 to 1815, and with only a couple of brief respites, Britain waged war against France. Given the historical significance of the French Revolution, it may be tempting to acquiesce in Harold Bloom's oddly elegiac belief that "the most important political event in early-nineteenth-century England was one that failed to take place: the repetition among London-ers of the revolution carried through by Parisians" (*Company* xiii). Instead of revolution we get Romantic poetry, which according to Bloom is the next best thing. Consoling conclusions, but while they affirm the importance of revolution to some (and by no means all) of the period's writers, they evade the material conditions that made radical writing so tremendous an act of re-sistance.[7] War was not just in the air. It was in the blood of patriotic Britons. If medicine normalizes the proper body, militarism nationalizes it, turning healthy bodies British through a steady diet of war with France. The ques-tion to put to Byron's poetry, then, is not how it reimagines revolution but how it makes resistance imaginable by troubling the forces of reaction.[8]

Byron was five when war erupted, twenty-seven when it ceased. His youth and early manhood witnessed the creation and mobilization of a corporate British fighting force to combat the enemy across the Channel. For its im-petus and its scale this undertaking was something new to the history of warfare. It made claims on civilian bodies as never before, subjecting them to new disciplines, privations, and norms, embodying in the process a new kind of human, the patriotic Briton. This incorporation of national and im-perial identity was the war's greatest victory, the carnal counterpart to the ideological triumph of constitutional monarchy. So while it is important to see in England's wars against republican and consular France the first his-torical instance of ideological rather than religious or territorial combat, it is equally important to remain alert to their corporeal effects. As Clive Emsley observes, "Nationalism became a motivating force behind the armies. . . . Peoples, rather than the mercenary armies of absolutist monarchs, marched to fight each other" (3). Bred by war to serve king, nation, and empire, Britons as a people come to incorporate a norm of embodiment as national as it was apparently natural. What medicine begins militarism vastly extends.

The forces that produce the patriotic Briton are manifold, but the collec-tive corporeal effects of militarism are easy enough to see. They can be encap-sulated in a single word: mobilization. War with France mobilized the British as a people, organizing their movements, concentrating their energies. This was not an effect confined to the military, although Britain's army and navy provided a model and even a means for civilian mobilization through their vastly increased size over the course of hostilities.[9] The year before war was declared, 1792, the British army numbered 45,000 (two thirds posted abroad), the British navy 16,000 (Emsley 11). By 1809 the army had increased to 300,000 regulars and the navy to 130,000 seamen and marines (Emsley 133).

Bodies were procured for service through the payment of bounties, balloting, or the navy's notorious press-gangs. Gentlemen could raise a regiment and thus acquire a command as natural born leaders of local patriots. One such, Henry William Paget, future Earl of Uxbridge, First Marquis of Anglesey, and hero of Waterloo (of whom more later), formed the battalion that became known as "the Staffordshire Volunteers," or the 80th Regiment of Foot. Paget's rank: lieutenant colonel. He drew his men primarily from the volunteers in his father's Staffordshire militia, but was particular about the bearing of his ensigns, stipulating that they be over five foot six, under thirty years old, "with a good countenance, straight, and wellmade. Each man to be carefully examined by a surgeon before he is attested'" (Anglesey 41). Obviously military service standardizes embodiment; the very word "embodied" means, militarily, the appointment of a unit of troops to active service. But Anglesey's preferences are important for what they reveal about the materiality of command. Leadership requires closer bodily conformity than regular soldiering, and its physical legitimacy is medically endorsed. Medicine and militarism join forces to embody British leadership.

But the physical appearance of soldiers is less important to the task of mobilization than coordinating their energies and actions. Foucault speaks with special clarity to this aspect of military preparation. A shift in eighteenth-century military practice away from the mass concentration of force to its tactical deployment through coordinated movements illustrates for him a mutation in the operation of power, its deployment through concrete techniques rather than general declarations.[10] The effect on the body is to manage it through the concentration and articulation of its forces in specific practices that assimilate its movements to those of other bodies. It takes forty distinct acts, for instance, to fire a muzzle-loading rifle. To shape a ragged band of provincial volunteers into steady, steely lines of mobile infantry requires the coordination of these acts in a series of techniques that maximizes their efficiency, accuracy, and destructiveness. Such techniques embody a union of energies, and such union of energies embodies a national identity. In its military deployment the body becomes the new natural thing that Foucault describes as "the bearer of forces and the seat of duration . . . susceptible to specified operations, which have their order, their stages, their internal conditions, their constituent elements. In becoming the target for new mechanisms of power, the body is offered up to new forms of knowledge" (*Discipline* 155). The pervasive militarism of life in the last decade of the eighteenth century materially embodies the patriotic Briton through the practice of a soldier's discipline.

The bodily effects of war do not remain confined to the battlefield. Foucault suggests that the population at home as much as the enemy abroad became in the eighteenth century the object of an army's operations. "Politics," he says, "sought to implement the mechanism of the perfect army, of the disciplined mass, of the docile, useful troop, of the regiment in the camp and in the field, on maneuvers and on exercises" (168). During the wars with France, the political implementation of military practices in Britain was hardly an accident. On the contrary, as the threat of invasion mounted it became state policy. Civil defense forces at the outset of hostilities were completely inadequate to that prospect, numbering less than 32,000 militia. That number was increased to about 65,000 by the Supplementary Militia Act of 1796, but the idea was not to arm the population so much as create within it a force of volunteer artisans and professionals overseen by an officer elite. As the war dragged on, however, and invasion forces gathered on the French coast first in 1797 and more frighteningly in 1803, it became clear that much more would be required. Britons must arm en masse, a conclusion the British government viewed with some trepidation. Colley describes the situation nicely: "Mobilizing these civilians presented an enormous challenge to the nerve and ingenuity of those in power. . . . In the face of economic distress, social upheaval and the lures of French Revolutionary doctrines, a major effort had to be made for almost a quarter of a century to encourage large numbers of men from a wide range of social backgrounds to take up arms in support of the British state" (*Britons* 287).

Britain needed a civil defense force and needed it fast. The first move was to find it, which led Parliament in 1800 to order the first census of Great Britain, justified by the belief that "in every war, especially in a defensive war, it must be of the highest importance to enroll and discipline the greatest possible number of men" (quoted in Colley 289). The strategy of numbering all citizens accompanied the more pointed tactic of identifying, by name and parish, able-bodied men. The Defense of the Realm Act of April 1798 required counties to interrogate all men between the ages of fifteen and sixty, determining their willingness to serve, the kind of service they could render, and the varieties of weapons they possessed. When repeated in 1803, the interrogation applied to men between the ages of seventeen and fifty-five. The results were an anatomy of popular patriotism that augured well for the mobilization of the public. While by no means each and every able-bodied Englishman was willing to take up arms for his country, and while patriotism varied from place to place, falling especially low where the importance of agriculture was especially high, the prospect of imminent invasion brought out the Briton in many, many men.

When the call came for volunteers (with the added threat of conscription if numbers flagged), the popular response was impressive. In early 1804 the size of the militia had risen to 176,000 while another 482,000 men had sworn readiness to repel an invasion with force. Many of the latter were drilling weekly in local volunteer regiments complete with state-issued firearms. The tradition of genteel civil defense gave way to the creation of a nation-at-arms that drew its members from the lower orders as much as the middling and elite. So pervasive and formative was the volunteer experience that it leads

Colley to conclude that "In Great Britain . . . it was training in arms under the auspices of the state that was the most common collective working-class experience in the late eighteenth and early nineteenth centuries, not labour in a factory, or membership of a radical political organization or an illegal trade union" (312). The embodiment of British national identity in popular military preparedness: it is in this sense that the army provides a practical model for citizenship. The mobilization of the British populace to repulse an impending French invasion turns state politics into a cold war waged internally against resistances to patriotism. The cultural production of the patriotic Briton illustrates with rare clarity what Foucault calls "the meticulous military and political tactics by which the control of bodies and individual forces was exercised within states" (168).

If the patriotic Briton, able-bodied and well-drilled, nationalized the proper body, the French enemy deviated from that norm physically as well as ideologically. John Bull was fleshy, robust, and virile, a meat-eating man-at-arms ready to die for his parliamentarially approved king. His French counterpart was lean, dry, and fey, a frog-eating fop pressed into service to promote tyranny. Physical differences incarnate national differences, legitimating combat in flesh and blood. What was true of medicine, that deviation from the proper norm reinforces its legitimacy, is true of militarism too, with this difference: where medicine assimilates the pathological to a norm, militarism eradicates it altogether. Krauts, nips, gooks, Charley: one objective of war is to destroy the enemy's deviant flesh. Their injury and extirpation is no mere collateral damage, the regrettable human cost of ideological victory, but the embodiment of that victory—in the enemy's evisceration. Elaine Scarry puts the point with force: war's "winning issue or ideology achieves for a time the force and status of material 'fact' by the sheer material weight of the multitudes of damaged and opened human bodies" (62). The triumph of British patriotism will be written in French flesh. Less subtly than medicine but with greater effect, war eliminates embodied otherness.

But it uses some of the same tactics, particularly at the level of representation. Wartime propaganda articulates with medical practice to promote a national norm of British embodiment. After his rise to power Napoleon became a convenient object of physical derision; his small stature, his classic profile, and even his vulgar nickname among the British, "Boney," define deviation from the national norm. Gillray's famous cartoons of "Little Boney" waving, perilously for him if no one else, a laughably huge saber put a comic twist on this figure of embodied otherness. But when invasion loomed likely, Napoleon's physical difference came to incarnate monstrosity. Handbills from 1803 and later consistently call him a monster, the Corsican monster, the monster of inhumanity. Military atrocities and imperial ambitions gave such names popular credibility, which Napoleon's bodily difference from the British norm only reinforced. By associating Napoleon with monstrosity, wartime

propaganda incarnates the menace of consular France in a manner that chimes
with the diagnostic conventions of the best medicine. For monstrosities are deviations that demonstrate the healthiness, even humanness, of a natural and
now national norm of embodiment. Hence the physical as well as ideological
force of diagnoses from wartime handbills such as the following:

> CAUTION TO JOHN BULL: The government of France is a monster that threatens
> the dissolution of its own and all other countries.

Or this one:

> BUONAPARTE'S CONFESSION OF THE MASSACRE OF JAFFA: But the consideration is, what
> a barbarian you have to fight!!! His word is nothing. He has no emotions. He is
> not a man, but a monster. . . . See with what indifference he tells of bloodshed!

Or another:

> BRITONS AWAKE. This relentless Tyrannt, this insatiable Monster of cruelty and
> ambition, this eternal enemy to the repose and happiness of all mankind, no lon-
> ger conceals his long buried . . . designs of annihilating this truly happy country.

Or finally, this "patriotic prayer":

> Monster! by heaven's mysterious will
> Perchance one fatal glory waits thee still:
> That gives thy crimes a brighter destiny!
> To fall on England's shore! By British hands to die!
> (*Biography V,* British Library)

These descriptions of Napoleon are typically by harum-scarum, but their invo-
cation of monstrosity gives them material force. The "Corsican Monster" is no
Halloween bugaboo; he and his legions menace the bodies of British patriots,
as another handbill demonstrates with a body count of civilians he's mown
down: 1,500 in Toulon, 6,000 in Paris, 1,000 in Lugo, 800 in Benasco, 3,800
in Jaffa (including 580 of his own soldiers), and 1,500 in Damnhour. This
monster is a menace to humanity, a deviation from all natural and national
norms.[11] The medical practices that substantiate such conclusions may not
be directly apparent in those handbills, but they reinforce the pervasive cultural conviction that France, incarnate in the monster Napoleon, disfigures
the health and wholeness of a Great Britain embodied in its patriotic civilian
population. In such cases war, or so the diagnosis goes, is the best and only
medicine.

If war eradicates monstrosities, and if Napoleon provides a ready instance, it might be well to reevaluate Byron's well-known identification with
Little Boney. It may not arise simply out of a sense of shared fate, although
Byron openly invites that conclusion. Given a cultural economy of proper
embodiment that codes deformity as monstrosity and codes monstrosity as

a national menace, Byron's radicalism and Napoleonic identifications are as much practices of flesh as habits of personality. Simon Bainbridge has recently gone far in addressing such questions historically, examining Byron's affinity for Napoleon in light of contemporary representations of his career.[12] But Byron's deformity inserts him in a very particular way into that economy, assimilating him to its deviations, monstrosities of form and force. Monster extraordinaire, Napoleon embodied the beyond of British patriotism. Byron stood beyond that pale too, on a prosthetic boot that complicates the embodiment of national identity.

"WERE YOU AT WATERLOO? . . . "

Waterloo was Napoleon's, well, Waterloo—the name has become synonymous with magnificent defeat. But Waterloo had a victor too—not Wellington's army so much as a patriotic nation mobilized by war. Great Britain emerged from twenty-two years of fighting France with an enhanced national identity and an increased imperial reach. And with the defeat of Little Boney came the triumph of nobility. Monarchy regained its throne throughout Europe and in England the gentry, landed or otherwise, reasserted its traditional right to rule. Colley sums up the social situation with morbid brevity: "Waterloo made the world safe for gentlemen again" (191). Not all gentlemen were pleased by such prospects, however. Byron for one saw only defeat in Waterloo: for Napoleon, for republicanism, for the promise of reform in Britain. His famous description in canto 3 of *Childe Harold's Pilgrimage* of that sacred field of British honor caused consternation among even his admirers for its complete refusal of the popular mood of eulogy, a mood Wordsworth and Southey had no trouble indulging.[13] Waterloo for Byron was a reactionary shambles, its heroic battle an imperial butchery. Blood, it turns out, is as good a fertilizer for crowns as for corn:

> How that red rain hath made the harvest grow!
> And is that all the world has gained by thee,
> Thou first and last of fields! king-making Victory? (*Works* 3: 82)

War in general and Waterloo in particular fulfill the embodiment of the patriotic Briton in slaughter. Byron measures patriotism with corpses and finds national identity terminal, as when he contrasts the duchess of Richmond's delicious festivities with their martial fruits a few days later:

> The earth is covered thick with other clay,
> Which her own clay shall cover, heaped and pent,
> Rider and horse,—friend, foe,—in one red burial blent!
> (*Works* 3:86)

Viewed not as the nation-at-arms but as bodies in combat, a mobilized people is a gathering of cadavers, its politics a meritocracy of blood. So much for the body of the patriot. National identity spells death.

Or worse. The body count at Waterloo was spectacular: 25,000 dead among the French, 17,700 among the British and their mercenary allies. The dead at least were at peace. The wounded remained splayed and groaning on the battlefield, some for upward of ten days. Among the British alone they numbered 9,528, and their suffering was beyond description (Cantlie 1: 391). Wellington's force, in the words of one history of military medicine, was "without any meaningful medical support at all" (Gabriel and Metz 2: 167). Of the 40 battalions that saw action (600 men each), only 22 had full medical support—one surgeon and two assistants. That gave 273 medics to attend the whole army, and a third of those had no formal medical training or combat experience. Because the swift deployment of Wellington's men left medical transports far in the rear, the wounded had to find their own way back to treatment, often in the arms of comrades. Even then attention was slow and recovery uncertain; by the end of June 5,000 men still languished in Belgian hospitals. "From any perspective," says the same account, "Waterloo was a military medical disaster of enormous proportions" (167). From the perspective of the wounded it was worse than hell, as the diary entry of a passing tourist suggests: "Coming from Waterloo passed forty waggons of wounded crying out. The men had been in cottages and not able to be removed before. Many died instantaneously, others were in a putrid state—a kind of living death" (quoted in Cantlie 1: 390).

On hearing of victory, British surgeons rushed across the Channel to the battlefield. Sir Charles Bell, the anatomist-aesthetician, arrived in early July, his enthusiasm for treating the wounded summed up in a letter to his friend and fellow surgeon John Thomson: "Johnny, how can we let this pass? Here is such an occasion of seeing gun shot wounds come to our very door. Let us go" (Cawthorne n.p.). Thomson accompanied Bell to the Continent, flashing operating instruments in place of a passport on landing and recording the whole experience in his clinically dispassionate *Report of Observations made in the British Military Hospitals in Belgium, after the Battle of Waterloo* (1816). An anthology of injuries, neatly categorized and classified, Thomson's report anatomizes British patriotism by way of the wounds of war. It reads like a catalog of available carnage, the direct marketing material of some gruesome wholesaler. Thomson identifies and describes different kinds of wounds (incised, punctured, contused/lacerated, and gunshot) and their bodily locations (head, face, neck, chest, belly, and extremities). He gives instances of each, rendering with clinical precision the disruption of flesh, the destruction of bone, the onset of post-traumatic infection. In discussing wounds of the thigh, for instance, he provides the following valuable information: "Several cases were to be seen in which large portions of the buttocks and of the thighs had been removed by cannon-ball. These wounds had at first a gangrenous look, and passed afterwards into a state in which they shewed but little disposition to heal" (125). Ouch. Cannonshot, grapeshot, gunshot, saber, bayonet: all put a dent in the armor of British embodiment. The wounds of Waterloo horrifically damaged and deformed the bodies of its veterans, as the series of macabre paintings that Bell made on the spot attests (Figure 30). Thomson's report doesn't simply record instances of injury, it legitimates them, becoming a kind of index of honorific national deformity. It produces a standard by which wounds and resulting deformities reinforce the norm of the proper body and the national identity it incarnates.

What is war but a wound machine? Waterloo, with its profligate carnage and ineffectual medicine, proves a painfully obvious instance of the way that machine works. If eradicating the deviant flesh of the enemy is one of war's objectives, damaging the body of the patriot is another. With the advent of ideological motivation and civilian mobilization, war between Britain and France becomes a contest of embodied nationhood in which even casualties are a weapon. The point of such warfare is as much to wound allies as to destroy enemies, the more of both the better. The strategic aim, in other words, of an army like Wellington's is not only to inflict injury, but *to be injured*. Louis Simpson's World War II description of life at the front is apt here too: "'Being shelled is the main work of the infantry soldier. Everyone has his own way of going about it'" (quoted in Scarry 81). The red coats, the long lines,

Figure 30. Soldier wounded at Waterloo, painted by Sir Charles Bell (11 August 1815). The Wellcome Library, London.

the steadfast nerve under fire: these are the active means of being shelled—acquiring wounds—under Wellington's command. Unfit for further service, the wounded were discarded on the battlefield, abandoned to the mysteries of regimental medicine.

But their wounds assured their importance to the cultural projects of nation and empire. The wounds of war become sites of national incarnation, apertures of flesh that graft the nation. Through the injury, the disfigurement, the scar, the treatment, the rehabilitation, the restitution, even the possible prosthesis, Britain comes again to be embodied, now in a deformity whose very abnormality reinforces national identity. Understood from this perspective, war with France serves the British body politic as a kind of ritual mutilation, the subjection of flesh (overwhelmingly of course that of the common laborer) to specific injury in order to produce national identity. Such identity arises not from a conscious sense of commonalty but from bodily mutilation, the wounds of war, inflicted first on the soldier's body, then transferred symbolically to the bodies of patriotic Britons through a semiotics of military service and sacrifice. In just this sense, Scarry describes the remarkable "literalness with which the human body opens itself and allows 'the nation' to be registered there in the wound" (112). A battle scar becomes a badge of belonging that incorporates the nation and testifies everywhere that "existence as a political being entails (not simply disembodied beliefs, thoughts, ideas but also) actual physical self-alteration" (112). Patriotism thrives by the wounds it inflicts and the mutilations it requires. Who in Britain were the most British of all? Those wounded at Waterloo, the first battle to be commemorated with its own badge of honor. "I have been at Waterloo. / 'Tis no matter what you do, / If you've been at Waterloo" (quoted in Emsley 171).

PRIMARY AMPUTATION

Byron understands that modern warfare produces bodies as it destroys them. Writing in *Don Juan* of the siege of Ismail, he affirms these productive effects:

> Here War forgot his own destructive Art
> In more destroying Nature; and the heat
> Of Carnage, like the Nile's sun-sodden Slime,
> Engendered monstrous shapes of every Crime. (*Works* 5: 390)

Waterloo produced such monsters too, often at the regimental surgeon's behest. Lacerations were stitched, fractures set, punctures probed, and shivered limbs sawn away. The art of military surgery created legions of monstrosities. Deformities of war are of a different sort than deformities of birth, however. They incarnate martial ideals that readily reinforce a national norm of embodiment. If Waterloo made a particular contribution to the advancement of medical knowledge, it was in the area of amputation. The sudden bounty of handy specimens proved to British surgeons what the French had long maintained: that if damaged limbs were to be amputated, sooner was better than later.

The clinical phrase was "primary amputation," and it meant getting the limb off before rather than after the onset of inflammation and fever. Thomson notes that nearly 500 amputations were performed on soldiers serving at Waterloo; later figures indicate that nearly half of them survived, an impressive number in an age before antibiotics (Cantlie 1: 392). Thomson also confirms the importance of primary amputation: "It has been generally admitted by military surgeons, that immediate amputation is required in almost all the injuries of the extremities occasioned by cannon-shot, and in many of those inflicted by musket-bullets" (232–33). He then lists six circumstances that unequivocally require amputation, including, quite reasonably, cases "where a limb has been shot off" (232). Military surgeons were flesh tailors, custom-cutting the patriotic body to preserve its health if not wholeness.

At Waterloo the demands on them were extreme. Bell operated for twelve hours a day, discovering that "'all the decencies of performing surgical operations were soon neglected; while I amputated one man's thigh there lay at one time thirteen all beseeching to be taken next. It was strange to feel my clothes stiff with blood and my arms powerless with the exertion of using my knife'" (Cantlie 1: 391). Bell's description shows that military surgery is a continuation of war, not its melioration, waged to preserve the life of the patriot's body but also to *create* wounds that embody the nation. This objective appears most openly in the behavior of one of Wellington's soldiers who was severely wounded at Obidos in 1808: "the patient was seated on a table, holding up the stump of his leg with both hands, and singing 'God save the King' in a lusty voice" (Brett-James 263). A grisly accompaniment to the hymn of crown and country, that stump incarnates a patriotism made possible by primary amputation.

This inhabitation of the flesh becomes complete with the addition of a prosthesis. Primary amputation prepares the body to receive the support it needs to return to normal life. While amputees were not always issued prosthetic limbs on discharge from service, amputations came to be performed with that end in mind. G. J. Guthrie, the expert field surgeon who accompanied Wellington on all his campaigns, argues for the importance of such considerations in *A Treatise on Gun-Shot Wounds, on Injuries of Nerves, and on Wounds of the Extremities Requiring the Different Operations of Amputation*, first published in 1815, then again in 1820 with added insights gleaned from the field at Waterloo. Guthrie deplores the insensitivity of most surgeons to the quality of their patients' peacetime lives. Of the two common methods of amputation, the flap and the circular incision, the former, which left a longer stump below the knee, was the commoner practice. But its effects on the amputee were troublesome because it required a prosthesis that limited mobility, fitting at the knee and exposing the stump:

> In the army . . . the soldier is discharged, with a common wooden leg, on which the stump is stretched out behind; and his circumstances in life seldom afterwards permit use of the knee. Here the good intentions of the surgeon are not only completely frustrated, but they prove prejudicial; for the length of stump behind is always inconvenient, and often gives rise to accidents, attended with much pain and distress. (389–90)

Guthrie prefers amputation by circular incision because it prepares the body for better support and ultimately greater happiness. The operation "is performed in the thick part of the leg; and the bone is usually sawed through about four inches from the patella, that, when the stump is healed, there may be sufficient length of bone left, to support with steadiness the weight of the body; and greater facility may be given to the motion of the leg" (391). The issue here is not merely the amount of weight that either kind of stump can comfortably bear, but the quality of mobility that becomes available through its articulation with prosthesis (Figure 31). By advocating a change in operations Guthrie is advocating a change in prostheses and therefore a change in the way the identity of the veteran comes to be embodied and symbolized. Is he to be an accident-prone shuffler or a sturdy patriot with a firm stance and a capable gait? A snug fit between stump and socket produces able, patriotic bodies.

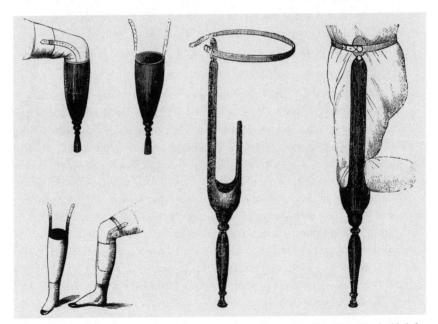

Figure 31. Prosthetic legs, early nineteenth century. Henry Heather Bigg, *On Artificial Limbs: Their Construction and Application* (1855). The Wellcome Library, London.

Lisa Herschback is absolutely right, then, to see that "the artificial limb was more than an object: it formed part of a system of intelligibility. In order to know what functions a leg would fulfill for the man, one had to know what functions the man would fulfill for the social body" (46). Herschback's subject is the American Civil War and its industrial production of both amputees and prostheses. The disabled veterans of Britain's foreign wars embody less an ideology of work and individual advancement, however, than patriotism pure and simple. They are Britons, and their prostheses prove it. Artificial replacements for limbs lost in the crown's service make the body's inhabitation by the nation permanent, substantiating rather than subverting an essentially British subjectivity.[14] The occasion prostheses otherwise might provide for opening the body toward otherness is contained by the role artificial limbs come to play in the cultural project of patriotic embodiment.

A pathetic instance of this effect appears in a letter published in the *Caledonian Mercury* about the time Britain and France were moving toward hostilities. The author is James Craigie, a member of the Royal Artillery, who saw action near Quebec:

> a cannon 18 pound shot from the rebel came and carried away both my hands; the right hand about an inch and an half below my elbow, and the left one about six inches and an half below the elbow.
>
> Thus I was rendered useless to my King, my country, and myself; but I gratefully acknowledge, that the Hon. Board of Ordnance has made provision for me; but alas! they could not make me useful to myself.
>
> Very lately, I heard of one Mr. Gavin Wilson in the Canon gate. I applied to him, and he has made me two jointed hands of leather, with which, besides writing these few lines to you, I can do a great many very useful things. (Lysons 2: 2, 154R)

Gavin Wilson was a bootmaker of some repute who pioneered the use of leather for prosthetic limbs.[15] He published Craigie's testimonial as part of an advertisement—the rest in rhyme—for his many clever wares, including "*Powder Flasks,* and *Porter Mugs,* / and Jointed *Leather Arms* and *Legs*." But the point to notice is that Craigie's sense of identity and self-worth comes through feeling useful to king and country as well as himself. Without the use of his arms he is incomplete—literally but symbolically too. Wilson's prostheses hand back his identity, restoring his usefulness as patriot and citizen. Materially and symbolically, artificial limbs revive and complete the body of the Briton mutilated in his Majesty's service. To use a prosthesis is to be useful once again to the projects of nation and empire.

And therefore to be used *by* them as well. Disabled veterans became carriers of embodied codes whose cultural function was to replicate patriotism. Discharge from military service on account of injury required a surgeon's evaluation, an official act that established the legitimacy of wounds received in battle. On the reverse of a veteran's discharge paper was printed the following N.B.: "When a Soldier has lost an Eye or Limb, or has been wounded or disabled in Service, the Discharge must particularly express the cause from whence proceeding, as when, where, and how it took place. Should any Mark remain in consequence, it is to be noticed in the Man's Description; the Surgeon, or Assistant Surgeon in his Absence, will sign his Name in the Margin." Medically sanctioned, the wounds of war transferred the patriotic body from military to civilian ranks. For the officer, that meant half-pay, plus a year's extra salary for a lost eye or limb. For the common soldier, it meant a paltry pension determined by degree of injury, length of service, and personal character.[16]

These determinations were made by the board of commissioners of Chelsea Hospital, where qualifying pensioners could live out their lives at the crown's expense. Chelsea's examination day ledgers read like the production reports of some grim factory of human disassemblage: "Increase Black, Laborer, Amputated left thigh at Waterloo; Charles Mason, Knitter, Wounded thighs, neck, left foot, breast at Waterloo; James McCabe, Laborer, Amputated right thigh at Waterloo; James Wright, Laborer, Lost his left leg below the knee at Waterloo" (*Chelsea Registers,* Oct.–Nov. 1815). All these disabled veterans (and the ledgers contain hundreds of names) return to a Britain largely unified by war with France. Their wounds, duly noted and remunerated, reinforce in their very deformity a national norm of proper embodiment. This is not to say that resistance to such a norm became unthinkable or that veterans never had such thoughts, only that a pervasive cultural project of embodiment put wounds to work as sites and symbols of nation and empire.

Prostheses advanced that project by literally materializing what was sacrificed for king and country, replacing living limb with an artifice that signified and solidified national identity. Consider in this regard the familiar iconographical tradition of representing the military pensioner with a peg leg, illustrated here by a print that shows army and navy vets swapping tales (Figure 32). Each has lost a limb, one wears a prosthesis, and the bodies of both memorialize military valor. Their wounds encode as they incorporate what it means to be a Briton. That this meaning has large cultural significance is the point of the print's subtitle: these maimed pensioners are living histories that circulate with the king's imprimatur to commemorate Great Britain. It is not simply that these bodies have been inscribed by ideologies of war that ultimately remain separate from them; rather they incarnate such codes and move according to their authority. The bodies of wounded veterans incorporate the nation, and where prostheses intervene they reiterate the Briton.

Figure 32. R. Dighton, *Descriptions of Battles by Sea and Land* (1801). The Wellcome
Library, London.

IMPERIAL LEGS

The most famous prosthesis in British history belonged to the First Marquess of Anglesey, William Henry Paget, veteran cavalry officer of the Peninsular war and hero of Waterloo. He lost his leg there to grapeshot, bearing
the wound with a nobleman's grace. He was atop his charger, consulting
Wellington after merciless hours of directing and rallying his ranks, when
shot smashed his right knee, splintering the joint. "By God, sir, I've lost my
leg!,'" is his laconic response, which on hearing, or so the story goes, Welling-

ton "momentarily removes the telescope from his eye, considers the mangled limb, says 'By God, sir, so you have!' and resumes his scrutiny of the victorious field" (Anglesey 149). Pip, pip, old boy. The noble Anglesey had been born to lead, and loss of limb was a matter of course. "The most perfect Hero that ever breathed" was removed from the battlefield to Brussels, where surgeons expeditiously amputated his leg (Capt. Horace Seymore, quoted in Anglesey 151). In the painting by C. F. Coene of an apocryphal visit of Wellington to Anglesey after the operation, the stump radiates a strange light, as if the stigma of some new power that now inhabits the bandaged flesh. The meeting between these heirs if not to the kingdom at least to the government of Great Britain prognosticates the postwar power of the gentry. Coene's painting illustrates handily the almost sacred role war wounds play in the embodiment of British national and imperial identity.

Anglesey returned to England *sans jambe*. The remains of his shattered limb were, with his approval, buried in a little wooden coffin in the garden of the house where the amputation took place. Apparently the shrine became a "lucrative source of revenue" (Timbs 182) to the owner, who erected a plaque in florid French commemorating "l'illustre et vaillant Comte Uxbridge, / . . . / qui, par son heroisme, a concouru au / triomphe de la cause du genre human" (Anglesey 150–51). Beneath the inscription someone scribbled in English a less elegant riposte: "Here lies the Marquis of Anglesey's limb; / The devil will have the rest of him" (Timbs 182). The devil had to wait, however, since Lord Paget stepped into a life of public service, one foot in Great Britain and the other forever planted on the Continent. On his return to London the prince regent declared "that he *loved* him . . . that he was his best officer and his best subject," and then made him a marquess. Anglesey became active in the House of Lords, was Lord High Steward at the coronation of George IV, served as Master-General of the Ordnance, and rose eventually to the post of Lord Lieutenant of Ireland. His career provides a perfect example of the way war with France and the battle of Waterloo in particular embodied the British patriot and then concentrated authority in the hands—and in some instance legs—of a ruling elite. As Colley sees it, Waterloo "could be cited as ultimate confirmation that those who dominated Great Britain owed their position to genuine distinction and devotion to duty, not just to birth or property—final proof that they were heroes indeed" (*Britons* 192). Anglesey's heroism, made flesh with the cut of a surgeon's bonesaw, qualified him along with worthies from all reaches of a united kingdom to lay material "claim to be the guardians of a 'national'—in the sense of British—culture." By 1819, as Colley notes, a journalist could observe that "'the manners of the nobility and gentry assimilate over the whole Kingdom'" (193).[17]

Anglesey's prosthesis only substantiated his heroism, nobility, and patriotism. It wasn't your average soldier's peg leg. An artisan named James Potts made a living crafting artificial limbs in Chelsea, where the hospital for pensioners provided him with plenty of work. In 1805 he patented the first wooden leg articulated at the knee, ankle, and toe joints, and in 1816 he made the first of several quite beautiful prostheses for Anglesey (Figure 33). Potts's work was top-notch, and he created a noble leg for a noble patriot. Unlike the familiar peg leg, whose crude artificiality materialized the blunt claims of patriotism on the bodies of commoners, Anglesey's leg was lifelike and elegantly sculpted. It embodied a much more intimate fit between man and nation. And it allowed greater ease of mobility, communicating enough limp to mark the hero, while concealing enough stump to confirm the gentleman. To the embodiment of national identity it adds the distinction of class privilege, a handcrafted prosthesis for a natural born British leader. The relative naturalness of such a leg incorporates social distinction, making Anglesey's wound something more than a common instance of national embodiment. It becomes the ideal that legitimates all those common cases and identifies war's deformities with a patriotic norm. Anglesey's idealized prosthesis assimilates its baser fellows, making his wound the barely visible type of more obvious mutilations. With its suppler joints and smoother movements, it articulates the Briton to wounded flesh, serving to affirm, materially and symbolically, the national culture that a patriot like Anglesey inherits in the wake of Waterloo.

In one of the ironies of cultural history the "Anglesey leg," as it came to be known, served as the model for the industrially produced prostheses fitted to the bodies of so many veterans of the American Civil War. If it is true, as Herschback argues, that the artificial limb in America came to stand for the implicit values of industrial capitalism—precision, uniformity, mechanical production, the transformative force of work—then perhaps it is no surprise that their model is an aristocrat's prosthesis. The cultural and material foundations of capitalist values are those of a British gentry that rose to power through military service. Industrialist social climbers in America and elsewhere put such values to their own profitable ends. The apparent democratization of the Anglesey leg might amount to the gentrification, in a sinister political sense, of the proper body. What seems a step ahead for bodily mobility might be a step behind for bodily freedom.

MUTILATIONS

That at least is how Byron read the cultural triumph of embodied patriotism. To a be Briton after Waterloo was for him a kind of open incarceration, the confinement of physical difference to a single national norm. The wounds of war were not birthmarks of empire but mutilations pure and simple, the self-inflicted carnal costs of imperial aggression. The annals of all tyranny cannot

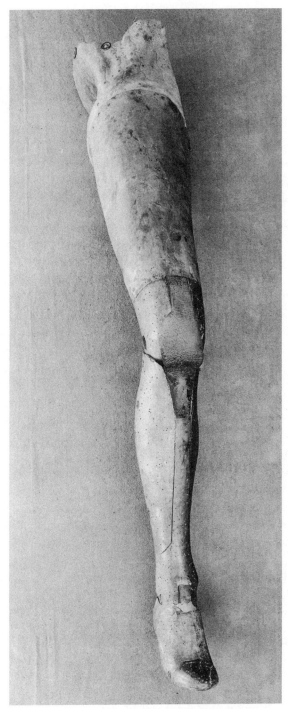

Figure 33. Wooden leg of the First Marquess Anglesey.
National Trust Photographic Library. Copyright The
National Trust.

"produce a reign / More drench'd with gore, more cumber'd with the slain!" than that of George III ("The Vision of Judgment," *Works* 6: 326), a claim Byron advances indirectly with his depiction of the siege of Ismail in cantos 7 and 8 of *Don Juan*. Seen apart from the imperatives of national allegiance, war seems a slaughtering of innocents, "nothing but a child of Murder's rattles" (*Works* 6: 366). As noted earlier, it breeds monsters by the "infinities of agonies" it inflicts, which Byron renders with mordant certainty:

> The groan, the roll in dust, the all-white eye
> Turned back within its socket,—these reward
> Your rank and file by thousands, while the rest
> May win perhaps a ribbon at the breast! (*Works* 6: 369)

The rewards of common soldiery are wounds embodying not the nation but the violence it wields against its people. Patriotism in this view secures tyranny by mutilating and eradicating the bodies of possible resistance. The ruling elite need their wounds too, of course, which is why Byron relates the facts concerning General Markow, who in earshot of "some groaning thousands dying near" showed such "sympathy for rank" that he "had his own leg broken" (6: 368). Such wounds are embodied hypocrisies that disguise domination with disfigurement.

The proper—patriotic—body incarnates a lie. That British culture seems intent on telling it is one of the points of *Don Juan*, summed up in a word of warning for those far from the field of battle: "Think how the joys of reading a Gazette / Are purchased by all agonies and crimes" (6: 403). Byron sees through the ruse of embodied patriotism to the privilege it feeds. The ruling elite consume the wounds of those mutilated in their service. Byron calls them "the hireling tribe / Who fatten on their Country's gore and debts" (6: 411). The body that rules Great Britain is not in fact that of the common patriot but that of a ravenous nobility, typified by a king who gets fat in the midst of famine: "Though Ireland starve, great George weighs twenty stone" (6: 403). Then there's Wellington, who also feeds off the national misfortune. Byron invokes this "best of cutthroats" at the outset of canto 9 to exemplify the carnivorous heroism that now rules. "War's a brain-spattering, windpipe-slitting art," after all, and really whets the appetite. So Byron sets Wellington to the heroic exploit of dinner, while noticing that not all patriots eat at the same table:

> Now go and dine from off the plate
> Presented by the Prince of the Brazils,
> And send the sentinel before your gate
> A slice or two from your luxurious means:
> He fought, but has not fed so well of late.
> Some hunger too they say the people feels . . . (6: 410).

An embodied patriotism leaves the people hungry and serves only to fatten their betters. Such is the force of proper embodiment, however, that it makes oppression bearable. Wounds won in the service of the crown, wooden legs worn for being British: the incorporations of national identity are powerful persuaders of human health and wholeness. Byron may view patriotism as incarceration and declare openly his "plain, sworn, downright detestation / Of every despotism in every nation" (6: 416), but as a nationalized norm the proper body proves too powerful to contest. Long live the embodied Briton— standing tall on imperial legs!

But is patriotism enough? Does it justify or compensate mutilation? That depends. Wounds incorporate identity differently for different classes of people—a social fact that a national norm of embodiment occludes. The experience of the common soldier just doesn't mean as much, culturally speaking, as that of his superiors. So when Thomas Hood, in his whimsical way, depicts the plight of a demobilized and disabled vet, he quietly, cunningly lodges a protest against the more common effects of patriotic embodiment:

> Ben Battle was a soldier bold,
> And used to war's alarms;
> But a cannon-ball took off his legs,
> So he laid down his arms! (81)

The army surgeons make Ben two new limbs, and the crown pays him for his troubles, but the money doesn't last and the legs won't love. Nelly Gray, his former sweetheart, spurns his renewed advances, swearing she'll "never have a man / With both legs in the grave!" (81). Good soldier that he is, Ben Battle asserts the patriotic virtues of duty and personal sacrifice:

> "O, Nelly Gray! O, Nelly Gray!
> For all your jeering speeches,
> At duty's call, I left my legs
> In Badajo's *breaches*!" (82)

But Nelly's no fool. Stumps are stumps and pegs are pegs. However dutifully mutilated, Ben has become too deformed to love.

His prostheses, for all their patriotic force, do not embody otherness in a way that would affirm Ben's life as one that matters. Like the war that necessitates them, they may work to eliminate physical difference, assimilating deformity to a patriotic norm. But when they fail, as in the case of this common soldier, bodies lose their cultural footing and social value. Penniless and loveless, Ben decides on suicide, cinches up a knot, "And, for the second time in life, / Enlisted in the Line" (82). Happily it's an easy task; all he has to do is kick his pegs out from under him. His death completes the ritual mutilation begun on the battlefield, finally eradicating difference in homage to a patriotic norm. Such are the effects of national identity on bodies of the least of Britons.

TRANSFORMATION

Then there's Byron. His prosthetic boot disrupts a patriotic norm of the proper body by neither correcting nor eradicating so much as simply covering deformity. The claims of medicine on his body had little lasting effect, a result Baillie prognosticates in an early letter to Byron's mother: "I found his foot in a much worse state than when I last saw it,—the shoe, entirely wet through and the brace around the ankle quite loose; I much fear his extreme Inattention will counteract every exertion on my part to make him better" (quoted in Eisler 55). As indeed it did. Byron's insouciance toward medical treatment allies him against its disciplinary aims and with the body in its deformity, its material difference, its articulation with prosthesis. In relation to these issues Byron's poetry and politics acquire physical urgency and force. The work that raises them most explicitly, of course, is *The Deformed Transformed* (1824), a play usually read in psychological terms as a dark meditation on the ways of the doppelgänger. But why take such pains to eliminate the obvious: its protagonist begins as a twisted, lame hunchback, physically deformed to the point that even his mother rejects him: "'Out hunchback!' . . . 'I was born so, mother'" (*Works* 7: 519). Psychoanalytically tempting as this beginning might be, the play makes more interesting sense in relation to Byron's therapeutic boots, the bodily drama of prosthesis they materialize, and confrontation with medicine and militarism they provoke.

For in those terms the play becomes a sustained protest against the norm of the proper body and its patriotic force. In thrall to his mother's bidding, Arnold wears his deformity like a set of chains: "I have no Home, no kin, / No kind—not made like other creatures, or / To share their sports or pleasures" (7: 520). The reason, obviously, is his physical difference, what he describes as "Deformity's dull, deadly, / Discouraging weight" (7: 531). It's easy enough to hear Byron behind these lines; they chime with his alleged confession to Lady Blessington: "my poor mother, and after her my schoolfellows, by their taunts, led me to consider lameness as the greatest misfortune, and I have never been able to conquer this feeling" (7: 733). But the sentiments Byron expresses register a problem that is social as well as psychological. When Arnold's mother taunts him she invokes, however inadvertently, contemporary medical evaluations of deformity: "Thou monstrous sport of nature" (7: 519). The phrase may be conventional, but even so registers the normalizing force of medical practice. For the apparent solution to Arnold's deformity is to view it as somehow interchangeable with perfect human health and wholeness. In

the weirdest beauty pageant in literature, Arnold gets to pick a better body
from among an array of ideal types:

> The greatest
> Deformity should only barter with
> The extremest beauty, if the proverb's true
> Of mortals, that extremes meet. (7: 530)

Arnold's choice of a scaled-down Achilles not only redeems deformity by assimilating it to a proper norm, it shows that norm to be ideologically loaded.

The Deformed Transformed exposes the cultural function of the proper
body. Medically and militarily, it advances a project of domination. On acquiring the best of bodies, Arnold turns immediately to warfare. He joins forces
with Charles Bourbon to sack Rome:

> Why!
> Thou art a conqueror; the chosen knight
> And free companion of the gallant Bourbon,
> Late Constable of France: and now to be
> Lord of the city which hath been Earth's lord
> Under its Emperors. (7: 540)

The proper body incarnates domination. Otherness, whether of deformity or
nationality, simply doesn't matter. Byron identifies proper embodiment with
historical tyranny and quietly indicts medicine and militarism as the means
of its operations.

Byron's alternative is twisted. Arnold's transformation occurs with the
help of a Stranger whose identity remains questionable throughout the play.
Perhaps he is the devil, perhaps an even darker spirit, but whatever he is, his
body materially deviates from the proper norm. He appears first out of a mist
as a tall black man, and on transforming Arnold into the shape of Achilles, he
changes *his* shape too—into Arnold's! Where Arnold disdains his monstrosity,
the Stranger accepts, affirms, and even consecrates it playfully: "I'm Caesar
and a hunch-back / Now" (7: 542). The Stranger resists the cultural imperative that compels Arnold to identify himself physically with a norm. Instead
the Stranger exploits the opportunity of his monstrosity to become, not merely
Arnold's constant needling companion, but a physical counterforce to an embodied norm that incarnates dominion.

In this the Stranger affirms the force of prosthesis to make different bodies matter. He is the genius of Byron's boots, the spirit of radical transformation in poetry and politics, cranky cousin of *Don Juan*'s narrator, and the
force of life that exceeds the human. The Stranger puts it best himself when
he responds to Arnold's plea for peace:

And where is that which is so? From the star
To the winding worm, all life is motion; and
In life commotion is the extremest point
Of life. (7: 541)

The force of prosthesis, as opposed to its medical or military function, turns life into a commotion of incommensurable matters: flesh, leather, iron, and earth. It opens toward otherness and transforms deformity, rendering the norm of the proper body an imperious archaism. So much for Achilles, so much for Sheldrake, so much even for Anglesley. But what of Byron, that abject stranger to the norm of the proper, patriotic Britons? Perhaps that question deserves another, asked best by Canguilhem: "To the extent that living beings diverge from the specific type, are they abnormal . . . or are they inventors on the road to new forms?" (141). That clever little dog in Seville knew the answer: Byron invents new forms by living his deformity. In Canguilhem's terms, he turns *normative,* becoming "capable of following new norms of life" (200). By insisting that such differences matter, Byron affirms the transformative life of monstrosities.

NOTES

INTRODUCTION

1. Jerome McGann's *Romantic Ideology* brought such innocence to an end long ago, as the many fine books published since in a historicist mode attest. For a representative sampling, see the Studies in Romanticism series of Cambridge University Press.

2. Mary Poovey provides an account of the process of social formation that gives rise to such a norm in *Making a Social Body*: "The last decades of the eighteenth century witnessed the first modern efforts to represent all—or significant parts—of the population of Britain as aggregates and to delineate a social sphere distinct from the political and economic domains" (8).

3. See Foucault, *Discipline and Punish*. For a very different description of liberal society in the eighteenth century, see Habermas, *The Structural Transformation of the Public Sphere*.

4. Macpherson provides a definitive account of the history and legacy of liberalism.

5. For a related discussion of Smith, see Poovey, *Social Body* 31–35.

6. Seltzer's *Bodies and Machines* provides a helpful account of the ways market culture coordinates bodies and their various meanings.

7. See *The Order of Things* 253–79.

8. See Anderson 5–6. On the emergence of nationalism in the eighteenth century, see also Hobsbawm, Thom, Colley, and Newman. I do not mean to suggest that British culture became totally homogenized at this time, but that a norm circulating with it at least made a common British identity available to very different groups in England, Scotland, and Wales.

9. See Simpson's *Romanticism, Nationalism, and the Revolt Against Theory,* especially chapters 2 and 3.

10. On caricature in the eighteenth century see Atherton, Caretta, and Paston.

11. See Bewell's *Romanticism and Colonial Disease,* chapter 3, for a discussion of this and other Gillray prints concerned with the politics of eating.

12. For an overview of the state of British medicine in the eighteenth century, see King. The work of the Porters, Roy and Dorothy, has refined that history, providing a bottom-up account of available medical treatment. See also in this regard the important contributions of Lawrence, as well as the more focused histories of Bynum, Loudon, Wear, and Cunningham and French. See Bewell's *Romanticism and Colonial Disease* for a discussion of the role colonial medicine plays in British culture of the Romantic period.

13. See Altick's survey of London shows for a discussion of Katterfelto and other renowned quacks, cranks, and curiosities.

14. While the pertinence of Foucault's work to British culture is contestable (as Roy Porter points out, for instance, England never saw the equivalent of a great confinement), its attention to the bodily effects of power provides an important example for cultural critics. Especially helpful in the present context are *The Birth of the Clinic, Discipline and Punish,* and *The History of Sexuality, Volume I.*

15. Derrida makes this gesture often, most famously perhaps at the end of "Structure, Sign, and Play in the Discourse of the Human Sciences" in *Writing and Difference.* For a position closer to my own, see Haraway's "The Promise of Monsters."

1. BUILDING BODIES

1. The Hunterian Museum, housed at the Royal College of Surgeons at 35–43 Lincoln's Inn Fields, London, is open to the public and well worth a visit. For the story of Hunter's resurrection of Byrne to medical fame and fortune, see also Fforde, "The Royal College of Surgeons of England," and Sawday, *The Body Emblazoned* 4–5.

2. Byrne's fear of the anatomists was as much a function of class as physique. Body snatchers, known in the eighteenth century as resurrectionists, did a brisk business, targeting in particular the corpses of the poor, who came to view anatomists and surgeons as purveyors of sacrilege. See Linebaugh, Marshall, Ruth Richardson, and Sawday.

3. On the emergence of capitalism, consumerism, and British national identity in the late eighteenth century, see Colley, Thompson, Barker-Benfield, Davidoff and Hall, and McKendrick et al. The problem of embodiment at that historical moment has begun to receive serious treatment in the work of Stafford, R. Porter ("Bodies"), Hunt, Bruhm, Kelly and von Mücke, Neveldine, and O'Connor. Grosz provides a good introduction to the many cultural and philosophical issues raised by the materialist turn to the body in recent theory and criticism, while Featherstone et al. advance an important sociological perspective, and Halberstam and Livingston offer an overtly postmodern approach. Much of this work can be seen as contributing to the cultural history of the human body inaugurated by the volumes edited by Feher et al. Some of the most interesting work to approach the body as a cultural artifact rather than natural object occurs under the rubric of disability studies, whose foremost theorist, Garland Thompson, can be credited with politicizing for cultural and literary criticism the problem of physical deformity. See in this regard the essays collected by Davis.

4. On the culture of monstrosity prior to the rise of modern medicine, see especially Park and Daston, Dudley Wilson, and Pender (the latter in Cohen, *Monster Theory*). Todd provides an extended account of the strange case of Mary Taft, who allegedly gave birth to monsters that bore an uncanny resemblance to rabbits.

5. For a full account of John Hunter's remarkable rise to distinction, see Kobler, Qvist, Peachey, and Dobson. Everard Home provides a succinct biographical sketch in his introduction to Hunter's *Treatise on Blood.*

6. The best introduction to Hunter's vitalist physiology and its difference from

traditional mechanistic anatomy comes in François Duchesneau's "Vitalism in Late-Eighteenth-Century Physiology." For an even more thorough discussion of the relation between anatomy and physiology in Hunter's work, see Cross. For a historical account of vitalism and Hunter's place in that tradition, see Thomas S. Hall.

7. In this Hunter advances the epistemic shift from representation to organic structure characteristic of late-eighteenth-century knowledge that Foucault documents in *The Order of Things*. See especially 226–32.

8. On the relationship between medicine and monstrosity in the eighteenth century see Dudley Wilson and Gilman (*Sexuality*). On the medicalization of monstrosity see Garland Thomson, Pender, and Park and Daston.

9. Baillie provides visual illustrations of such monstrosities, most strikingly of a hydrocephalic child, in his companion publication, *A Series of Engravings*.

10. On the cultural function of the museum as a site of public—and disciplinary—pedagogy, see Bennett.

11. In this it anticipates the operation of the public museum as Bennett decribes it, allowing visitors "to identify with power, to see it as, if not directly theirs, then indirectly so, a force regulated and channelled by society's ruling groups but for the good of all: this was the rhetoric of power embodied in the exhibitionary complex—a power made manifest not in its ability to inflict pain but by its ability to organize and coordinate an order of things and to produce a place for the people in relation to that order" (67).

12. See Introduction.

13. See especially *Discipline and Punish* 135–69, and Thomson, *Bodies* 38–41.

14. For a discussion of the political register of the term "monstrosity" in Britain at the time of the French Revolution, see Hirsch. For a full assessment of radical print politics in the early decades of the nineteenth century, see Gilmartin.

15. Perhaps this explains T. J. Wooler's title for his radical publication, *The Black Dwarf*, whose 1817 title page sports an image of a small black man and a goat-legged satyr.

2. TROUBLING MEASURES

1. This tradition begins with Coleridge (ever in need of a little healing), becomes institutionalized by Mill and Matthew Arnold, and lives on in humanist critics such as Abrams, Geoffrey Hartman, and Don Bialostosky.

2. For a full account of Whytt's innovations and a discussion of their implications for literature, see Bruhm and De Almeida. G. J. Barker-Benfield and Richardson discuss the cultural effects of eighteenth-century advances in neurophysiology.

3. See *British Romanticism and the Science of the Mind*.

4. On Brown and his unusual approach to neurophysiology, see De Almeida and W. F. Bynum.

5. Eventually Wordsworth cut this passage from the "Preface." So much for miracles of a physical nature.

6. The passage just quoted comes from a long section Wordsworth added in 1802 that goes out of its way to refer the effects of meter to reason, as if to assure that the

"certain laws" that "metre obeys" (phrases from the 1800 "Preface") are grounded in mind and not body. Meter governs poetry's physiological effects, guaranteeing their rationality.

7. For a full account of this full-figured man, see Bondeson 237–60, and for a semiotic assessment of his physical difference, see O'Connor 177–78.

8. The nationalist force of these effects appears even more brazenly in the cartoon titled *Two wonders of the World, or a Specimen of a New Troop of Leicestershire Light Horse* (George #10570), which has the massive Lambert astride a charger bearing down with saber in hand on an appropriately frightened Napoleon (George 8: 437). Lambert in uniform makes a ponderable Briton.

9. See Laqueur's "Bodies, Details, and the Humanitarian Narrative" as well as Gilman's *Difference and Pathology* for a similar discussion in a broader context and O'Connor for a brief discussion of Miss Biffin. To appreciate the kind of cultural work deviant flesh comes to perform in the late eighteenth and early nineteenth centuries, see the six volumes of *The Wonderful and Scientific Museum*.

10. Bartholomew Fair has received a wealth of critical treatment, especially regarding its Renaissance incarnations. The pioneering work of Stallybrass and White is indispensable here, but see also Bristol, Marcus, Mullaney, and Burt. On the Fair's history, Morley (*Memoirs*) is masterly.

11. For additional late-eighteenth- and early-nineteenth-century descriptions of Bartholomew Fair, see Ben Johnson the Younger, *Bartholomew Fair; A Musical Drama,* "Biographical Sketch of Richardson the Showman," and *The Adventures of George and Henry Otley.*

12. Foucault interestingly links museums to fairs as opposite forms of heterotopia, the former based on an endless accumulation of time and the latter on its instantaneous loss. See "Spaces" 26.

13. On the history and implications of the licensing of popular festivals, see Bristol, Burt, and Marcus.

14. See Bennett 17–102. If there is a limitation to Bennett's powerful analysis it is in his commitment to the notion of "governmentality," which leads him to view all transformative social practices as coopted in advance.

15. However surreptitiously, the spirit of the place lives on in the Peace Memorial erected on the former site of Bartholomew Fair. When I visited the small, circular green in the summer of 1999, it was littered with empty cans of Crest Super 10% and a big-bellied man was sleeping off his binge on a bench. Presiding over the scene was the Peace Monument itself, a statue of a woman in a toga, on whose head some wag had placed a blaze-orange traffic cone. Long live the Cockney Carnival!

16. For an account of the fizzled Bartholomew Fair uprising and its political implications, see Worrall's important book.

17. Readings of *Frankenstein* are legion, but few of them take the monster's physical deformity seriously. See Mellor (*Shelley*) for a comprehensive discussion—from a feminist perspective—of *Frankenstein* and science, Levine for a more traditional view, and Marshall for an inventive historical approach. For a psychoanalytic tour de force around the problems of mourning and melancholia, see Rickels 277–303.

18. Of the many important books on the issue of gender and British Romanticism, particularly pertinent to this discussion are Mellor, *Gender* and Poovey, *Proper Lady,*

especially chapter 1. Poovey's notion of the proper lady provides a model, conceived primarily in ideological terms, for the cultural norm of the proper body discussed here.

19. Hirsch argues that Shelley advocates a radical reconstruction of the family in *Frankenstein* in a manner oblivious to the traditional liberal division between public and private spheres.

3. POSSESSING BEAUTY

1. Gilman provides an account of Baartman's role in pathologizing female sexuality in *Difference and Pathology* 76–108. See also Bennett 77–78.

2. Goldberg, Gilroy, and Dyer each provide an important conceptual starting point for thinking about the relationship between race and Enlightenment rationality. For an intellectual history of this tradition, see Hannaford. For selections from some of the originary texts of raciology, see Augstein. For the relationship between race and medicine, see Ernst and Harris. For issues specific to the problem of race during the Romantic period, see Richardson and Hofkosh, and the volumes in Kitson and Lee, *Slavery, Abolition, and Emancipation: Writings in the British Romantic Period*. For the history of the slave trade in England, see Walvin, *Black Ivory*.

3. See Honor for a discussion of the racial—and racist—implications of Camper's "discovery." Goldberg parses the implications of Enlightenment assumptions for the emergence of racial difference in *Racist Culture*.

4. In *The Mismeasure of Man* Stephen Jay Gould shows how the measurements of an ostensibly disinterested science can validate and therefore legitimate cultural assumptions.

5. According to Barry Baldwin, Reynolds's example of the relative beauty of whites and blacks has a pre-Socratic source: Xenophanes of Colophon, who ridicules the relativism of religious custom in similar terms.

6. Richard Wendorf recently published the first extended monograph on Reynolds's portraits. For further discussion of Reynolds, see Barrell's *The Political Theory of Painting*. For a sweeping overview of portraiture as a genre in the eighteenth century, see Marcia Pointon's *Hanging the Head*.

7. Reynolds's young black sitter may have been Francis Barber, Dr. Johnson's beloved servant, or Reynolds's own faithful but nameless black servant, or even Omai. According to David Manning, "There is no firm evidence for any of these but it may be significant that when the picture's first owner, Sir George Beaumont, who knew Reynolds well, lent it to be exhibited at the BI it was catalogued as 'Black servant of Sir Joshua'" (1: 498). I prefer to emphasize the anonymity of Reynolds's subject and therefore the absence, in this portrait of a young black man, of the one thing a portrait is supposed to preserve, a unique identity.

8. Among the many critical texts that examine Blake's visual art, see in particular Bindman, Mitchell, and Viscomi.

9. See Ward, "'Sir Joshua and his Gang': William Blake and the Royal Academy."

10. A speculation, but not an incredible one. I have reversed the image of the face to show it as Blake might have seen it while engraving. When he engraved these plates,

he was working from Stedman's watercolors, but because all but seven have been lost, it is impossible to tell how much liberty Blake took with the original images.

4. BAD HABITS

1. However tempting it may be to describe Coleridge as an opium *addict,* historical accuracy requires other terms: opium eater, laudanum habitué, and so forth. *Addiction* as a physiocultural concept emerged later in the nineteenth century, the effect of a multiplicity of forces, including a rising medical profession, a growing antipathy toward things "oriental," a militant Quaker moralism, the introduction of the syringe. I therefore cannot follow those, like Alina Clej, who simply transpose the concept of addiction backward and apply it anachronistically to Romantic writers. In fact, Coleridge becomes one of the early architects of the concept. On the question of narcotics and addiction in the nineteenth century, see Clej, Leask (*British Romantic Writers*), Milligan, Harding, Parssinen, Musto, Berridge and Edwards, and Ronell, as well as some of the essays in *Beyond the Pleasure Dome,* ed. Vice, Campbell, and Armstrong.

2. Anyone interested in coming to terms with Coleridge in all his complexity should begin with Barfield's *What Coleridge Thought.* A good biography is indispensable too, such as Bate's, or more recently Richard Holmes's magnificent two-volume *Coleridge.*

3. Medical treatment has obviously changed since Coleridge's day. Before the advent of germ theory later in the nineteenth century and the rise of bacteriology as a science, opium was routinely used to treat the symptoms of a wide range of illnesses. Afterward, it came to be viewed as a superfluous, even dangerous, medicament. See Bewell's *Romanticism and Colonial Disease* for a fascinating discussion of Coleridge's opium use in the context of cholera treatment.

4. See *Of Grammatology,* part II, chapter 2.

5. See Sallis, *Crossings,* especially chapter 2. See too Deleuze, *Nietzsche and Philosophy*; Heidegger; and Scott.

6. With the exception of Heidegger, Sallis is the first to read the Dionysian, not in dialectical terms, but as an image for the coming to presence of life that exceeds images.

7. This poem has produced many pages of criticism. See in particular Magnuson, "Kubla Khan"; DePaolo; and Bahti.

8. I in no way mean to diminish the importance of tracing the "intertextuality" of "Kubla Khan," especially the work of Lowes and Shaffer. But the poem's language interrupts and transforms that of its forerunners.

9. As it does in Hegel, Lacan, or De Man, where loss becomes lack and serves as an a priori condition of experience, producing a transcendentalism of the negative.

10. The best readers of Coleridge's "Rime" include Brisman, Ferguson, Williams, Paglia, and Cavell.

11. The regulative gloss that Coleridge added to the "Rime" in 1817 only exaggerates this effect. The definitive treatment of the gloss comes in McGann's "The Meaning of the Mariner."

12. Foucault's reminder is germane here: "The Problem is not changing people's consciousness—or what's in their heads—but the political, economic, institutional re-

gime of the production of truth. . . . The political question, to sum up, is not error, illusion, alienated consciousness, or ideology; it is truth itself" (*Power/Knowledge* 133).

13. On the asylum in the late eighteenth century, see Porter, *Anatomy of Madness, Mind-Forged Manacles,* and *A Social History of Madness.*

5. Crazy Body

1. "Alle Vorurtheile kommen aus den Eingeweiden," (*Ecce Homo* 279). See Kaufmann's translation, 240.

2. De Quincey criticism has been something of a growth industry of late, stimulated by John Barrell's justly renowned psychocultural study, *The Infection of Thomas De Quincey.* To sample the range of recent criticism, see in particular McDonagh; Rzepka, *Sacramental Commodities;* Clej; and Leask, *British Romantic Writers* and "Universal Aesthetic."

3. The world is soon to have an authoritative edition of De Quincey, edited by Lindop. Until it arrives, David Masson's fourteen-volume *Collected Writings* (1896–97) remains the best approximation. I will refer to it except when quoting De Quincey's *Confessions,* for which I cite Aileen Ward's Signet Classics edition.

4. I attribute to De Quincey the implications and effects of his translation—with embellishments—of an essay in German on Kant's final illness by Ehregott Wasianski. De Quincey published his memoir under his own name and thereby claimed as an effect of his authorship the trick of testing critical philosophy against the imperatives of flesh. As will become clear, much of De Quincey's other work chimes with this materialist critique of transcendentalist pretensions. Critics such as Rzepka would attribute De Quincey's memoir entirely to Wasianski. It seems to me a bit late in the day to maintain so innocent a sense of authorship. To paraphrase Heraclitus, nobody (re)produces the same text twice.

5. On Kant's reputation in England generally and De Quincey's part in crafting it, see Wellek, *Immanuel Kant, Confrontations,* and *History,* as well as Ashton.

6. On the status of the body in Kant's third *Critique,* see Krell, *Contagion* 6–15. Kant may have a feeling for pleasure and pain, but his allegiance to the supersensible protects him against the body's "dire forces" (Krell, *Contagion* 7).

7. The one article to examine seriously the implications of eating to the opium eater concludes that De Quincey's strange dietary habits indicate an unusual affliction: male anorexia (Plotz).

8. I thus diverge from Charles Rzepka's insistence that subjectivity displaces the body in De Quincey's work ("Body").

9. For a reading of De Quincey's *Confessions* hostile to these conclusions, see Russett 233–34.

10. In *The Birth of the Clinic,* Michel Foucault describes the modus operandi of medicine, its legitimation of "a generalized medical consciousness, diffused in space and time, open and mobile, linked to each individual existence, as well as to the collective life of the nation, ever alert to the endless domain in which illness betrays, in its various aspects, its great, solid form" (31).

11. Foucault defines this practice in the third volume of his *History of Sexuality* (*Care*). I suggest we view De Quincey's ethic of maintenance as an instance of care for the self rather than as evidence of the deviance of addiction.

6. MOTHER FLESH

1. See Laqueur's *Making Sex* for the full argument. Of related interest are the essays in *The Making of the Modern Body*. Schiebinger's *Nature's Body* and Jordanova's *Sexual Visions* approach the relationship between sex, science, and politics from a feminist perspective.

2. Laqueur and McLaren both attest to the emphasis on female orgasm in traditional theories of conception.

3. For traditional accounts of the history of obstetrics, in which the (masculine) profession arises to manage the suffering of pregnant women, see Shorter and O'Dowd and Phillipp. Accounts that stress the problems of power and gender include those of Moscucci, Murphy-Lawless, Wilson (*Making*), and many of the essays in Bynum and Porter's collection.

4. Adrian Wilson nicely parses the varieties of eighteenth-century midwifery that eventually became consolidated under the specialty of obstetrics in "William Hunter and the Varieties of Man-Midwifery."

5. On the importance of William Hunter to the history of modern obstetrics, see the essays in Bynum and Porter. Details of Hunter's life are available in Peachey, Illingworth, and the memoir written by Samuel Foate Simmons and Hunter's brother John.

6. Henderson and Jordanova ("Gender, Generation, and Science") discuss the implications of Hunter's book for women's bodies and their appropriation by obstetrics in the late eighteenth century.

7. See Moscucci and Murphy-Lawless for the story of the victory of obstetrics over the traditionally female practice of midwifery. The rear-guard action fought by Elizabeth Nihell in her *Treatise in the Art of Midwifery* (1760) makes for invigorating reading, given her vituperative rejection of Smellie's (to her mind) nefarious forceps. Female midwives were still around in the 1790s, but the monied trade preferred man midwives, especially in the cities. Many expert women were relegated to subordinate positions in the lying-in hospitals that were founded to address the needs of poorer women.

8. On Wollstonecraft's feminism see Lorch and Gary Kelly. In describing it I prefer the term "liberal" to "radical," since Wollstonecraft retains fundamental allegiances to the political theory of possessive individualism that MacPherson associates with Locke and his liberal heirs. On the question of gender identity in the late eighteenth century, see Poovey (*Proper Lady*), Barker-Benfield, and Mellor (*Romanticism and Gender*). Mellor's collection of essays (*Romanticism and Feminism*) takes a literary look at feminist issues of the period.

9. On Wollstonecraft's death, see Jones's meticulous discussion as well as Godwin's firsthand account and the description in Tomalin's biography.

10. Jones provides a helpful detailed contrast of regular obstetric practice then and now.

11. See Mellor's *Mary Shelley* for a full discussion of the feminist implications of *Frankenstein*; see also Poovey (*Proper Lady*) and Johnson.

7. IMPERIAL LEGS

1. The material history of prosthetics has not received much attention, partly because, as material, prostheses were summarily discarded after use. Philips's history of Blanchford and Sons, Ltd., artificial limb manufacturers, offers the best introduction to the subject, but see also McGavigan's dissertation on artificial limbs as well as Bigg's Victorian-era assessment of their various forms and functions.

2. For modern medical diagnoses of the possible cause of Byron's lameness, see Kemble and Morrison. Byron's body was exhumed in the early years of the twentieth century, in part to settle the question of his deformity. The skeleton was intact but to the surprise of the examiners one of Byron's feet had been cut off and the bones were resting at the bottom of his coffin. Of the many fine critical studies of Byron, particularly germane to the discussion here are Kelsall, Foot, Christensen, and McGann's *Fiery Dust* and *Don Juan in Context*.

3. In this you could view the prosthesis, à la Derrida, as a material *supplement,* which is the gist of Wills's position. See *Of Grammatology,* part II.

4. For a quick description of the disciplinary character of medicine in the late eighteenth century, see "The Politics of Health in the Eighteenth Century" in *Power / Knowledge*. See *Discipline and Punish* for the full historical argument.

5. Witness in this regard the dedication that prefaces the humble trussmaker's first publication: "In Gratitude / For the Knowledge I Acquired / from the Instructions / of the Greatest Anatomist of his Age, / Who Approved of this Work, / And (had he lived) / would have permitted it to be inscribed to him / The Following Pages / (however unworthy) / are dedicated to the memory of / D. William Hunter, F.R.S. etc. / by the Author."

6. See Foucault's discussion of illegalities and delinquency, *Discipline and Punish* 257–92.

7. This is true even of the critical sort of historicism that made ideology the object of inquiry, as in McGann's important polemic, *The Romantic Ideology*. Thankfully, the historicist turn that book called for has begun to acquire a concrete, even materialist cast. See especially Marilyn Butler, Bainbridge, and Magnuson *(Reading)*. For a general introduction to the problem of Romanticism as a historical category in England, see Day.

8. See Bruhm for a related discussion of the relationship between Byron's deformed foot, pain, and warfare. Examining the martial "vicissitudes of pain" allows Byron to "transform his tyrannically painful body into an agent of freedom" (143).

9. On the social effects of military mobilization in Britain in the late eighteenth and early nineteenth centuries, see Emsley, chapters 2 and 6, and Colley, *Britons* chapter 7, "Manpower."

10. See the chapter "Docile Bodies" in *Discipline and Punish* for Foucault's discussion of the relation between modern soldiery and the circulation of power.

11. Not surprisingly, perhaps, William Hone hilariously parodies the execrations

even the mention of Napoleon gave rise to as late as 1820 in his "Bonapartephobia, or Cursing Made Easy to the Meanest Capacity," a pamphlet "shewing how to nickname and curse Napoleon, to the best advantage, upon all occasions." Here's the learned Dr. Slop holding forth: "No sooner is a piece of successful villainy achieved by the *Monster,* than our print-shop exhibits the *iron countenance* of NAPOLEON THE GREAT!—the *portrait* of that execrable *Villain!* that *bare-faced* Villain! that *daring* Villain! That *perjured* Villain!—that *Disgrace of the Human Species!*—the *Corsican!* . . . This *Monster in a human shape, on his blood-stained throne!* this *abhorred* Monster! this *accursed* Monster!—this Viper of *Corsica!* . . . There is not a street in London, in which at least *ten* individuals would not joyfully pay their *hundred pounds each, to see this Monster* HANGED" (6–7, 8, 9).

12. Although this identification is a literary commonplace, Bainbridge provides a scrupulous historical account of its vicissitudes. See his chapter 4.

13. See Southey's *The Poet's Pilgrimage to Waterloo* and Wordsworth's "Thanksgiving Ode," as well as Bainbridge's discussions of these nationalist eulogies, 160–77.

14. O'Connor describes the prosthetic economy in Victorian culture in more utilitarian than nationalist terms, since the mass-produced prosthetics of the later nineteenth century engineered "a fiction of physical wholeness in the interest of recuperating the laboring male body" (105).

15. According to Philips, Wilson was the first after Ambrose Pare (1509–90) to attempt a prosthetic leg with a knee joint. He fashioned the leg from hardened leather, designing a joint that could be fixed while sitting, flexed while walking. See Philips 30.

16. Hall has compiled a description of the injuries and compensations of all officers who served during the Peninsular campaigns, many of whom saw action at Waterloo too. See his companion to Sir Charles Oman's history of the Peninsular war. Common soldiers were remunerated at a much lower rate than officers for their injuries, fixed primarily by the extent to which they would be able to contribute to earning their own living. The first degree of injury was the worst, as described by the *Regulations of 14 Nor. 1829 for granting pensions to discharged soldiers*: "Men losing *two Limbs* or *both Eyes,* from Wounds, or being so severely wounded as to be *totally incapable* of earning a livelihood & to require the assistance and care of some other person" (6). A sergeant with such wounds could receive three shillings six pence a day, a private as much as two shillings.

17. It should be noted that political reform gains momentum as the nineteenth century proceeds from the increasingly apparent contradiction between the proper bodies of the social elite and the unkempt flesh of the working class.

WORKS CITED

Abrams, M. H. *Natural Supernaturalism: Tradition and Revolution in Romantic Literature*. New York: Norton, 1971.

Altick, Robert. *The Shows of London*. Cambridge: Harvard University Press, 1978.

Anderson, Benedict. *Imagined Communities: Reflections on the Origin and Spread of Nationalism*. London: Verso, 1991.

Anglesey, George Charles Henry Victor Paget. *One-Leg: The Life and Letters of Henry William Paget, First Marquess of Anglesey, K.G., 1768–1854*. London: Jonathan Cape, 1961.

The Annual Register. London, 1758– .

Aristotle. *The Complete Works of Aristotle: The Revised Oxford Translation*. 2 vols. Edited by Jonathan Barnes. Princeton: Princeton University Press, 1984.

Arnold, Thomas. *Observations on the Nature, Kinds, Causes, and Prevention of Insanity*. 2d ed. London, 1806.

Ashton, Rosemary. *The German Idea: Four English Writers and the Reception of German Thought, 1800–1860*. Cambridge: Cambridge University Press, 1980.

Atherton, Herbert M. *Political Prints in the Age of Hogarth: A Study of the Ideographic Representation of Politics*. Oxford: Oxford University Press, 1974.

Augstein, Hannah Franziska. *Race: the Origins of an Idea, 1760–1850*. Bristol: Thoemmes Press, 1996.

Bahti, Timothy. "Coleridge's 'Kubla Khan' and the Fragment of Romanticism." *Modern Language Notes* 96 (1981): 1035–50.

Baillie, Matthew. *The Morbid Anatomy of Some of the Most Important Parts of the Human Body*. 2d. ed. London, 1797.

———. "Of a remarkable deviation from the Natural structure in the Urinary Bladder and Organs of Generation of a Male." *Transactions of a Society for the Improvement of Medical and Chirurgical Knowledge*. London, 1793.

———. *A Series of Engravings Accompanied with Explanations which are Intended to Illustrate the Morbid Anatomy of Some of the Most Important Parts of the Human Body*. London, 1799.

Bainbridge, Simon. *Napoleon and English Romanticism*. Cambridge: Cambridge University Press, 1995.

Bakhtin, Mikhail. *Rabelais and His World*. Translated by Helene Iswolsky. Bloomington: Indiana University Press, 1984.

Baldwin, Barry. "A Classical Source for Reynolds on the Relativity of Beauty." *Notes and Queries* 41 (1994): 208–09.

Barfield, Owen. *What Coleridge Thought.* Middletown: Wesleyan University Press, 1971.

Barker-Benfield, G. J. *The Culture of Sensibility: Sex and Society in Eighteenth-Century Britain.* Chicago: University of Chicago Press, 1992.

Barrell, John. *The Infection of Thomas De Quincey: A Psychopathology of Imperialism.* New Haven: Yale University Press, 1991.

———. *The Political Theory of Painting.* New Haven: Yale University Press, 1996.

Bartholomew Fair: or the Adventures of George and Henry Otley. London, 1810.

Bartholomew Fair; a Musical Drama, as Performed at the Cobourg Theatre. London, 1823.

Bate, Walter Jackson. *Coleridge.* New York: Macmillan, 1968.

Beddoes, Thomas. *Hygiea or Essays Moral and Medical on the Causes Affecting the Personal State of our Middling and Affluent Classes.* 4 vols. Bristol, 1802.

Bell, Sir Charles. *The Anatomy and Philosophy of Expression as Connected with the Fine Arts.* London, 1847.

Bennett, Tony. *The Birth of the Museum: History, Theory, Politics.* London: Routledge, 1995.

Berridge, Virginia, and Griffith Edwards. *Opium and the People: Opiate Use in Nineteenth-Century England.* London: Allen Lane, 1981.

Bérubé, Michael. *Life as We Know It: A Family, a Father, and an Exceptional Child.* New York: Pantheon, 1996.

Bewell, Alan. "An Issue of Monstrous Desire: *Frankenstein* and Obstetrics." *Yale Journal of Criticism* 2, no. 1 (1988): 105–28.

———. *Romanticism and Colonial Disease.* Baltimore: Johns Hopkins University Press, 1999.

Bigg, Henry Heather. *On Artificial Limbs, their Construction and Application.* London, 1855.

Bindman, David. *Blake as an Artist.* Oxford: Oxford University Press, 1978.

"Biographical Sketch of Richardson the Showman." *Bentley's Miscellany* 1 (1837): 182–84.

Biography V. Separate Events 1803. Projected Invasion of England. British Library. 806.k.1.

Blake, William. *The Complete Poetry and Prose of William Blake.* Edited by David V. Erdman. Newly rev. ed. Berkeley: University of California Press, 1982.

Bloom, Harold. *The Visionary Company: A Reading of English Romantic Poetry.* 1961. Ithaca: Cornell University Press, 1971.

Bondeson, Jan. *The Two-Headed Boy, and Other Medical Marvels.* Ithaca: Cornell University Press, 2000.

Brett-James, Antony. *Life in Wellington's Army.* London: Allen & Unwin, 1972.

Brisman, Leslie. "Coleridge and the Supernatural." *Studies in Romanticism* 21 (1982): 123–59.

Bristol, Michael D. *Carnival and Theater: Plebian Culture and the Structure of Authority in Renaissance England.* London: Methuen, 1985.

Brown, John. *Elements of Medicine.* 2 vols. Edited by Thomas Beddoes. London, 1795.

Bruhm, Steven. *Gothic Bodies: The Politics of Pain in Romantic Fiction.* Philadelphia: University of Pennsylvania Press, 1994.

Buchan, William. *Domestic Medicine.* 2d American ed. Philadelphia: Cruikshank, 1774.

Burke, Edmund. "Letter I.—On the Overtures of Peace, 1796." *The Works of Edmund Burke, with a Memoir.* 3 vols. New York: Harper, 1859. II: 214–47.

———. *Reflections on the Revolution in France.* Edited by L. G. Mitchell. Oxford: Oxford University Press, 1993.

Burt, Richard. *Licensed by Authority: Ben Jonson and the Discourses of Censorship.* Ithaca: Cornell University Press, 1993.

Butler, Judith. *Bodies That Matter: On the Discursive Limits of "Sex."* New York: Routledge, 1993.

———. *Gender Trouble: Feminism and the Subversion of Identity.* New York: Routledge, 1990.

Butler, Marilyn. *Romantics, Rebels, and Reactionaries: English Literature and its Background, 1760–1830.* Oxford: Oxford University Press, 1981.

Bynum, W. F. *Science and the Practice of Medicine in the Nineteenth Century.* Cambridge: Cambridge University Press, 1994.

———, and Roy Porter, eds. *William Hunter and the Eighteenth-Century Medical World.* Cambridge: Cambridge University Press, 1985.

Byron, George Gordon, Lord. *Byron's Letters and Journals.* Edited by Leslie A. Marchand. 13 vols. Cambridge: Harvard University Press, 1973–82.

———. *Lord Byron: The Complete Poetical Works.* Edited by Jerome J. McGann. 7 vols. Oxford: Oxford University Press, 1980– .

Camper, Petrus. *The Works of the Late Professor Camper on the Connnexion between the Science of Anatomy and the Arts of Drawing, Painting, Statuary, Etc., Etc.* Translated by T. Cogan. London, 1794.

Canguilhem, Georges. *The Normal and the Pathological.* Translated by Carolyn R. Fawcett and Robert S. Cohen. New York: Zone, 1989.

Cantlie, Sir Neil. *A History of the Army Medical Department.* 2 vols. Edinburgh: Churchill Livingstone, 1974.

Carretta, Vincent. *George III and the Satirists from Hogarth to Byron.* Athens: University of Georgia Press, 1990.

Cavell, Stanley. *In Quest of the Ordinary: Lines of Skepticism and Romanticism.* Chicago: University of Chicago Press, 1988.

Cawthorne, Terence. "Sir Charles Bell." *King's College Hospital Gazette.* Summer 1952, n.p.

Chelsea Registers, 1702–1917. Public Record Office, WO97.

Chrichton, Alexander. *Inquiry into the Nature and Origin of Mental Derangement.* London, 1798.

Christensen, Jerome. *Lord Byron's Strength: Romantic Writing and Commercial Society.* Baltimore: Johns Hopkins University Press, 1993.

Clarke, John, M.D. *Practical Essays on the Management of Pregnancy and Labour; and the Inflammatory and Febrile Diseases of Lying-In Women.* London, 1793.

Clej, Alina. *A Genealogy of the Modern Self: Thomas De Quincey and the Intoxication of Writing.* Stanford: Stanford University Press, 1995.

Cohen, Jeffrey Jerome, ed. *Monster Theory: Reading Culture.* Minneapolis: University of Minnesota Press, 1996.

Coleridge, Samuel Taylor. "Biographia Literaria." *Samuel Taylor Coleridge*. Edited by H. J. Jackson. Oxford: Oxford University Press, 1985.

———. *Collected Letters of Samuel Taylor Coleridge*. 6 vols. Edited by Earl Leslie Griggs. Oxford: Clarendon, 1959.

———. *The Collected Works of Samuel Taylor Coleridge*. 12 vols. Edited by Kathleen Coburn et al. Princeton: Princeton University Press, 1969.

———. *The Complete Poetical Works of Samuel Taylor Coleridge*. 2 vols. Edited by E. H. Coleridge. Oxford: Clarendon, 1912.

———. *The Notebooks of Samuel Taylor Coleridge*. 4 vols. Edited by Kathleen Coburn. Princeton: Princeton University Press, 1957.

———. *The Table Talk of Samuel Taylor Coleridge*. Edited by T. Ashe. London: George Bell & Sons, 1903.

Collection of 77 Advertisements, 1680–1700. British Library. N.Tab.2026125.

Colley, Linda. *Britons: Forging the Nation, 1707–1837*. New Haven: Yale University Press, 1992.

———. "Whose Nation? Class and National Consciousness in Britain, 1750–1830." *Past and Present* 113 (1986): 96–117.

Cottle, Joseph. *Reminiscences of Samuel Taylor Coleridge and Robert Southey*. 1848; reprint, Westmead: Gregg International, 1970.

Cross, Stephen J. "John Hunter, the Animal Oeconomy, and Late-Eighteenth-Century Physiological Discourse." *Studies in History of Biology* 5 (1981): 1–110.

Cullen, William. *A Methodical System of Nosology*. Translated by Elead Lewis. Stockbridge, 1808.

Cunningham, Andrew, and Roger French, eds. *The Medical Enlightenment of the Eighteenth Century*. Cambridge: Cambridge University Press, 1990.

Davidoff, Leonore, and Catherine Hall. *Family Fortunes: Men and Women of the English Middle Class, 1780–1850*. London: Hutchinson, 1987.

Davis, Lennard J., ed. *The Disability Studies Reader*. New York: Routledge, 1997.

Day, Aidan. *Romanticism*. London: Routledge, 1996.

De Almeida, Hermione. *Romantic Medicine and John Keats*. Oxford: Oxford University Press, 1991.

De Certeau, Michel. *The Practice of Everyday Life*. Translated by Stephen Rendall. Berkeley: University of California Press, 1984.

Deleuze, Gilles. *Kant's Critical Philosophy*. Translated by Hugh Tomlinson and Barbara Habberjam. Minneapolis: University of Minnesota Press, 1984.

———. *Nietzsche and Philosophy*. Translated by Hugh Tomlinson. New York: Columbia University Press, 1983.

———, and Félix Guattari. *Anti-Oedipus: Capitalism and Schizophrenia*. Translated by Robert Hurley, Mark Seem, and Helen R. Lane. Minneapolis: University of Minnesota Press, 1983.

Denman, Thomas. *An Introduction to the Practice of Midwifery*. 2 vols. London, 1787.

DePaolo, Charles. "Coleridge and the Cities of the Khan." *The Wordsworth Circle* 13 (1982): 3–8.

De Quincey, Thomas. *The Collected Writings of Thomas De Quincey*. 14 vols. Edited by David Masson. London: A & C Black, 1896–97.

———. *Confessions of an English Opium Eater and Other Writings*. Edited by Aileen Ward. New York: Signet, 1966. 21–111.

Derrida, Jaques. *Of Grammatology*. Translated by Gayatri Chakravorty Spivak. Baltimore: Johns Hopkins University Press, 1976.

———. *Writing and Difference*. Translated by Alan Bass. Chicago: University of Chicago Press, 1978.

Dictionary of National Biography. 22 vols. London: Oxford University Press, 1920.

Dobson, Jessie. *John Hunter*. Edinburgh: Livingstone, 1969.

Duchesneau, François. "Vitalism in Late Eighteenth-Century Physiology: The Cases of Barthez, Blumenback, and John Hunter." In Bynum and Porter, 259–296.

Dyer, Richard. *White*. London: Routledge, 1997.

Eaves, Morris. *The Counter-Arts Conspiracy: Art and Industry in the Age of Blake*. Ithaca: Cornell University Press, 1992.

Eisler, Betina. *Byron: Child of Passion, Fool of Fame*. New York: Knopf, 1999.

Emsley, Clive. *British Society and the French Wars, 1793–1815*. London: Macmillan, 1979.

Equiano, Olaudah. *The Interesting Narrative and Other Writings*. Edited by Vincent Carretta. New York: Penguin, 1995.

Ernst, Waltraud, and Bernard Harris. *Race, Science, and Medicine, 1700–1960*. London: Routledge, 1999.

Featherstone, Mike, Mike Hepworth, and Bryan S. Turner, eds. *The Body: Social Process and Cultural Theory*. London: Sage, 1991.

Feher, Michael, Ramona Nadaff, and Nadia Tazi, eds. *Fragments for a History of the Human Body, Part One*. New York: Zone, 1989.

Feldman, Paula R., ed. *British Women Poets of the Romantic Era: An Anthology*. Baltimore: Johns Hopkins University Press, 1997.

———, and Theresa M. Kelly, eds. *Romantic Women Writers: Voices and Countervoices*. Hanover: University Press of New England, 1995.

Ferguson, Frances. "Coleridge and the Deluded Reader: 'The Rime of the Ancient Mariner'." *Post-Structuralist Readings of English Poetry*. Edited by Richard Machin and Christopher Norris. Cambridge: Cambridge University Press, 1987.

Fforde, Cressida. "The Royal College of Surgeons of England: A Brief History of its Collections and a Catalogue of Some Current Holdings." *World Archaeology Bulletin* 6 (1992): 22–52.

Foot, Michael. *The Politics of Paradise: A Vindication of Byron*. New York: Harper and Row, 1988.

Foucault, Michel. *The Birth of the Clinic: An Archaeology of Medical Perception*. Translated by A. M. Sheridan Smith. New York: Vintage, 1973.

———. *The Care of the Self*. Translated by Robert Hurley. New York: Vintage, 1986.

———. *Discipline and Punish: The Birth of the Prison*. Translated by Alan Sheridan. New York: Vintage, 1979.

———. *The History of Sexuality, Volume I: An Introduction*. Translated by Robert Hurley. New York: Vintage, 1978.

———. "Of Other Spaces." *Diacritics* 16 (1986): 22–27

———. *The Order of Things: An Archaeology of the Human Sciences*. New York: Vintage, 1973.

————. *Power/Knowledge: Selected Interviews and Other Writings, 1972–1977.* Edited by Colin Gordon. New York: Pantheon, 1980.

Gabriel, Richard A., and Karen S. Metz. *A History of Military Medicine.* 2 vols. New York: Greenwood Press, 1992.

Gallagher, Catherine. "The Body Versus the Social Body in the Works of Thomas Malthus and Henry Mayew." In Laqueur and Gallagher, 83–106.

George, M. Dorothy. *Catalogue of Political and Personal Satires Preserved in the Department of Prints and Drawings in the British Museum.* Vols. 5–11. London: British Museum Publications, 1978.

Gerzina, Gretchen. *Black London: Life before Emancipation.* New Brunswick: Rutgers University Press, 1995.

Gillman, James. *The Life of Samuel Taylor Coleridge.* London: W. Pickering, 1838.

Gilman, Sander. *Difference and Pathology: Stereotypes of Sexuality, Race, and Madness.* Ithaca: Cornell University Press, 1985.

————. *Sexuality: An Illustrated History, Representing the Sexual in Medicine and Culture from the Middle Ages to the Age of AIDS.* New York: Wiley, 1989.

Gilmartin, Kevin. *Print Politics: The Press and Radical Opposition in Early-Nineteenth-Century England.* Cambridge: Cambridge University Press, 1996.

Gilroy, Paul. *Against Race: Imagining Political Culture beyond the Color Line.* Cambridge: Harvard University Press, 2000.

Godwin, William. *Memoirs of the Author of "A Vindication of the Rights of Woman."* Edited by Gina Luria. New York: Garland, 1974.

Goldberg, David Theo. *Racist Culture: Philosophy and the Politics of Meaning.* Oxford: Blackwell, 1993.

————. *The Racial State.* Oxford: Blackwell, 2002.

Gould, Stephen Jay. *The Mismeasure of Man.* Rev. ed. New York: 1996.

Grosz, Elizabeth. *Volatile Bodies: Toward a Corporeal Feminism.* Bloomington: Indiana University Press, 1994.

Guthrie, G. J. *A Treatise on Gun-Shot Wounds, on Injuries of Nerves, and on Wounds of the Extremities Requiring the Different Operations of Amputation.* 2d. ed. London, 1820.

Habermas, Jürgen. *The Structural Transformation of the Public Sphere: An Enquiry into a Category of Bourgeois Society.* Translated by Thomas Burger with Frederick Lawrence. Cambridge: MIT Press, 1989.

Halberstam, Judith, and Ira Livingston, eds. *Posthuman Bodies.* Bloomington: Indiana University Press, 1995.

Hall, John. *The Biographical Dictionary of British Officers Killed and Wounded, 1808–1814.* London: Greenhill, 1998.

Hall, Stuart. "Variants of Liberalism." In *Politics and Ideology,* ed. J. Donald and Stuart Hall. Milton Keynes: Open University Press, 34–69.

Hall, Thomas S. *Ideas of Life and Matter: Studies in the History of General Physiology, 600 B.C.–1900 A.D.* 2 vols. Chicago: University of Chicago Press, 1969.

Hannaford, Ivan. *Race: The History of an Idea in the West.* Baltimore: Johns Hopkins University Press, 1996.

Haraway, Donna. "The Promises of Monsters: A Regenerative Politics for Inappropriate/d

Others." In *Cultural Studies*, ed. Cary Nelson, Lawrence Grossberg, and Paula A. Treichler. New York: Routledge, 1992.

Harding, Geoffrey. *Opium Addiction, Morality, and Medicine*. London: Macmillan, 1988.

Haslam, John. *Observations on Insanity*. London, 1798.

Hayles, N. Katherine. *How We Became Posthuman: Virtual Bodies in Cybernetics, Literature, and Informatics*. Chicago: University of Chicago Press, 1999.

Hayter, Alethea. *Opium and the Romantic Imagination*. Berkeley: University of California Press, 1968.

Hazlitt, William. "Mr. Coleridge." *William Hazlitt: Selected Writings*. Edited by Ronald Blythe. Harmondsworth: Penguin, 1970.

Heidegger, Martin. *Nietzsche: Volumes One and Two*. Translated by David Farrell Krell. New York: HarperCollins, 1991.

Henderson, Andrea. "Doll-Machines and Butcher-Shop Meat: Models of Childbirth in the Early Stages of Industrial Capitalism." *Genders* 12 (1991): 100–19.

Herschback, Lisa. "Prosthetic Reconstructions: Making the Industry, Remaking the Body, Modelling the Nation." *History Workshop Journal* 44 (1997): 23–57.

An Historical Account of Bartholomew Fair; Containing a View of its Origin, and the Purposes it was first instituted for. Together with a Concise Detail of the Changes it hath undergone in its Traffic, Amusements, etc., etc. London, 1810.

Hirsch, David A. Hedrich. "Liberty, Equality, Monstrosity: Revolutionizing the Family in Mary Shelley's *Frankenstein*." In Cohen, 115–42.

Hobsbawm, E. J. *Nations and Nationalism since 1780*. Cambridge: Cambridge University Press, 1990.

Hofkosh, Sonia. "Tradition and the *Interesting Narrative*: Capitalism, Abolition, and the Romantic Individual." In Richardson and Hofkosh, 330–44.

Holmes, Richard. *Coleridge*. Vol. 1. New York: Viking, 1990. Vol. 2. New York: Pantheon, 1999.

Hone, William. *Bartholomew Fair Insurrection; and the Pie-Bald Poney Plot!* London, 1817.

———. *Buonapartephobia, or Cursing Made Easy to the Meanest Capacity*. London, 1820.

———. *The Every-Day Book; or Everlasting Calendar of Popular Amusements*. 2 vols. London, 1826.

Honor, Hugh. *The Image of the Black in Western Art*. Vol. 4. Cambridge: Harvard University Press, 1989.

Hood, Thomas. *Selected Poems of Thomas Hood*. Edited by John Clubbe. Cambridge: Harvard University Press, 1970.

Hunt, Lynn, ed. *The Invention of Pornography: Obscenity and the Origins of Modernity, 1500–1800*. New York: Zone, 1993.

Hunter, John. *Essays and Observations on Natural History, Anatomy, Physiology, Psychology, and Geology, being Hunter's Posthumous Papers*. Edited by Richard Owen. 2 vols. London: Van Voorst, 1861.

———. *Lectures on the Principles of Surgery*. London, 1837. Vol. 1 of *The Works of John Hunter*. Edited by James F. Palmer. 4 vols.

———. *Observations on Certain Parts of the Animal Oeconomy*. 2d ed. London, 1786.

———. *A Treatise on the Blood, Inflammation and Gunshot Wounds*. Edited by Everard Home. Philadelphia, 1796.

Hunter, William. *An Abstract from Dr Hunter's Lectures on the Gravid Uterus*. Ms. College of Physicians Library, Philadelphia.

———. *The Anatomy of the Human Gravid Uterus*. London, 1774.

———. *Two Introductory Lectures, Delivered by Dr. William Hunter, to his Last Course of Anatomical Lectures, at his Theatre in Windmill-Street*. London, 1784.

Illingworth, Sir Charles. *The Story of William Hunter*. Edinburgh: Livingstone, 1967.

John Johnson Collection of Printed Ephemera. Bodleian Library. Oxford.

Johnson, Barbara. "My Monster/My Self." *Diacritics* 12 (1982): 2–10.

Jones, F. Wood. "John Hunter's Unwritten Book." *The Lancet* 261 (1951): 778–80.

Jones, John. *The Mysteries of Opium Revealed*. London, 1701.

Jones, Vivien. "The Death of Mary Wollstonecraft." *British Journal for Eighteenth-Century Studies* 20 (1997): 187–205.

Johnson, Ben the Younger. *A Descriptive Poem of Bartholomew-Fair, for the Instruction and Amusement of Youth of Both Sexes*. London, circa 1780.

Jordanova, Ludmilla J. "Gender, Generation, and Science: William Hunter's Obstetrical Atlas." In Bynum and Porter, 385–412.

———. *Sexual Visions: Images of Gender in Science and Medicine between the Eighteenth and Twentieth Centuries*. Madison: University of Wisconsin Press, 1989.

Kant, Immanuel. *Anthropology from a Pragmatic Point of View*. Translated by Mary Gregor. The Hague: Martinus Nijhoff, 1974.

———. *The Conflict of the Faculties*. Translated by Mary Gregor. New York: Abaris Books, 1979.

———. *Critique of Judgment*. Translated by J. H. Bernard. New York: Hafner Press, 1951.

———. *Observations on the Feeling of the Beautiful and the Sublime*. Translated by John T. Goldthwait. Berkeley: University of California Press, 1960.

Kelley, Robin D. G. *Yo' Mama's Disfunktional!: Fighting the Culture Wars in Urban America*. Boston: Beacon, 1997.

Kelly, Gary. *Revolutionary Feminism: The Mind and Career of Mary Wollstonecraft*. New York: St. Martins, 1992.

Kelly, Veronica, and Dorothea von Mücke. *Body and Text in the Eighteenth Century*. Stanford: Stanford University Press, 1994.

Kelsall, Malcolm. *Byron's Politics*. Sussex: Harvester, 1987.

Kemble, James. "Byron: His Lameness and Last Illness." *Quarterly Review* 257 (1931): 234–43.

King, Lester. *The Philosophy of Medicine: The Early Eighteenth Century*. Cambridge: Harvard University Press, 1978.

Kitson, Peter, and Debbie Lee et al., eds. *Slavery, Abolition, and Emancipation: Writings in the British Romantic Period*. 8 vols. London: Pickering and Chatto, 1999.

Kobler, John. *The Reluctant Surgeon: A Biography of John Hunter*. New York: Doubleday, 1960.

Krell, David Farrell. *Contagion: Sexuality, Disease, and Death in German Idealism and Romanticism*. Bloomington: Indiana University Press, 1998.

———. *Infectious Nietzsche*. Bloomington: Indiana University Press, 1996.

Kristeva, Julia. *Powers of Horror: An Essay on Abjection*. Translated by Leon S. Roudiez. New York: Columbia University Press, 1982.

Laqueur, Thomas. "Bodies, Details, and the Humanitarian Narrative." In *The New Cultural History*, edited by Lynn Hunt, 176–205. Berkeley: University of California Press, 1989.

———. *Making Sex: Body and Gender from the Greeks to Freud*. Cambridge: Harvard University Press, 1990.

———. "Orgasm, Generation, and the Politics of Reproductive Biology." In Laqueur and Gallagher, 1–41.

———, and Catherine Gallagher, eds. *The Making of the Modern Body: Sexuality and Society in the Nineteenth Century*. Berkeley: University of California Press, 1987.

Lawrence, Christopher, ed. *Medical Theory, Surgical Practice: Studies in the History of Surgery*. London: Routledge, 1992.

———. *Medicine in the Making of Modern Britain, 1700–1920*. London: Routledge, 1994.

———. "The Nervous System and Society in the Scottish Enlightenment." *Natural Order: Historical Studies of Scientific Culture*. Edited by Barry Barnes and Steven Shapin. London: Sage, 1979.

Leask, Nigel. *British Romantic Writers and the East: Anxieties of Empire*. Cambridge: Cambridge University Press, 1992.

———. "Toward a Universal Aesthetic: De Quincey on Murder as Carnival and Tragedy." In *Questioning Romanticism*, edited by John Beer. Baltimore: Johns Hopkins University Press, 1995.

Lefebure, Molly. *Samuel Taylor Coleridge: A Bondage of Opium*. New York: Stein and Day, 1974.

Levinas, Emanuel. *Totality And Infinity: An Essay in Exteriority*. Translated by Alphonso Lingis. Pittsburgh: Duquesne University Press, 1969.

Levine, George, ed. *One Culture: Essays in Science and Literature*. Madison: University of Wisconsin Press, 1987.

Lindop, Grevel. *The Opium Eater: A Life of Thomas De Quincey*. London: J. M. Dent, 1981.

Linebaugh, Peter. "The Tyburn Riot against the Surgeons." In *Albion's Fatal Tree: Crime and Society in Eighteenth-Century England*, edited by Douglas Hay et al. New York: Pantheon, 1975.

The Literary Gazette and Journal of the Belles Lettres. London, 1824.

Lloyd, David. "Race under Representation." *Oxford Literary Review* 13 (1991): 62–94.

Locke, John. *Two Treatises of Government*. Edited by Peter Laslett. 2d. ed. Cambridge: Cambridge University Press, 1967.

———. *Essay Concerning Human Understanding*. Edited by John W. Yolton. 2 vols. London: Dent, 1961.

Lorch, Jennifer. *Mary Wollstonecraft: The Making of a Radical Feminist*. New York: St. Martins, 1990.

Loudon, Irvine. *Medical Care and the General Practitioner, 1750–1850*. Oxford: Clarendon, 1986.

Lowes, John Livingston. *The Road to Xanadu*. Boston: Houghton Mifflin, 1927.

Lysons, Daniel. *Collectanea; or, A Collection of Advertisements from the Newspapers . . . [1661–1840]*. 5 vols. British Library, 1889. e.5.

Macpherson, C. B. *The Political Theory of Possessive Individualism: Hobbes to Locke.* Oxford: Oxford University Press, 1962.

Magnuson, Paul. "'Kubla Khan': That Phantom World So Fair." In *Critical Essays on Samuel Taylor Coleridge,* edited by Leonard Orr. New York: G. K. Hall, 1994.

———. *Reading Public Romanticism.* Princeton: Princeton University Press, 1998.

Malthus, Thomas. *On Population.* Edited by Gertrude Himmelfarb. New York: Modern Library, 1960.

Manning, David. *Sir Joshua Reynolds: A Complete Catalogue of His Paintings.* 2 vols. New Haven: Yale University Press for the Paul Mellon Centre for Studies in British Art, 2000.

Marchand, Leslie A. *Byron: A Biography.* 3 vols. New York: Knopf, 1957.

Marcus, Leah S. *The Politics of Mirth: Jonson, Herrick, Milton, Marvell, and the Defense of Old Holiday Pastimes.* Chicago: University of Chicago Press, 1986.

Marshall, Tim. *Murdering to Dissect: Grave-Robbing, Frankenstein, and the Anatomy Literature.* Manchester: Manchester University Press, 1995.

Marx, Karl. "Commodities." *The Portable Karl Marx.* Edited by Eugene Kamenka. New York: Viking, 1983.

McDonagh, Josephine. *De Quincey's Disciplines.* Oxford: Clarendon Press, 1994.

McGann, Jerome J. *Don Juan in Context.* Chicago: University of Chicago Press, 1976.

———. *Fiery Dust: Byron's Poetic Development.* Chicago: University of Chicago Press, 1968.

———. "The Meaning of the Mariner." *Critical Inquiry* 8 (1981): 35–67.

———. *The Poetics of Sensibility: A Revolution in Literary Style.* Oxford: Clarendon, 1996.

———. *The Romantic Ideology: A Critical Investigation.* Chicago: University of Chicago Press, 1983.

McGavigan, Brigit. "Artificial Limbs and Amputation in Victorian Britain." Diss. The Wellcome Institute for the History of Medicine, 1996.

McKendrick, Neil, John Brewer, and J. H. Plumb. *The Birth of a Consumer Society: The Commercialization of Eighteenth-Century England.* Bloomington: Indiana University Press, 1982.

McLaren, Angus. "The Pleasures of Procreation: Traditional and Biomedical Theories of Conception." In Bynum and Porter, 323–42.

Mellor, Anne K. *Mary Shelley: Her Life, Her Fiction, Her Monsters.* New York: Routledge, 1989.

———. *Mothers of the Nation: Women's Political Writing in England, 1780–1830.* Bloomington: Indiana University Press, 2000.

———. *Romanticism and Gender.* New York: Routledge, 1993.

———, ed. *Romanticism and Feminism.* Bloomington: Indiana University Press, 1988.

Milligan, Barry. *Pleasures and Pains: Opium and the Orient in Nineteenth-Century British Culture.* Charlottesville: University of Virginia Press, 1995.

Mitchell, W. J. T. *Blake's Composite Art: A Study of the Illuminated Poetry.* Princeton: Princeton University Press, 1978.

Morley, Henry. *Memoirs of Bartholomew Fair.* London: Chapman and Hall, 1859.

———. *Scrapbook.* British Museum C70.h.6(2).

Morrison, A. B. "Byron's Lameness." *The Byron Journal* 3 (1975): 24–31.

Moscucci, Ornella. *The Science of Woman: Gynaecology and Gender in England, 1800–1929.* Cambridge: Cambridge University Press, 1990.

Mullaney, Steven. *The Place of the Stage: License, Play, and Power in Renaissance England.* Chicago: University of Chicago Press, 1988.

Murphy-Lawless, Jo. *Reading Birth and Death: A History of Obstetric Thinking.* Bloomington: Indiana University Press, 1998.

Musto, David. *The American Disease: The Origins of Narcotic Control.* New Haven: Yale University Press, 1973.

Neveldine, Robert Burns. *Bodies at Risk: Unsafe Limits in Romanticism and Postmodernism.* Albany: SUNY Press, 1998.

Newman, Gerald. *The Rise of English Nationalism: A Cultural History, 1740–1830.* London: Weidenfeld and Nicolson, 1987.

Nietzsche, Friedrich. *Beyond Good and Evil: Prelude to a Philosophy of the Future.* Translated by Walter Kaufmann. New York: Vintage, 1966.

———. *The Birth of Tragedy and The Case of Wagner.* Translated by Walter Kaufmann. New York: Vintage, 1967.

———. *Ecce Homo. Nietzsche: Werke.* Edited by Giorgio Colli and Mazzino Montinari. Part 6, vol. 3. Berlin: De Gruyter, 1967. 253–372.

———. *The Gay Science.* Translated by Walter Kaufmann. New York: Vintage, 1974.

———. *On the Genealogy of Morals and Ecce Homo.* Translated by Walter Kaufmann and R. J. Hollingdale. New York: Vintage, 1967.

———. "On Truth and Lying in an Extra-Moral Sense." *Friedrich Nietzsche on Rhetoric and Language.* Edited and translated by Sander L. Gilman, Carole Blair, and David J. Parent. New York: Oxford University Press, 1989. 246–57.

Nihell, Elizabeth. *Treatise on the Art of Midwifery: Setting Forth Various Abuses Therein, Especially as to the Practice of Instruments.* London, 1760.

O'Connor, Erin. *Raw Material: Producing Pathology in Victorian Culture.* Durham: Duke University Press, 2000.

O'Dowd, Michael J., and Elliot E. Phillipp. *The History of Obstetrics and Gynaecology.* New York: Parthenon, 1994.

Paglia, Camille. *Sexual Personae.* New York: Vintage, 1991.

Paine, Thomas. *Political Writings.* Edited by Bruce Kuklick. Cambridge: Cambridge University Press, 1989.

Pargeter, William. *Observations of Maniacal Disorders.* London, 1792.

Park, Katharine, and Lorraine J. Daston. "Unnatural Conceptions: The Study of Monsters in Sixteenth- and Seventeenth-Century France and England." *Past and Present* 92 (1981): 20–54.

Parssinen, Terry M. *Secret Passions, Secret Remedies: Narcotic Drugs in British Society, 1820–1930.* Manchester: Manchester University Press, 1983.

Paston, George. *Social Caricature in the Eighteenth Century.* New York: Benjamin Blom, 1968.

Pateman, Carole. *The Sexual Contract.* Stanford: Stanford University Press, 1988.

Paulson, Ronald. *Breaking and Remaking: Aesthetic Practice in England, 1700–1820.* New Brunswick: Rutgers University Press, 1989.

Peachey, George C. *A Memoir of John and William Hunter.* Plymouth: Brendon and Sons, 1924.

A Peep at Bartholomew Fair; Containing An Interesting Account of the Amusements and Diversions of that Famous Metropolitan Carnival. London, c. 1810.

Pender, Stephen. "'No Monsters at the Resurrection': Inside Some Conjoined Twins." In Cohen, 143–67.

Philips, Gordon. *Best Foot Forward: Chas. A. Blanchford & Sons, Ltd. (Artificial Limb Specialists), 1890–1990.* Cambridge: Granta, 1990.

Pinel, Philippe. *Treatise on Insanity.* Translated by D. D. Davis. Sheffield, 1806.

Plato. *Ion.* Translated by Lane Cooper. *Plato: The Collected Dialogues.* Edited by Edith Hamilton and Huntington Cairns. Princeton: Princeton University Press, 1961.

Plotz, Judith. "On Guilt Considered as One of the Fine Arts: De Quincey's Criminal Imagination." *The Wordsworth Circle* 19 (1988): 83–88.

Pointon, Marcia. *Hanging the Head: Portraiture and Social Formation in Eighteenth-Century England.* New Haven: Yale University Press for the Paul Mellon Centre for Studies in British Art, 1993.

Poovey, Mary. *Making a Social Body: British Cultural Formation, 1830–1864.* Chicago: University of Chicago Press, 1995.

———. *The Proper Lady and the Woman Writer: Ideology as Style in the Works of Mary Wollstonecraft, Mary Shelley, and Jane Austen.* Chicago: University of Chicago Press, 1984.

Porter, Dorothy, and Roy Porter. *Patient's Progress: Doctors and Doctoring in Eighteenth-Century England.* London: Polity, 1989.

Porter, Roy. *The Anatomy of Madness: Essays in the History of Psychiatry.* London: Tavistock, 1985.

———. "Bodies of Thought: Thoughts about the Body in Eighteenth-Century England." In *Interpretation and Cultural History,* edited by Joan H. Pittock and Andrew Wear. London: Macmillan, 1991.

———. *Mind-Forged Manacles: A History of Madness from the Restoration to the Regency.* London: Athlone Press, 1987.

———, ed. *The Popularization of Medicine, 1650–1850.* London: Routledge, 1992.

———. *A Social History of Madness: The World Through the Eyes of the Insane.* New York: Weidenfeld and Nicolson, 1988.

Qvist, George. *John Hunter, 1728–1793.* London: Heinemann, 1981.

Regulations of 14 Novr. 1829 for Granting Pensions to Discharged Soldiers. London, 1829.

Reynolds, Sir Joshua. *The Discourses of Sir Joshua Reynolds, P.R.A.* London: Macmillan, 1924.

———. "To the Idler, Saturday, Nov. 10, 1759." *The Works of Sir Joshua Reynolds, Knight, Late President of the Royal Academy.* Vol 2. London: 1801.

Richardson, Alan. *British Romanticism and the Science of the Mind.* Cambridge: Cambridge University Press, 2001.

———, and Sonia Hofkosh, eds. *Romanticism, Race, and Imperial Culture, 1780–1834.* Bloomington: Indiana University Press, 1996.

Richardson, Ruth. *Death, Dissection, and the Destitute.* London: Routledge, 1987.

Rickels, Laurence A. *The Vampire Lectures.* Minneapolis: University of Minnesota Press, 1999.

Ronell, Avital. *Crack Wars: Literature, Mania, Addiction.* Lincoln: University of Nebraska Press, 1991.

Rousseau, Jean-Jacques. *Emile, or On Education*. Translated by Allan Bloom. New York: Basic Books, 1979.

Russett, Margaret. *De Quincey's Romanticism: Canonical Minority and the Forms of Transmission*. Cambridge: Cambridge University Press, 1997.

Rzepka, Charles. "The Body, the Book, and 'the True Hero of the Tale': De Quincey's 1821 *Confessions* and Romantic Autobiography as Cultural Artifact." In *Studies in Autobiography*, edited by James Olney. New York: Oxford University Press, 1988.

———. *Sacramental Commodities: Gift, Text, and the Sublime in De Quincey*. Amherst: University of Massachusetts Press, 1995.

Sallis, John. *Crossings: Nietzsche and the Space of Tragedy*. Chicago: University of Chicago Press, 1991.

Sawday, Jonathan. *The Body Emblazoned: Dissection and the Human Body in Renaissance Culture*. London: Routledge, 1995.

Scarry, Elaine. *The Body in Pain: The Making and the Unmaking of the World*. Oxford: Oxford University Press, 1985.

Schiebinger, Londa. *Nature's Body: Gender and the Making of Modern Science*. Boston: Beacon, 1993.

Schneider, Elizabeth. *Coleridge, Opium, and Kubla Khan*. Chicago: University of Chicago Press, 1953.

Scott, Charles. *The Question of Ethics: Nietzsche, Foucault, Heidegger*. Bloomington: Indiana University Press, 1990.

Seltzer, Mark. *Bodies and Machines*. New York: Routledge, 1992.

Shaffer, E. S. *"Kubla Khan" and the Fall of Jerusalem*. Cambridge: Cambridge University Press, 1975.

Shaviro, Steven. *The Cinematic Body*. Minneapolis: University of Minnesota Press, 1993.

Sheldrake, Timothy. *An Essay on the Various Causes and Effects of the Distorted Spine*. London, 1783.

———. "Mr. Sheldrake on Distortions of the Feet. Lord Byron's Case." *The Lancet* (1828): 779–82.

———. *A Practical Essay on the Club-Foot*. London, 1798.

Shelley, Mary. *Frankenstein, or The Modern Prometheus*. Edited by James Rieger. New York: Bobbs-Merrill, 1974.

Shorter, Edward. *Women's Bodies: A Social History of Women's Encounter with Health, Ill-Health, and Medicine*. 1982. New Brunswick: Transaction, 1991.

Simmons, Samuel Foate, and John Hunter. *William Hunter, 1718–1783: A Memoir*. Edited by C. H. Brock. Glasgow: University of Glasgow Press, 1983.

Simpson, David. *Romanticism, Nationalism, and the Revolt against Theory*. Chicago: University of Chicago Press, 1993.

———. *Wordsworth's Historical Imagination: The Poetry of Displacement*. New York: Methuen, 1987.

Smith, Adam. *The Essential Adam Smith*. Edited by Robert L. Heilbroner with Laurence J. Malone. New York: Norton, 1986.

Stafford, Barbara. *Body Criticism: Imaging the Unseen in Enlightenment Art and Medicine*. Cambridge: MIT Press, 1991.

Stallybrass, Peter, and Allon White. *The Politics and Poetics of Transgression*. London: Methuen, 1986.

Thom, Martin. *Republics, Nations, and Tribes*. London: Verso, 1995.

Thompson, E. P. *The Making of the English Working Class.* New York: Vintage, 1963.

Thomson, John. *Report of Observations made in the British Military Hospitals in Belgium, after the Battle of Waterloo.* Edinburgh, 1816.

Thomson, Rosemarie Garland. *Extraordinary Bodies: Figuring Physical Disability in American Culture and Literature.* New York: Columbia University Press, 1997.

———, ed. *Freakery: Cultural Spectacles of the Extraordinary Body.* New York: New York University Press, 1996.

Timbs, John. *English Eccentrics and Eccentricities.* London: Bentley, 1866.

Todd, Dennis. *Imagining Monsters: Miscreations of the Self in Eighteenth-Century England.* Chicago: University of Chicago Press, 1995.

Tomalin, Claire. *The Life and Death of Mary Wollstonecraft.* New York: Harcourt Brace Jovanovich, 1974.

Trelawney, Edward John. *Trelawney's Recollections of the Last Days of Shelley and Byron.* Edited by Edward Dowden. London: Milford, 1941.

Vice, Sue, Matthew Campbell, and Tim Armstrong, eds. *Beyond the Pleasure Dome: Writing and Addiction from the Romantics.* Sheffield: Sheffield Academic Press, 1994.

Viscomi, Joseph. *William Blake and the Idea of the Book.* Princeton: Princeton University Press, 1993.

Walvin, James. *Black Ivory: A History of British Slavery.* Washington: Howard University Press, 1994.

———. *Slavery and the Slave Trade: A Short Illustrated History.* Jackson: University Press of Mississippi, 1983.

Ward, Aileen. "'Sir Joshua and his Gang': William Blake and the Royal Academy," *Huntington Library Quarterly* 52 (1989): 75–95.

Warner, Michael. *The Trouble with Normal: Sex, Politics, and the Ethics of Queer Life.* Cambridge: Harvard University Press, 1999.

Wear, Andrew, ed. *Medicine in Society: Historical Essays.* Cambridge: Cambridge University Press, 1992.

Wellek, Rene. *Confrontations: Studies in the Intellectual and Literary Relations Between Germany, England, and the United States during the Nineteenth Century.* Princeton: Princeton University Press, 1965.

———. *A History of Modern Criticism, 1750–1950.* Vol. 3. New Haven: Yale University Press, 1965.

———. *Immanuel Kant in England.* Princeton: Princeton University Press, 1931.

Wendorf, Richard. *Joshua Reynolds: The Painter in Society.* Cambridge: Harvard University Press, 1996.

White, Charles. *An Account of the Regular Gradation in Man, and in Different Animals and Vegetables; and from the former to the latter.* London, 1799.

Williams, Anne. "An I for an Eye: 'Spectral Persecution' in 'The Rime of the Ancient Mariner'." *PMLA* 108 (1993): 1114–27.

Wills, David. *Prosthesis.* Stanford: Stanford University Press, 1995.

Wilson, Adrian. *The Making of Man-Midwifery: Childbirth in England, 1660–1770.* Cambridge: Harvard University Press, 1995.

———. "William Hunter and the Varieties of Man-Midwifery." In Bynum and Porter, 343–69.

Wilson, Dudley. *Signs and Portents: Monstrous Births from the Middle Ages to the Enlightenment.* London: Routledge, 1993.

Wollstonecraft, Mary. *Collected Letters of Mary Wollstonecraft.* Edited by Ralph M. Wardle. Ithaca: Cornell University Press, 1979.

———. *Mary and Maria.* Edited by Janet Todd. London: Penguin, 1991.

———. *A Vindication of the Rights of Woman.* Edited by Carol H. Poston. 2d ed. New York: Norton, 1988.

The Wonderful and Scientific Museum: or Magazine of Remarkable Characters; including all the Curiosities of Nature, from the Remotest Period to the Present Time, Drawn from every Authentic Source. 6 vols. London, 1803.

Wordsworth, William. *The Prelude: A Parallel Text.* Edited by J. C. Maxwell. New Haven: Yale University Press, 1981.

———. *Selected Poems and Prefaces.* Edited by Jack Stillinger. Boston: Houghton Mifflin, 1965.

Worrall, David. *Radical Culture: Discourse, Resistance, and Surveillance, 1790–1820.* Detroit: Wayne State University Press, 1992.

Yeats, William Butler. *Selected Poems and Two Plays of William Butler Yeats.* Edited by M. L. Rosenthal. New York: Macmillan, 1962.

Young, George. *A Treatise on Opium.* London, 1853.

Žižek, Slavoj. *The Sublime Object of Ideology.* London: Verso, 1989.

INDEX

Paul Youngquist is associate professor of English at Penn State University. He is the author of *Madness and Blake's Myth,* and he has also written essays on British Romanticism, science fiction, and black music.